# Fragments of Death,
# Fables of Identity

# New Directions in Anthropological Writing
## *History, Poetics, Cultural Criticism*

GEORGE E. MARCUS
*Rice University*

JAMES CLIFFORD
*University of California, Santa Cruz*

GENERAL EDITORS

# Fragments of Death, Fables of Identity

*An Athenian Anthropography*

Neni Panourgiá

THE UNIVERSITY OF WISCONSIN PRESS

The University of Wisconsin Press
114 North Murray Street
Madison, Wisconsin 53715

3 Henrietta Street
London WC2E 8LU, England

Library of Congress Cataloging-in-Publication Data
Panourgia, E. Neni K. (Eleni Neni K.), 1958–
Fragments of death, fables of identity: an Athenian anthropography /
Neni Panourgiá.
268 pp.        cm. — (New directions in anthropological writing)
Includes bibliographical references and index.
ISBN 0-299-14560-3 (alk. paper).
ISBN 0-299-14564-6 (pbk.: alk. paper).
1. Ethnology—Greece—Athens. 2. Ethnology—Greece—Athens—Methodology.
3. Death—Social aspects—Greece—Athens.
4. Funeral rites and ceremonies—Greece—Athens.
5. Athens (Greece)—Social life and customs.
I. Title. II. Series.
GN585.G85P35        1995
306'.09495'12—dc20—95-6196

Τοῦ Στάθη

In a life that is no longer disfigured, that no longer prohibits,
in a life that would no longer cheat men out of their dues
—in such a life men would probably no longer have to hope, in vain,
that this life would after all give them what it had so far refused.
For the same reason they would not have to fear so greatly
that they would lose this life, no matter how deeply this fear
had been ingrained in them.
—Theodor W. Adorno,
   *The Jargon of Authenticity*

# Contents

# Contents

# Illustrations

# Acknowledgments

Every text, inevitably, bears the marks of many actors, many authors, multiple eras and places. I wrote this text in many places, under various circumstances, and among different people who marked the development of my thought and the questions asked (but not necessarily answered) here. Athens, Bloomington, Boulder, Salt Lake City, New York City, and Princeton are the places where it found its shape and form.

My first thanks, posthumous but no less deep and heartfelt, go to those whose deaths, literally, created the circumstances for the conception and production of this text. I write in memory of Katerina Baskákē, Petroula Gourgourê, Télēs Labrinidis-Labrikidis, Evangelia Panourgiá, Panayês Petrópoulos, Léngō, Théklē, and Tássos Sideris, Yiôrgos Panourgiás, Tássos Panourgiás, and the many patients at the Anti-Cancer Institute of Athens and their families.

My family, nuclear and extended alike, provided me with emotional, intellectual, and financial support (even when they did not exactly agree with my approaches) and unsparing critique of the anthropological and ethnographic praxis. Pierre Cachia is family, and I could never express to their true proportions my love, gratitude, and deepest respect for him. My parents, Kōnstantinos Panourgiás and Dēmētra Tsakálou-Panourgiá, taught me how to love, respect, and acknowledge humanity and how to fight for what I think is right. But I am particularly grateful to them for teaching me not to break the world down along gender lines, for always allowing me to do what a son would have been allowed to do, for combating racism, prejudice, and discrimination. My sister, Lea, and her two sons, Oréstēs and Iásōn, have provided me with a home, an embrace, and unfailing love and support under sometimes excruciatingly trying circumstances. This book is a gift to all of them.

I could never thank enough my teachers who allowed me to take to intellectual paths whose destinations none of us really knew. We all survived well. Early on, Kitsa Metaxá, the late Ted Petrides, Markos Dragoumis, the late Panayiotēs Zaronis, the late James Folsom, and Kia Karayianni all kindled and fed my interests and passion for learning. To Michael Herzfeld go my deep thanks for supporting me during my studies and for elevating the level of discourse in the field of modern Greek anthropology. Anya Peterson Royce and Ray DeMallie pushed for an ethnographic approach when other approaches seemed to occupy my mind, and William Hansen allowed me to plunge into the ancient Greek ways of death and emerge again. I thank them for their help. Dr. Lynn Lyons, at the University of Utah Medical School, made it all worthwhile.

I am also indebted to the staff of the Third Surgical Clinic at the Anti-Cancer Institute, especially its chief, Dr. Pericles Vassilopoulos, who took an interest in my project and coaxed me to continue. Dr. G. Rigatos, chief of the First Pathology Clinic at the Institute, has had an even greater influence on my work through our exchanges concerning psychosocial oncology, thus helping to situate my research within a broader biomedical context, and through his steady supplying of relevant bibliographic references.

Equally critical in the formulation of many of the approaches taken in this book was the Dissertation Support Group of the Anthropology Department at Indiana University, to which I belonged during the time that this text was still in its dissertation stage. To its members at the time—Patricia Clay, Barbara Santos, Cathy Siebold, James Wafer, and Petronella Wafer—I owe more than I can express. They painstakingly went over very early, very rough drafts, offered alternative theories, and critiqued the ones I presented. Many other people have offered me support, a critical eye and ear, or simply an embrace (of sorts) when one was needed. I could not possibly name them all, but I will identify a few. I have greatly profited from my relationships with Robert Fagles, Beatrice Grabowski, Gregory Jusdanis, Nea Meyers-Herzfeld, Liana Theodoratou, and Cathy Winkler. Deep thanks of a different order go to Sérgios Alexópoulos, Laoura Meletopoulou, Evi Tsintzou and Yiôrgos Klōnárēs, Sotêrēs and Katerina Tsoukala-Voyadji, and Hara T. Tzavella-Evjen and Harold Evjen.

Many of the questions addressed here were originally presented at various meetings on modern Greek studies, and I have profited greatly from my interaction with those colleagues. Vassilis Lambropoulos has patiently discussed many theoretical issues with me and offered guidance. Artemis Leontis has presented fresh approaches to matters I had considered complete. Eva Konstantellou probed, questioned, and supported me at times of self-questioning, elation, and despair. Charles Stewart read the first text, asked questions that I did not want to answer, and supplied me with valuable bibliographic references. Julie Hunter, almost Socratically, pointed out issues that needed to be addressed further. Steve Frangos, the brother I never had, has never ceased to be as close as a phone call whenever I needed him, be it for the procurement of obscure references, for moral and emotional support, or for direly needed bibliographic material.

A number of people outside the field of modern Greek studies were kind enough to look at this text, or portions of it, and offer invaluable advice. Aristeidis Baltas, Ruth Behar, Eduardo Cadava, Eugenia Georges, Edward Mitchell, Robert Reed, Miles Richardson, and Edith Turner have all contributed to the making of this book. I have gained tremendously from their wisdom, and I feel lucky to have met them in my intellectual wanderings.

To George Marcus goes my deepest appreciation for the faith he showed in my project from the beginning, and for inviting me to submit it for publication in the series when all I could show him was the first chapter of an unfinished dissertation. He has influenced my thought from the beginning of my anthropological career and as series editor allowed me to tread into uncharted territory. Rosalie Robertson, senior editor at the University of Wisconsin Press, with her patience, perseverance, and vision for the series, has made pathfinding smoother. Angela Ray's meticulous and inspired copyediting has been a gift. The readers' reports scratched deeply beneath the surface, and there was not one of their comments that I did not find helpful. This text is better for their contribution.

Framing all this, through his longtime friendship, his love, his companionship, and his intellect is Stathis Gourgouris. He is an inspiration and a stimulation. Parts of this text are largely a product of our discussions, and his presence permeates these pages, which he has corrected, questioned, challenged, and so tenderly supported. I cannot thank him enough for this, any more than I can thank him for his existence.

Chapter 1 appeared in an earlier form as "A Native Narrative," *Anthropology and Humanism* 19, no. 1 (June 1994):40–51. The section "The Subject" in chapter 4 appeared in an earlier form as "Death by Cancer: Local and Unlocal Knowledge," *Psycho-Oncology Letters* 1, no. 3 (Sept. 1990):24–28. The song "The Fucking Fifties" in chapter 3 comes from *Songs for Naughty Children* by Loukianós Kēlaēdhónēs. I thank him for going over the song and clarifying points. The poem "Hyperchómenoi," presented as an epigraph to chapter 10, was translated by its author, Hara T. Tzavella-Evjen, and I use the translation here with her kind permission.

# Directions for Reading

Experimentations are usually defamiliarizing, and this experimental ethnography shall not escape that. I have experimented with form and content, so I feel I should offer some guidelines as to how to read this.

The book is divided in three parts, the first and third growing out of the middle one, which constitutes the main narrative. In Part I we will go from a general consideration of what constitutes the anthropological subject and the anthropological object to the negotiation of this notion by anthropologists who consider themselves objects and "natives" who consider themselves subjects, and the range within which this reconsideration takes place. In the second part, as if using a camera, we will focus on this reconceptualization as it is formed on the occasion of a single death. And in Part III we will see the ways in which ritual, with its almost geocultural texture, serves as the perfect medium through which the assertion over subjecthood, objecthood, and individuality is being made. Not coming from the culture exclusively, nor existing exclusively in its space, ritual, through memory, manages to draw the individual in an almost personal relationship that allows for the negotiation of cultural and social prescriptions, urging the actors to conduct their lives by sliding through the constraints of existence. There is no conclusion in this project, only an Epimython, which should be taken literally: it is an afterthought on the mythology of life.

I always find it more illuminating if I read the notes to a chapter in the beginning, before the chapter. The idea of footnotes and endnotes appears limiting to me because it does not do justice to the importance of the noting text. I do, however, recognize the difficulty of including this type of discursive exegesis in the main text (because of the difference in style), but I also acknowledge the need for further explication. Therefore, at the end of each segment, I present short texts as additions that are meant to complete, expand, and augment the main discussion, as well as to offer advance notice of future problematics.

In earnest Greco-Western spirit, I have opted to call these additions *parerga*, a term in the tradition that encompasses the historical and discursive development of social, philosophical, and critical thought since the Enlightenment, which acts upon the entire discipline of anthropology, from its methodology to its epistemology.

*Parergon* means a work alongside another, main work. The initial appearance of the term occurred in *Philotheou Parerga,* written by the voivode of Wallachia, Nikólaos Mavrokordatos, probably between 1716 and 1718. The manuscript was submitted for registration to the librarian to the king of France, Abbé Bignon, by the royal ambassador of France in Constantinople, the Marquis de Bonnac, in July 1719. The text, which was conceived as an addition to the previous work of Nikólaos and as a guide of conduct for his son, was a first attempt in Greek at the authorship of a novel, in the form of a treatise on optimal behavior by the subjects of a state in relationship to their ruler. The endeavor falls in line with the project of enlightened despotism, which sought to create a paternal relationship between the hegemon and his subjects under a cloak of symbiosis and cooperation. It also addresses the responsibilities that rulers have toward their subjects and the ethical dilemmas they face in exercising their authority. Along with the writings of his father, Alexandros Mavrokordatos, Nikólaos' oeuvre constitutes the canon of the Phanariot society (that is, the portion of Greek-speaking, Eastern Orthodox Ottoman subjects who managed to elevate themselves into the highest-ranking places within the empire, through their cosmopolitanism, polyglot achievements, and Western education and culture, making themselves indispensable to the government of the Christian minorities of the empire). The work was finally published in Vienna in 1800.

The term in English first appeared in Ayliffe's *Parergon Juris Canonici Anglicani; or, A Commentary by Way of Supplement to the Canons and Constitutions of the Church of England* (1726). The title makes perfectly clear that both the word and the idea of parergon appeared at the moment of transition from a religious to a secular discourse, which characterizes the age of the Enlightenment. It is not accidental that, although this work concerns questions of canonicity and constitutionality in the Church, it does so within a resolutely legal framework.

The most illustrious treatment of the parergon came with Immanuel Kant, first in his *Critique of Practical Reason,* published in 1788, and then in a very long note in his second edition of *Religion within the Limits of*

*Reason Alone* (1794). In his *Critique* Kant develops the idea of the parergon along the lines of adornment, embellishment, and ornamentation
(*Zierathen*) of the work. The parergon, then, is that which is an adjunct,
not an intrinsic constituent in the representation of the object. Still, as
Jacques Derrida points out (1987:53), even as an adjunct, the parergon
manages to augment the delight of taste. For Kant the frames of pictures
or the drapery on a statue could be parerga. Thus part of the object but not
a member of it, the parergon is neither outside nor inside the *ergon*, the
work. Thus situated, the parergon falls into that analytical space so much
favored by us anthropologists, the space of liminality.

In the second edition of his *Religion*, Kant makes the idea of the parergon even more attractive for future anthropologists. The relevant note is
appended to a "General Remark" that closes the second part. Each part
comprises a parergon that concerns a parergon. There are four "General
Remarks," which Kant describes as being "in some measure *parerga* on
religion; they are not integral parts of it but they verge on it [*aber strossen
doch an sie an:* they touch it, push it, press it, press against it . . . ]" (in
Derrida 1987:53). In this passage, through a seemingly infinite segmentation of the commentary, Kant connects the idea of the parergon with the
idea of reflective faith, and it is this particular reflectivity that will concern
us here, in the present endeavor.

Almost a half century after Kant's death, the idea of parerga was explored again, this time by Arthur Schopenhauer. The author states explicitly that the writings in his *Parerga and Paralipomena* (1851) are subsidiary
to his more systematic works and that they have been brought together
because they cannot find a place in those works. The *Parerga and Paralipomena* deals primarily with philosophical issues that seek to position the
subject vis-à-vis death, the subject's existence, and the legal system.

Not intending to belabor the point, I should also draw attention to the
fact that inherent in the idea of the parergon is the logic of the supplement.
Derrida should be credited for developing this idea by connecting anthropology and the logic of the supplement in the work of Claude Lévi-Strauss.
He approaches *Tristes tropiques* from within the operative framework of
Lévi-Strauss, who seeks to place his work on a direct line of descent from
Jean-Jacques Rousseau. Thus *Tristes tropiques* is viewed as "at the same
time *The Confessions* and a sort of supplement to the *Supplément au voy-
age de Bougainville*" (Derrida 1976:107). Derrida continues his reflections
on the supplement by pointing out that the supplement inevitably makes
its presence both apparent and necessary by emphasizing its absence from
the main structure. The supplement replaces and intervenes (*tient-lieu*);

its presence is as dangerous to the structure as its absence is (see Derrida 1976:141–64, 269–316).

In step with this spirit, I acknowledge a bias of mine toward the Greek derivation of terms rather than the Latin, not for nation(al)istic reasons—that would be too easy and not a terribly sagacious explanation—but because I honor the beginnings of our discipline, which sprang out of the nineteenth-century philhellenic philological tradition.

The main narrative (Part II) is preceded by a list of characters with altered names, not to obscure their identities to you, the readers, but to protect our identities (mine and theirs as actors) from ourselves. Likewise, I do not refer to them by their relative kinship terms, for two reasons. First, I have a lot of aunts and uncles, and after a while identification becomes difficult. Second, these people have lives and relationships beyond my kinship ties to them. They have social personae by which they have simultaneous multiple social identities; in referring to them only by their relative kinship terms, I would be assuming the central role in their lives, and that is neither true nor correct. What is correct, however, is that some people are related only through me. Those relationships will become apparent in the narrative.

In my precarious position as an ethnographer-interlocutor, I often found myself torn between my ethnographic analysis of a situation and my simultaneous acting in it; the result is a new position, that of the communicative agent between the two. I found it essential to establish dialogues with myself in my attempt to breach the space between experience and analysis. This led me to assume an added identity. It is not important which of the characters is me, because when I speak under another name I have assumed my identity as an actor, a position which is inevitably informed by my ethnographic training. What I add in those passages is, to misquote Clifford Geertz, my own piece of "traditional knowledge." In this way I avoid the chasm between the analytical "we" and the analyzed "they," but at any given moment I can be "we" and I can be "they." Throughout the text I will give you the appropriate clues to let you know who is counted among whom.

xxii

# Note on Transliteration

I have looked at many attempts to create a systematic approach to transliteration, and the one I find most agreeable (with minor adjustments) is the one used by Robert Fitzgerald in his translation of the *Odyssey*, which keeps most of the complexities of Greek orthography. Furthermore, through that system of transliteration, the affinities between certain Greek words and words in the Romance languages become more apparent. I find this method to be reader-friendly. In this book I retain most of the Greek diphthongs and two-lettered vowels, as well as the double consonants, and I make an effort to indicate long and short vowels. I have also opted to use accent marks, which indicate the stress in a word. The only instance in which I have not used accent marks is when a two-lettered vowel is used (such as in *eipe*); in these cases it should be assumed that the accent falls on the second vowel of the cluster. I use accent marks on all proper names, except for those which already have an established spelling in European languages. Pronunciation of vowels in transliterated words follows this scheme:

e *or* é = (short *e*) as in *E*dgar  
ê = (long *e*) as in *i*nto, accented  
ē = (long *e*) as in *i*nto, not accented  
o = (short *o*) as in Orêstēs, not accented  
ó = (short *o*) as in *O*tto, accented  
ô = (long *o*) as in *au*to, accented  
ō = (long *o*) as in *au*tomaton, not accented  
i = (short *i*), as in *i*n  
y i = (soft and long *g*), as in the Spanish *fuego*

Double consonants have the same value in pronunciation as single ones.

# Note on Photographs

There is a conspicuous absence of funeral photographs in this text which needs to be addressed. Until the middle of the century funeral photographs were very common, and usually they were the only ones taken of people, along with their wedding pictures. Since the civil war of 1944–1949, however, funeral photographs ceased to be taken partly because of fear of identification of the dead by the government forces. Eventually funeral photography fell into disuse, reserved only for notables, and then involving only the photographing of the casket and the funeral, not of the dead person.

# Fragments of Death,
# Fables of Identity

# 1

# Promythion

## OBJECT AND SUBJECT

### *Ethnographic Opportunism (Mine)*

Kai psychê
ei méllei gnôsesthai autên
eis psychên
autê vleptéon

ton xéno kai ton exthró ton eidhame ston kathréftē

And psyche
if she is to know herself
she ought to look
into psyche

the stranger and the enemy we saw them in the mirror
—George Seferis, "Argonauts"

On 28 August 1986, Léngō, Myrtô's sister, had been on her way to visit her dying grandfather, but stuck in Athens traffic, she did not get to his apartment until shortly after he had died. The undertaker, however, was there and had already displayed the cover of the coffin at the entrance of the building, to inform the neighbors that a death had occurred. Léngō, even before she came into the apartment, immediately guessed that the cover of the coffin signaled her grandfather's death and nobody else's. At the entrance she met the undertaker, who offered her his condolences. She came upstairs drenched in tears and shaking. "I had been expecting it, Neni, all

3

this time," Léngō said as I held her "But I didn't want to find out about it in such a way—seeing that crow downstairs! And the coffin cover! He didn't say anything, but he had that smile on his face, that peevish goatlegged man [*o katsikopódharos*]."

Moving along in anthropological time, later that evening, when I was alone, a thousand thoughts raced through my mind. I pondered Léngō's complaint about having learned something so intimate, so painful, so private as her grandfather's death through agents, the first as inanimate as the medium that would contain the dead body (the coffin cover), the second as detached and distant as the professional who mediated between the containment and the interment, on one hand, and her emotional universe, on the other (the undertaker).

The understanding of things pertaining to death, in Athens, revolves around one main issue, that of the immediacy of the dead to the survivors, which should guarantee the immediacy of the transference of knowledge pertaining to the dead person, excluding intermediaries, agents of information, and representatives of the commercialization of death rituals. Léngō wanted—indeed, she understood it as her right and privilege as a granddaughter—to learn about her grandfather's death through a member of the immediate family, preferably through a beloved member of the immediate family. She certainly did not want to learn it through the undertaker, whom, as she said later during the funeral, she considered a parasite, someone "making money through other people's pain." Hence she cried in her sister's embrace, constructing the intimacy and immediacy of which she had been deprived.

The truth of the matter is that the undertaker did make a cultural blunder. He should have first ascertained that all family members had been notified of the death before he displayed the coffin cover at the entrance to the building. In his eagerness to please Léngō's mother, who had been a longtime patron of the funeral parlor and a friend of the proprietor's father, the undertaker arrived at the house within minutes after he had been summoned. He chanced upon Léngō as she was coming in and he was placing on the outside wall the death announcement. He even offered his condolences to her. All of his actions were proper; only his timing was wrong. Had he waited until all had been notified, his actions would have been correct. He would have acted as the intermediary between the family and the outside world. In fact, however, he became an intermediary between the family members who knew and Léngō, who did not. Her lack of knowledge was registered (to her) as an exclusion from the totality of the

4

family. And it only happened because she lived farther away than anyone else, because traffic was too heavy.

What struck me most, at the time, were the resemblances of the concepts associated with this situation to anthropology and anthropologists, to ethnographers and also their implication for ethnography. I thought of all the discussions I had read pertaining to the issues of agency, containment, interpretation, rituals, and cultural constructs. I was in the thick of my fieldwork, midway through it. I rushed to my old diaries. In the one from 1974 I found an entry containing a biting criticism of representation. My grandmother Evangelia Panourgiá had told me a story about an event that had happened during the 1921 Greek expedition against Turkey in Asia Minor. "One day," she said, "during the war, Eléni [one of her closest friends] and I decided to go to the movies. Your grandfather and Eléni's husband were both in the army, in the same regiment, at Eskişehir. So we thought we'd go to the movies to spend our afternoon. We got into the theater, and the newsreel started showing before the film itself. Then as we were watching footage from the war, they showed a sequence from a battle between the Greek infantry and the Turkish cavalry. And there, in the middle of it, appeared Eléni's husband, on foot, being killed by a Turk on his horse. The Turk was on his horse, and he raised his sword and with a swoop brought it down on Eléni's husband. Almost split him in half. She had no idea her husband had died. That's how she found out."

If one should not learn about the death of a loved one through the professional who will dispose of the beloved body, one should certainly not have to learn about such a death through the media, in the public space, through a piece of transparent celluloid. Sometimes, though, as in the moment of war, the image travels much faster than the printed word and is addressed to the anonymous masses of media viewers. The distance between the beloved body and the receiver of the news becomes thus impossible to cross, exposed as it is to public viewing, when it is understood that the opposite should happen: the distance between the announcement, the announcer, and the object of the news should be equal to that between the object and the subject of the news.[1] In other words, the closer the relationship with the dead, the more intimate and private the announcement should be, so that the horror of death, of existence, will not become a matter of public (hence casual) exchange and will not obliterate the intimacy and immediacy of private and personal knowledge. The reification and objectification of the image (the dead body memorialized in the media, in the script, on the celluloid) strip the moment of anything that is human, creating an object for observation which is hardly understood as also an object of intimacy.

This representation is not far removed from the anthropologist's "body of knowledge," where cultural structures and systems of thought are usually understood as a *res,* an object to be represented, explained, dismantled, stripped to its structural skeleton, its bare bones, so to speak, a body that will expose its inner mechanisms.

"So, how is it for you?" I used to be asked while a first-year graduate student of anthropology. "How do you find accounts of Greece or what the Greeks are like? Do you find them objective?" Objective? I find them interesting and sometimes accurate, many seem funny, and just as many are hurtful. I usually feel uncomfortable when my identity is made into an object and when I experience the collectivization of the representation ("Greeks do this" or "Greeks are that"). But objectivity has not been among my concerns. It seems, however, that objectivity has been the standing theme in the framing of anthropological praxis and theory.

Ethnographic writing is usually marked by a familiar and familiarizing introduction which acts as the visualizing agent for what is to follow, a visualization of the physical environs as seen through the eyes of the ethnographer. It is sometimes exotic, sometimes other, sometimes modern, depending on the ethnographer's ideological, theoretical, and political stance on the issue (see Friedman 1987; Faubion 1993; Marcus 1982; Rabinow 1982; Fabian 1983; and Sontag 1969). It is an attempt at—and often the successful attainment of—a description, a representation, a hermeneusis, an interpretation, of a culture. Sometimes it is self-reflexively, in Stephen Tyler's words, an "evocation . . . transcendent . . . neither by theory nor practice, nor by their synthesis," as it "describes no knowledge and produces no action. It transcends instead by evoking what cannot be known discursively or performed perfectly, though all know it as if discursively and perform it as if perfectly" (1987:199).

This ethnographic opening, sometimes descriptive, sometimes discursive, sometimes textualized, is always contextualized and usually followed by a recounting of the researcher's feelings about having finally arrived at the place he or she will call home for the next twelve to eighteen months, a place which still resonates and reminds the scholar only too painfully of the long hours spent at a library or in a classroom preparing for this, of the arduous experience of writing grants, of the endless hours spent in efforts to secure permits, to obtain official stamps attesting to the desperate need for the research, to establish a linguistic aptitude. George Marcus makes it resolutely clear that regardless of ideology, politicization, theoretical position, or the topic of an ethnography, the ethnographer should "give a sense of the conditions of fieldwork, of everyday life (Malinowski's 'imponderabilia')," of some proof of actually "hav[ing] been there" through the discussion of "micro-process," of holism, and of cultural translation. Nevertheless, he concedes that "there are no standard ways—particularly now—in which an ethnographer accomplishes these tasks" (1982:168). Thus he anthropologized Paul Feyerabend's "anything goes" (1975:295) and legitimated alternate ethnographic voices, while allowing for Tyler's "polyphonic texts" (1987:203).

It is immediately apparent from such an introduction that the place—modern, other, or exotic—visited for the first time or revisited for the umpteenth time, is a foreign place, exuding the insecurities of anything new and the excitement of the unknown. The reader is immediately positioned opposite something interesting. As readers, we know from the beginning that what follows is an out-of-the-ordinary encounter for the author-writer, and we hope that this extraordinary experience will be transmitted and transcended, that we will partake in a minute and exoteric way of this otherness. We will be enriched.

How does one, then, introduce this reversal of ethnographic situations, of fieldwork at home, where the positions of the analyst ethnographer and the interlocutor are occupied by "the savage 'I' "? (de Certeau 1985a:67). This is not a generalized idea of home, not a generic place situated (spatially, symbolically, and temporally) somewhere in one's generic culture, as Marilyn Strathern's " 'auto'-anthropology" (1987:16) or Kirsten Hastrup's "fieldwork among friends" (1987:94) have established.[2] It is not even, solely, Victor Turner's sense of home as the "tradition of the Western European culture" (1992:35). Rather, it is a specific home, the ethnographer's home, an actual rather than a classificatory family, in the midst of one's longtime friends. The implications and the ramifications of such fieldwork are endless and, I would argue, as frightening and painful as "allo"-anthropology. One does not need to learn the language, does not need to obtain visas and permits, does not need an invitation to conduct one's research, as Martin Yang put it eloquently and tactfully in 1945. But one should demonstrate to everyone involved (professors, committees, actors, family) that one's research project is an important one, is not frivolous, is not the excuse for an extended visitation of home. The stakes are high.

First, the problems are of the most immediate, practical nature: institutional funding is extremely limited for this type of research, as Anthony Jackson reminds us (1987:8). To an extent this is justifiable, since the "natives," us, the "auto-anthropologists," can work through our own systems with some degree of privileged knowledge and procure funds that might be totally unavailable to "strangers"; our families, friends, and acquaintances constitute but a few, significant examples of this. Second, one must deal with the issue of justification of the research, especially in the eyes of one's family (parents, in particular), who may have vocal reservations about a young, healthy, capable, well-educated individual such as their daughter or son sitting around for a year, sometimes taking notes, sometimes tape-recording, researching issues which often puzzle them or appear to be of no importance or epiphenomenal of their culture.[3] Third, one is faced with the inevitable trepidation of winning or losing one's family or friends. If all goes well and the research outcome is to the satisfaction of family and friends, the ensuing result is a stronger, tighter relationship. But what if all does not go well and the outcome is not very pleasing to the "subjects"? There is not a chance here of the luxury anthropologists often accord themselves of not allowing a translation of their work into the subjects' language, or of never returning to the field. The results will be known, the ethnographers will return to their "field," someone's feelings will be hurt, someone else will be offended, certain relationships will be irreparably severed.

Those and other thoughts, fears, and trepidations, as well as feelings of exhilaration, overwhelmed me when I arrived at the Athens airport for the first year of my fieldwork. At that time I expected to study the social and political ramifications of a marginal urban musical genre, the *rembétika*, a cultural manifestation which was as foreign to my cultural and political praxis as it would have been for any non-Greek researcher. After the first few months at it, it became clear to me that I was not doing fieldwork "at home," as I had started out to do, but was studying the Other at my home. That had not been my intention.

There is nothing wrong with the idea of the Other, at least on the surface. Intrinsically, it seems that the Other has replaced the "exotic" as an analytical and classificatory device, but this is the present modus operandi of anthropology, and in our search for a replacement of both classifications we would have to redefine the discipline. My concern here is not with a replacement of the Other or with a redefinition of anthropology, but rather with the other view of anthropology, that which is behind the reflexive mirror. I, the anthropologist, the subject, and I, the "native," the object, am exploring and presenting the view that exists before and beyond my two *I*s. I, the native, am looking at the anthropologist that I am, looking back at the native, with the gaze that is part of the collective gaze of my subject (which is my cosmos).

This reflects an interest prompted by Sartre's interrogation of the new anthropology, where "the questioner, the question, and the questioned are one" (1963:177) and where, as answered by Foucault's project, the body of the scholar is the summation of the social, political, and ideological conditions that engulf it. It is the moment when the personal and the private become political and public, thus interrogating the constructed separation of the two. It is also the moment when this body becomes the nodal point of interchangeable social personae, of the acquisition of multiple identities, and the viewing of the world, of one's experience of life, through a stereoscopic vision. Hence, the issue is not whether an inside anthropologist will present something ethnographically "better" or "truer" than a noninsider, but rather whether some different light, just as bright and illuminating, can shine on the culture at hand.[4] The challenge is great. It is the ultimate in self-reflexivity, but the line between self-reflexivity and self-absorption is thin. Once this line is crossed, the praxis becomes omphaloscopic (navel-gazing in anthropological argot, from *omphalos*), and Stanley Tambiah has already warned us that "there is a danger we will do too much of this navel watching" (in Wilford 1990). Even this interior vantage point is not freed of the conventions of otherness; it is not, a priori, a statement of sameness between the researcher and the researched, but it becomes, a fortiori, an individual (yet not necessarily personal) mark of identity.

The ethnographer still does not know whether or not "the entrance to another existence" and the appropriation of the "other side" of evocation will really constitute and legitimate claims to "interiority," which often remain outside the field even of this privileged perspective (see Irigaray 1985). Undoubtedly, the greatest fear in taking this position is that one might become the personification of hubris to one's discourse.

Here we embark on a search for the self as the subject and the object, although, as Gilbert Durand has pointed out, "when we make ourselves the object of our own subjectivity" not only do we become "paradoxical" but we are also obliged to realize that these distinctions are fictitious, "since subject and object both participate in the same action, the verb that unites them" ([1969] 1973:236). Hence, we look for the self in the self through its delineation of the Other, a venture which inevitably leads us to the Other in the familiar and the self. There are many new configurations in this recent search for the new subject, the nonmystified, nonreified new self. The results show in new, reflexive, sensitive ethnographies and theoretical texts,

9

which question not only the outcome of ethnographic research and authorship but also the techniques and methodology of anthropological inquiry. Furthermore, Marcus points out, these new ethnographies attempt to explain life in other cultures through the dismantling of the group experience and its reassemblance as personal experience viewed within the context of "shared ideas and assumptions" (1991b:10).[5]

The search for the new subject also shows in the "anthropology at home" project, which admittedly is better equipped theoretically and espouses a more liberal and less hegemonic ideology than the "native" anthropology trend of the 1970s (I use the notion of hegemony as developed by Gramsci). The latter research was undertaken in India, Africa, and Brazil by native—that is, dominant culture—anthropologists who researched minority groups in their own countries. It was, however, an endeavor which placed the native anthropologist in the position of the tool, of the intermediary (between the native culture and the epistemological center of its analysis) who would produce information on those aspects of the culture that were inaccessible to foreign researchers, not necessarily viewed as a professional but rather as a trained insider (see Jones 1970). It is precisely this logic that prompted one of my teachers in graduate school to tell me that I would never be able to produce anything theoretically sound, since "it is known that Greeks don't possess abstract thought."

Even the "anthropology at home" methodology, however, takes the uniformity of a culture for granted, in its general premises, just as it takes for granted that native anthropologists have a priori knowledge of their culture. It remains uncritical of its own "orientalizing" processes.[6] Furthermore, this position does not acknowledge the possibility that interiority does not necessarily follow inclusion. One can be included in some ways in a group without being accorded the privileged interiority that will give one a different perspective. Therefore, even a native anthropologist might not have access to inside information if the anthropologist is not included fully in the group, whichever the group might be. And as David Hayano has pointed out, there is no easy way to determine precisely how one as an anthropologist identifies oneself or the groups to which one belongs (1979:100; see also Limón 1991:116).

Families and family alliances are not free of these restrictive relationships either. Although one might be a member of a family—a daughter, let us assume for the sake of this argument—one will not, a priori, be included in all aspects and intimate relationships of that family, whereas a nonfamily member who has been accorded inclusiveness might. Or in Yang's terms, "being born and brought up among the people does not automatically qualify a person as an interpreter" (1972:72). In other words, simply by being of the country/culture/group/family, one is not automatically guaranteed infinite and interminable self-knowledge, except when one is consciously and deliberately counted as "one of ours," the Greek *dhikós* (an extremely problematic term, and not only because of its untranslatability).[7]

When Strathern was at Cambridge, she conducted "auto" research in Elmdon, a village in Essex. Although one could argue that she might find the environs, the social and cultural praxis, and the language of Elmdon as familiar to her as those in Cambridge, one could hardly accept that Strathern was "at home" in Elmdon as she would have been at Cambridge. Her work was not an "auto-anthropology" (her term), an anthropological inquiry and exploration into her cultural/political/ideological self, as the *auto* part of the term implies; it was as much an *allo-*, a *hetero-*anthropology as my research on the *rembétika* would have been.[8] Therefore, the epistemological and theoretical limitations she acknowledges as being associated with auto-anthropology actually belong to the established, traditional ethnographic hetero-experience. The limitations and trepidations of true auto-anthropology are situated elsewhere. Strathern's primary objection to "auto"-anthropology, however, is that "the indigenous anthropologist . . . is not contributing to *self-knowledge* in any straightforward sense. He/she is not in a position to *reauthor* events, and thus set his/her version alongside other *proprietary* narratives; nor is he/she as a writer utilizing the conceptual resources of *that society* as the foundation of description" (1987:29; my emphasis).

Here we see that there is one legitimate knowledge, one accepted truth, one method of obtaining gnosis which awaits to be unlocked, revealed, interpreted, stripped of the native's contrivances, that of the heteroanthropologist. We have the subscription to one absolute truth, which is invisible to the native eye and is rendered epiphanous only through the intervention, the marking of it, by the foreign anthropologist. We also have the allusion to the incompatibility of the subject's way of knowing with that of the scientist, and that objectivity belongs to the domain of the outsider, not the insider (see Tedlock 1991). In this scheme, there is hardly a place for Geertz's "relative contexts" of knowledge (1983:66). Knowledge here is unrelative; it only exists on the level of the native, which is a level that cannot be transcended by the anthropologist, that cannot be shared, and is therefore noncommutative. This knowledge becomes static and unidimensional, a body to be observed, analyzed, described, and accounted for. One cannot but wonder, however, about the reality of these limitations.

Strathern's concern is with the ability of the anthropologist to take up

11

a position in a culture in an objective enough way as to be able to uncover the contrivances of the culture, to see that which is hidden, and "to produce knowledge of anthropologists as contrivers: first, as participating in a social life which rests on contrivance; and second, as active contrivers in constructing knowledge about that social life" (1987:29). From this perspective all anthropologists are not only viewed as accomplices of a cultural scheme to mislead each other, but they are stripped of their right to share their "conceptual resources" with those of "that culture" as members of "that culture." Strathern looks for "objective" accounts in ethnographic writing and questions the abilities of "auto"-anthropologists to produce such results—a legitimate concern, if one entertains the idea of objectivism.

In its search for scientific legitimacy, anthropology became entangled in the scientistic search for a *res,* an "object," and for an "objective" methodology. It is a great wonder that anthropologists who have written some of the most sensitive, de-objectifying, and multivocal works in the discipline (*Tristes tropiques,* for example) have also written some of the most objectifying, dissecting, and detached accounts (*The Elementary Structures of Kinship*). In light of Durand's "paradoxical" relationship of subject to object, it seems that it is only correct for us to try to uncover the Other, the "object" outside of ourselves. All in all, human existence and praxis are intrinsically transitive, in the grammatical sense of the word. We need objects that will be the recipients of our actions. But they also are our mirrors, and "like all mirrors, these reflections are not always accurate" (Myerhoff 1978:32). When we look at a mirror, our reflection becomes our inverted and posed object (until the mirror cracks or breaks, when we see a multiplicity of our reflection, fragments of our identity).

We face, then, a possible objectivity, a neo-objectivity, one that is legitimated by modernity, an objectivity which views the concept of otherness as a frivolous, elitist, and truistic construction (Friedman 1987:163–65). It is the objectivity that the Moroccan novelist and psychiatrist Ben Jelloun is so strongly fighting against; it is the attempt to "create an objective self—stripped of its subjectivity, its needs quantifiable and known: the dream of modernity" (Rabinow 1982:181). However, as George Lakoff and Mark Johnson (1980) have argued, the conceptual opposite of objectivity should not necessarily be subjectivity, since binary thought is not the inevitable predicament of humanity.[9] Furthermore, they argue that the binary opposition of objectivism versus subjectivism should only be viewed as an inside argument of objectivists and subjectivists, since the two intellectual and ideological traditions came into existence with the almost exclusive purpose of refuting each other. The rest of us can think in metaphors.

12

Whether as a subject, as an object, or as the inescapable metaphor (human existence) that binds both together, humanity deserves the right and the privilege to be communicated, perhaps translated (sometimes even interpreted), from every possible angle, that of the "native" included, so that we will finally attain the ever-elusive heteroglossic and polyphonic texts we desire.[10] Finally, the only position that perhaps can be maintained is the activity of the action entailed in the sub-*ject* and the ob-*ject,* in the fluidity of its transposable existence.

Let me now return to narrative time and give one last illustration of this fluidity, which will also take us back to where we started (my grandfather's death) and which will reveal my two *I*s.

An hour or so before my encounter with my sister, Léngō, on 28 August 1986, in Athens:

My grandfather would die any minute now. My mother, Dêmētra, had summoned Nikólas, the family doctor. They came into my grandfather's room, where Myrtô and I had been sitting all day. Dêmētra tried to feed some milk to him. He mechanically swallowed it. Myrtô became impatient and chased her and the doctor out of the room. They came back after a while. Still nothing. They left again. Myrtô moved over to his bed and started caressing his hand. "Pappou," she said, "Pappou, do you hear me? Do something, Pappoulê." He took four deep breaths, turned his eyes, and died. It was almost four o'clock in the afternoon. I stood there looking at this person who in a split second was transformed from alive to dead, from a personality to a corpse, from a name to a body, this person whom I had dearly loved all my life, who had marked me as a person, who had placed me in a separate category from the rest of his grandchildren. I stood there, stunned, unable to move, to do anything, even to cry, even to close his eyes. Then I remembered Nikólas, the doctor, waiting with Dêmētra in her apartment next door. I had to summon him. He had to prepare the death certificate. I wanted Myrtô with me, but we didn't want to leave Grandfather totally alone—as if it really mattered. We went for the doctor together. Nikólas came in alone, soon followed by Dêmētra, and checked for vital signs. Then he asked me to do the same, which I did. It was a strange feeling, feeling for a pulse in a warm body that had none. The incongruity of it startled me. Nikólas confirmed the death. He looked at me and said, "You are very composed." I could not say anything. I could not explain to him at the moment that had I not assumed this anthropologically informed "composure" I would have broken down with grief, anger, and despair, something which, inevitably, happened later.[11] Of course to this day Dêmētra, my mother, questions the truth and objectivity of my account, insisting that she and the doctor were also present when my grandfather died, that the rest is a figment of my disturbed imagination.

Here I am, *I,* Neni, the anthropologist, putting my assumed anthropological self forth in my attempt to break the news to my other self, my other (just as real) persona, Myrtô, the granddaughter. Here is the anthropologist, the broker of news, assuming the role of the coffin cover, the fragment of transparent celluloid, placed there, that piece of detached self, to accept the brunt of the moment.

PARERGA

1. Sudnow (1967) has presented an erudite analysis of the structure of transmission of information about the death of relatives in the United States, according to kinship distance, degree of closeness and familiarity with the deceased, the relative ages of the survivors, and the social standing of the individual. Thus, Sudnow notes, the names of accident victims are not broadcast over the media before their relatives are informed of the death, and more distant relatives are not told about a death before the members of the immediate family are informed. Conversely, in the case of well-known individuals, such as John Kennedy, the public might learn about the death much earlier than the extended family of the deceased.

In this age of late capitalism and galloping private enterprise, however, it is difficult to speak with any degree of certainty about ethical conduct and cultural expectations. Greece acquired her first privately owned broadcasting stations in the early 1990s. This means that every news item falls, inevitably, within the scope of viewers' and listeners' ratings. Among other things, this situation has produced a new conceptualization not only of what constitutes a news item (*eidēsē*) but also, more important, of the power and status that the news item bestows upon the news media. In the fall of 1994 a tragic traffic accident happened in the center of Athens which illustrates most effectively this particular point. The driver of a city bus lost control of his vehicle and ran over a number of people waiting at the stop to board it. This resulted in six dead and about two dozen injured people. The crews of the major private television channels arrived at the scene within minutes of the accident and, aided by their helicopters hovering over the area, started their special broadcasts. They showed the scene, interviewed a number of witnesses and the loiterers, and then began to speculate about the identity of the dead. One crew found three identity cards and their corresponding voting booklets, which belonged to the same family, and hastened to announce that all three individuals were dead. It so happened

14

that only one of the people (the father) was actually dead. The other two (the mother and the son) were at home watching the news when they were informed, in such a public manner, that not only was their husband and father presumed dead, but so were they. This conduct prompted a reprimand from the minister of press and information, who reminded the men and women of the news media that no announcements should be made regarding the death of any citizens before their identity has been established and their families have been notified. The answer that came from the channels was stunning: any death that becomes known becomes public and, hence, a news item, and any news item upgrades the ratings; hence it is considered absolutely ethical and within the norms of professional conduct for news channels to act in the manner they did.

2. Hastrup employs the category of "friends" not to define a group of people preexisting her fieldwork in Greenland, but rather to describe the new set of alliances that were formed during the course of her fieldwork. Although there is really no reason to doubt the intensity and sincerity (in a way, the "authenticity") of these relationships, we cannot ignore the fact that they were formed as a result of the ethnographer's presence in another culture. Such an encounter almost invariably entails hegemonic relationships. We should also take into account the ambivalent feelings that the Danish have always expressed (privately) toward their dominion over the island. Presumably all ethnographers can claim that they go away from the field site having formed some friendships, some enmities, and some relationships of indifference. This framework, however, is not the one that interests me here.

Strathern treats Sussex as home, positioning the British culture within the framework of "home" as opposed to the framework of "away" (e.g., the Colonies, the ethnographic field). In the case of a British anthropologist (i.e., a citizen of a former colonial power), this scheme is inevitably a reminder of the colonial roots of anthropology. British and other European literature of the colonial era has shown that within the discourse of the colonial powers abroad (India, Africa, the Caribbean, prerevolutionary America), even families who had lived in the colonies for generations used the designation "home" only for the locus of the metropolis (Great Britain) and not for the general topos of the colony. Certainly the authors I have in mind range from Rudyard Kipling to E. M. Forster and Joseph Conrad.

Furthermore, as Altorki (1982:168) notes, it should not be taken for granted, or even considered plausible, that "an anthropologist from country X, born and raised in a city" and with an educational level higher than that of the people among whom she conducts field research, could be classified as an indigenous anthropologist, in the strict sense of the term, when studying illiterate peasants.

I should also note that here I am addressing only Strathern's article in the Jackson 1987 collection. This discussion does not extend to, incorporate, or take into account the rest of Strathern's work, which, although impressively progressive and thorough, is not pertinent to the discussions at hand.

For succinct analyses of the intimate relationship between anthropology and colonialism, see David Scott's intricate treatment of the issue (1991, 1992). Scott makes a convincing argument that not only should the notion (and study) of specific cultural practices by anthropologists be viewed through the institutionalized discursive analysis of the Other (1991), but also that anthropology will be furthered only when its practitioners realize, problematize, and abandon the assumed distant and transparent relationship between subject and object (1992a, b). Marcus also asserts that "our discussions of the self along cross-cultural planes of 'otherness' are always and inevitably a kind of colonial discourse," since, he argues, those discussions always take place away from the context that has produced them, thus domesticating the voice of the Other to preexisting and always imposed opinions and interests (1991a:16).

3. Video recording, a relatively new technique in ethnographic documentation, is much more easily accepted in Greece since it is not associated with any specific profession, as is note taking (usually associated with the medical, legal, and financial establishments) or tape recording (the trademark of anthropologists, folklorists, and journalists).

Video recording has become an integral part in the marking of rituals and celebrations by actors themselves, as the ownership of VCRs has increased from 2 percent of the total Greek population in 1983 to 10 percent in 1986 (survey in Tsoucalas 1987:311). Thus, video recording permeated the life of Greeks in the 1980s to such an extent that the hegemonic position retained by the other two recording practices has been neutralized. For an inspired analysis of what Alexiou has termed "radiophonic orality" (the radio's intervention in folktale-telling), see Alexiou 1984–85.

4. Or as Hayano has said, "an insider's position is not necessarily an unchallengeable 'true' picture; it represents one possible perspective" (1979:102).

5. On the new ethnographies and theoretical texts, see Rabinow 1977; Marcus and Fisher 1987; Taussig 1987; Tyler 1987; Domínguez 1989; Richardson 1990; and Seremetakis 1991. See Rabinow 1982 for an anthro-

pologically centered analysis of the reified self. See also the ongoing discussions on the issue as they appear in "Notes and Queries of the Broader Implications of the Current Interest in the Study of 'The Self' for the Conduct of Cross-Cultural Research," *Anthropology and Humanism Quarterly* 16, no. 1 (March 1991):10–36.

6. *Orientalizing* here, corresponding with Said's usage, means the process employed by analysts (and applied to their subjects under analysis) whereby generalized characteristics (languages, types, mentalities) are attributed to cultures which do not, on their own, acknowledge these categories as being commonly shared. Furthermore, Said argues, these categories are underlined by "the rigidly binomial opposition of 'ours' and 'theirs,' with the former always encroaching upon the latter (even to the point of making 'theirs' exclusively a function of 'ours')" (1979:227). Therefore Strathern's willingness to adopt Elmdon as "home" for a group of students from Cambridge is doing just that, whereas we are left with serious doubts as to the willingness of the Elmdoners to subscribe to this view of the world.

7. As Thumb notes, "in modern Greek there is no special adjectival pronoun denoting possession; it is supplied by the genitive of the conjunctive pronoun placed after the noun; thus, *o patéras mou:* my father" ([1910] 1964:89). *Dhikós* (pl. *dhikoi*) on its own cannot denote possession; it needs the qualifying conjunctive pronoun to lend it possessive qualities. When used alone, *dhikós* denotes emotional proximity (as Thumb points out, "the feminine *dhikia* means 'my wife,' 'my beloved' " [90]); inclusion in a special group (as the expression *ela dhikia mou* indicates) or its complete and ironic opposite (as in the identical expression *ti léei e dhikia sou?* which indicates complete rejection from the special group); and/or the extended, bilateral, beloved kindred, as in the case of the term *dhikoloyiá* (see Seremetakis 1991:25). The terms *dhikós* or *dhikoloyiá* are not used as opposites to the "not one of ours," *xénos*. The term *xénoi* (in the plural) is also used for houseguests who are not members of the immediate, nuclear family. *Xénos* is actually the opposite of *dhikós mas* or, more accurately, *dhikoi,* as Herzfeld has pointed out in connection with his discussion about race (1980a:290) and as Danforth has discussed in regard to the distinction between "insider" and "outsider" (1989:171). In other words, the operative logic here is not one of exclusion but one of inclusion.

8. Strathern (1987) introduces the term *"auto"-anthropology* to describe research conducted by anthropologists of a Western (dominant) culture on the subalterns of that culture. It is not clear whether she would have applied the term to what Hayano (1979) called auto-ethnography or

ethno-sociology to describe the work done by (subaltern) ethnographers in their own social and cultural environment. The terms *allo-* and *hetero-anthropology* are part of my answer to the terminological (and taxonomic) quandary that results from the original proposition of these terms.

This introduction of terms seems to underline a profound bewilderment in anthropology as to which terminology best applies to "nontraditional" (read: non-Western) anthropology. Apart from the apparent epistemological need for naming—and thus for classification—what is evident here is the difficulty that anthropology faces in accepting its own alterity as an organic part of its identity. In this light, the fact that Strathern implies a shift in focus from "auto-ethnography" (which refers to the methodology) to "auto-anthropology" (which refers to the theory of the discipline) further disqualifies this type of anthropological inquiry, by presenting it not merely as methodologically invalid but also as fundamentally incompatible with the epistemological grounds of anthropology.

This point, however, should be set apart from Pratt's venturing into the terminology. Pratt proposes to call Felipe Guaman Poma de Ayala's *Nueva Corónica* an autoethnographic text, that is, a text in which people undertake to describe themselves in ways that engage in a dialogue with representations others have produced about them (1991:35). Auto-description, however, even as a reaction to a previous allo-description, cannot be taken as ethnography (in the current use of the term) when it does not operate within the intellectual and epistemological directives of the discipline, a discipline deeply rooted in the Western intellectual tradition.

The point is that if we are prepared to accept as legitimate anthropological inquiry all inquiry that has the social and cultural entity *anthropos* as its subject, there is no need for the invention of new terminology.

9. The dominant epistemological discourse (that is, objectivity sought in anthropological analysis) is such that even researchers who have succeeded in freeing their approaches of other discursive and theoretical conventions, and have placed themselves in the dual position of subject and object, still concern themselves with the issue of objectivity. Yang (1945, 1972) and Seremetakis (1991), almost fifty years apart in their writings, seek to convince their readers that their research is truly objective. In this book I take a clear stance toward intersubjectivity (in the terms that Tedlock framed it in 1991).

Domínguez is right on the mark when she addresses the ambivalence that usually informs people's position toward subjectivity, especially when subjectivity is taken—in nonspecialized discussions, she says—to be "a question of point of view," which removes the question from the parameters of its epistemological validity. Thus, Domínguez explains, subjectivity is taken as "individuated though not necessarily so, referring to opinion and perspective though rooted in experience, opposed (usually) to 'fact' (through the positing of objectivity as its opposite) though not necessarily invalid" (1991:13).

10. I use *heteroglossia* along the lines of Bakhtin's definition of the term. For Bakhtin (1981) heteroglossia is the condition that inevitably characterizes every utterance because of complex settings and contexts. Thus a text, any text, cannot but operate as the summation of the multiple contexts that have converged for its creation—historical, social, environmental, cultural, physiological—and which render its meaning simultaneously momentary and indefinite. As Tsitsipis notes (1993:66n), for Bakhtin context is never taken as something fixed; its signification is constantly shifting. Thus, no two accounts can ever be the same, not even accounts by the same researcher, since the contexts that are the points of reference of these accounts are always shifting and changing, never the same, never static. This reading of the notion of heteroglossia legitimates each ethnographic account and praxis (that of the Western ethnographer on a non-Western culture and all possible rearrangements and transpositions of this relationship) as they dovetail within ethnographic theory. Such a reading dispenses with their hitherto canonized mutual exclusion. Bakhtin acknowledges the fact that any systematic episteme (linguistics in his case, anthropology in ours) must actively suppress heteroglossia in order to arrive at conclusions. I, however, prefer to heed Clifford (1983) when he advocates resisting the apparent need to suppress heteroglossia and favors actively engaging in the authorship of heteroglossic ethnographies. By all accounts, it's an experiment.

For a convincing analysis of Bakhtin's dialogized heteroglossia and its applicability to anthropology and linguistics, see Tsitsipis 1993.

11. Cutileiro noted a similar composure when he wrote that "in order to be able to survive and describe the life of some of my fellow-countrymen I had, as it were, to impersonate an Oxford anthropologist" (1971:vii).

# Part I

# FRAGMENTS OF COSMOS

Ἐκεῖ ποὐ φύτρωνε φλισκούνι κι ἄγρια μέντα
κι ἔβγαζε ἡ γῆ τό πρῶτο της κυκλάμινο,
τώρα χωριάτες παζαρεύουν τά τσιμέντα
καί τά πουλιά πέφτουν νεκρά στήν ὑψικάμινο.

Κοιμήσου Περσεφόνη, στήν ἀγκαλιά τῆς γῆς,
στοῦ κόσμου τό μπαλκόνι ποτέ μήν ξαναβγεῖς.

There, where pennyroyal and wild mint
would start their germination
and earth would grow her very early cyclamen,
it's the cement now that peasants go on haggling
and birds drop dead in the iron-furnace tower.

Sleep, Persephone, in the embrace of the earth,
never again appear on the balcony of this world.
    —Nikos Gatsos, "Persephone's Nightmare"

# 2

# The Anthropologist

## GYPSIES AND ORGANZA

Let me begin in a way that has become rather standard in the study of our (human) condition: by telling you a biographical story—with which this whole endeavor is replete—that situates my position toward alterity within the context of modern Greece.

When I was a child my parents would tease me, saying that they had taken me from the Gypsies, as a way of explaining to me why I was so much darker skinned than anyone else in the family. Now it so happens that I am, admittedly, rather dark for a Greek. As a matter of fact, those who know me well are convinced that some Damascene blood must be flowing in my veins. My parents' whole joke might have very well remained on a humorous level if they had not decided to take it a step further and thus, somehow, become responsible for my anthropological proclivities.

On Sunday mornings, season in and season out, my parents would take my sister, Lea, and me for a ride in the country. In the winter we would be dressed in woolen trousers and suede jackets; in the summer, in beautiful starched white, powder blue, or pink organza, hand-embroidered by our grandmother, with stiff petticoats underneath, white socks, and white bows in our hair. Lea, with her alabaster, almost translucent skin, hazel eyes, and blond curls, looked as if she belonged in a Renaissance painting. I did not. We would take the winding coastal road from Athens to Loutraki, passing first through the ancient sacred grounds of Eleusis, now inhabited by Arvanites and engulfed by refineries, shipyards, and iron smelting furnaces. Then we would drive through Mégara. Mégara was a powerful city in ancient times, with its own currency, its own army, even its own colonies. Mégara is no longer a powerful city. Its economy is now reduced to

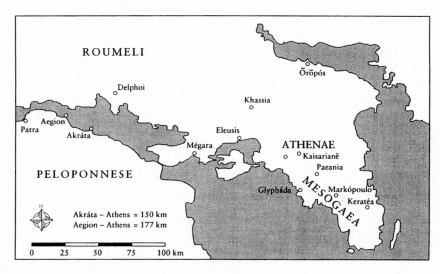

Map of Attica and Northern Peloponnese

chicken husbandry and the supply of manual laborers to the nearby cement factories, steel mills, and oil and gas refineries. In the 1960s, however, the refineries were not there, and the plain of Mégara was still the space of a single crop: olives. The olive groves of Mégara had been renowned since ancient times—they are mentioned by Pausanias—and had sustained the area financially throughout the centuries. The junta of 1967–74 cut down the groves in 1973, to the last tree, planning to build there some sort of factory.[1] They never did. The plain stands empty and barren, as if awaiting a future it cannot see.

But when I was a child the groves were still there—thick, dark, silvery, moving in the wind, beautiful. From the crest of the hill the road brought us right into the groves, surrounded by the trees. To the left the groves extended all the way to the sea, right across from the island of Salamis; to the right they reached all the way to the hills, where the chicken coops were. And there, underneath the trees, in this serene and idyllic landscape, lay my terror: the Gypsies. I saw tents and tents, and more tents, seemingly without end. Smoke came out of these tents, children ran around half naked, women in colorful skirts went about their chores, food simmered in pots out in the open, clothes dried on the tree branches, horses and donkeys milled about. And then my parents would say, jokingly, "Neni, that's your *soï*," which meant "That's *your* family."[2] They continued, "Now, if you are not a good girl, we'll give you back to them." I would look at my

24

starched organza or my woolen trousers, I would look at my sister's angelically oblivious face, and I would look at the expanse of this colorful humanity on either side of the road. I knew that there was no choice for me. No matter what my parents said, I knew I did not belong with the Gypsies.[3] But the fear was deeply rooted. (I later realized, of course, that my fear did not stem from the Gypsies, the Tsiggánoi—for whom my parents had managed to create a sense of affinity in me—but from, on the one hand, the anxiety over the possibility of separation from my family and, on the other, the realization that, even if I were given away, my sister would still remain as their daughter. In a nutshell, it was the oedipal complex confounded by sibling rivalry.)

As I grew older I heard other remarks about my skin color. One of my father's friends called me Creole. I had no clue about what the word meant, but it sounded suspiciously close to the Greek word for meat (*kréas*) and the word for mole (*kreatoeliá*). I was terrified. A few years later someone else said that I looked like Josephine Baker. At least this was a name; I could recognize that a person lurked somewhere behind it. I asked my father who she was. He told me she was a famous singer and added, "I think she's Creole." Then my father, the everlasting source of information in my life, finally explained to me, around the age of sixteen, what *Creole* meant. (The truth in this matter—what Creole is and whether Josephine Baker was really Creole or not—is, at this point, inconsequential.)

I knew all along, however, that we were Arvanites. It was something that would always come up in my mother's teasing or angry comments regarding either Lea and me or our father, along with his whole side of the family. "Arvanitika kefália" (Arvanitic brains, heads, dispositions), she would say, meaning that we were stubborn, difficult, unruly. Or that is what I knew until the summer of 1990.

## ARVANITES?

In the spring of 1990, with the opening of the Albanian borders and the demise of the Communist political and social structure there, Albanians started coming into Greece, first as political refugees and subsequently as immigrants. That summer I gave the first draft of this text to members of my family to read. One day at lunch, my father's brother turned to me and very affectionately and didactically tapped the crown of my head and asked me why I classified the family as Arvanites. I looked at my father, who looked back at me in a peculiar way, and at my mother (not an Arvanitissa), who looked at me, stunned, and shrugged her shoulders. Only the four of us were at the table, and I realized immediately that I would have to pull this snake out of its hole on my own, as the Greek expression goes.

I said that I had always known that we were Arvanites, and as I said that I realized that not only was I falling into a tautology, but the more I spoke the deeper I would be dragged into a tautological discourse, because that is inevitably the discourse of identity. One is something because one *is* something. There is no logical way around it. I continued, nevertheless, and I decided to employ my anthropological training (read: intellectual and epistemological ploys) in order to face my father and my uncle, both engineers, who were challenging not only my anthropological gnosis (as "natives") but also my own "native" identity (again as "natives"). Then my father, very annoyed, said: "I thought that you can ascribe a specific ethnicity only to people who have been members of an ethnic group for at least two hundred years. We have not been Arvanites for that long."

That is true. The way that we "became" Arvanites was through the marriage of a Hassiôtēs maiden (an Arvanitissa from an old Attikan family) to a Panourgiás (not an Arvanitēs) after the War of Independence of 1821–29. Therefore, technically speaking, my father was correct: we had not been Arvanites for more than two hundred years. I was intrigued, however, at the time frame that he had proposed as the basic parameter of one's inclusion into an ethnic group. I asked about the significance of the two centuries, and he replied that generational memory goes that far back. "If you can't trace your line into the group all the way back to that original generation of two hundred years ago, then you are not of that group."

Who are the Arvanites, then? Maybe we should answer the question with another question: What is known about them? The answer is, Very little. The best treatment of the subject comes from Era Vranousē, especially in her 1970 article about the terms *Albanians* and *Arvanites*. In her exhaustive research of the issue, Vranousē painstakingly traces the development of the uses of the two terms from their first appearance in the works of Byzantine historiographers through the uses of these works by later historical writers (nationalist and not) in Greece, Albania, and Bulgaria.

Vranousē shows that the first mention of the terms appears in the work of Michael Attaliatēs, who wrote in 1079–80 the history of the years 1034–40. In his text Attaliatēs uses the term *alvanoi* twice, and *Arvanites* once. Vranousē shows that the term *Arvanitai* used by Attaliatēs indeed refers to the Byzantines who lived in the area of Arvanon, in Illyria, whereas the term *alvanoi* (translated *albani* in the Latin text) is a term of exclusion: *alvanoi* (*albani*), she claims convincingly, is the medieval term for foreigners (1970:225–27). She traces to the term *albani* the English term *alien*

26

and the French term *aubain*. Thus, she claims, various medieval writers used the term *albani* in opposition to the term *Latini,* which indicated the native population (that is, the Byzantines).[4] In Attaliatēs' text, Vranousē says, these albani, the foreigners, were the Normans who had settled in Lombardy and who, after assisting the Byzantines in their war against the Arabs, were led by the Byzantine colonel Maniakēs to an uprising against their former allies.

*Arvanites* is the term originally used to denote those who came from the city of Arvanon (or Alvanon, according to later sources) in Illyria, called in the Byzantine era Dyrrháchion and in ancient times Epidhamnos. The term conforms to the grammatical rules of the Greek language that govern the structure of nouns and adjectives denoting place of origin. By the middle of the thirteenth century the term had been established as the signifier of the corresponding ethnic group in Illyria.[5] Vranousē attributes the use of the term *Alvanoi,* as an equivalent to the term *Arvanites,* to the antiquarian scholars of the fourteenth century who considered the use of the cluster *rv* vulgar and opted for its transformation into the more pleasing (to them) *lv,* having misread and misinterpreted the original distinction in the use of the two terms by Attaliatēs and Anna Komnena.

By the fourteenth century Orthodox Christian Arvanites had made their way into the Greek *théma* of the Byzantine Empire, which largely comprised the land that now constitutes Greece. They came first to Attika as early as 1383, when Ramón de Villanova was commissar of the duchy of Athens and Hypáttē, and in subsequent times some of them settled in the Peloponnese. They did not complete their immigration until 1579, when Sultan Murat III offered them land in Athens, thus removing them from the Peloponnese, where they had been engaging in acts of aggression against the Turks (Michael-Dede 1987:117), and transforming them into landowners in Attika. From then on Arvanites occupied the Attikan plains from the area of Mesogeia in the southeast to the northwestern areas of Phylê and Khassiá. Thus, the Arvanites were already inhabiting Athens when the city became the capital of Greece in 1834. By that time the Arvanites had intermarried with the newcomers to Athens, and they continued to intermarry even afterward, especially with people from the upper strata of the new Greek and Bavarian government. Eventually they, like the Vlachs, ceased to be counted as a separate ethnic group.[6]

All this leads us to the pestering question of identity—personal, national, individual, ethnic, especially as it has been formulated lately, as a question of epistemology. From post-structuralism to postmodernism the question has led us to the interrogation of the subject: the disciplinary subject (Who is the anthropologist, the literary critic, the philosopher?), the national subject (Who is the Greek, the Bosnian, the South African?), the cultural subject (Who is the "native," the prodigy, the object of inquiry?). All in all, who can claim culture, critical thought, logos, and discourse? Who can claim knowledge, history, tradition, and/or modernity? It is thus that the question of identity, primarily as the experience of one's relation to one's (personal/national/collective) past, has been central in the debates about Greece, native and foreign, throughout her history. From the essays of Adamantios Korais and the scholars of the Enlightenment (both Greek and European) to the minor essays of Jacob Philipp Fallmerayer and their echoes in the racist writings of the Third Reich, we Greeks have been entangled in the debate over identity even at the level of daily discourse.[7] Why deal with Greece, then? Because of her importance as the major cultural baggage of Western civilization (as the Alan Bloom camp would have us believe) or because of her importance as a minor entity? Or is there something else, something much deeper and more complex than ancient splendor versus modern obscurity?

In order for Greece to be delivered her independence from the Ottomans by the great powers of the enlightened West, Greece had to prove not only that she could become a modern nation but, somehow, that Greece, under the Oriental patina of the Ottoman subject, was always already the primal modern entity. Or alternately, Greece could have followed Ludwig von Maurer's advice, who, in 1836, said that "all the Greeks have to do in order to be what they used to be is to mimic the Germans" (in Tsiomis 1985b:144). And the Greek intellectuals understood only too well that in order for them to be considered European they first had to prove that they were as "Greek" as the rest of the Europeans. In this game—the game of their country's existence as an independent nation—what mattered was their essence proved through the circuitous identification of the past through the modern, and not the other way around. What needed to be proved, in the first place, was their modernity, and the only way of proving that was through the proof of their ancient pedigree. To an extent that was precisely what the Greeks tried to do, but in their mimicking they attempted to incorporate not only the Germans but also the French and the English, in essence the totality of the European entity.

As Gregory Jusdanis points out, this condition set in motion the apologetic process of "purposeful modernization" and carved the future "of the modernizing project in a society unprepared for it" (1991:xii). This process, Jusdanis argues, constitutes one of the earliest attempts of modernization outside the realm of what is today Western Europe. The first issue that had to be dealt with in this "modernizing project" included not only the issue of national unification but also, along the lines of the nationalist ideology that was sweeping Western Europe as the most radical and revolutionary concept, the issue of the singularly ethnic sovereign state. In other words, in order for Greece to be considered modern, Greece had to be inhabited by Greeks, whatever the term was construed to denote. Within this framework, tradition (the coexistence of ethnically diverse subjects of the Ottoman Empire) and modernity (one nation, one state) came to be understood as diametrically opposite to each other. This conceptual opposition precipitated a number of other binarisms, such as cultural introversion/ extroversion, East/West, progressive/conservative, ancient/contemporary, urban/rural, local/national. These operated not necessarily on the level of local organization of everyday life, but they became the paradigms of analysis of the modern Greek condition.

"I went to Greece a few years ago and loved it," my American guest, a classicist whom I was meeting for the first time, told me. "But I still can't understand this obsession of the Greeks with antiquity. Why do they stay glued to it, instead of accepting who they are today?" "Who are the Greeks today?" I asked. There was silence—a silence that betrayed the perpetual uneasiness that informs the intellectual's understanding of modern Greece.

What is this modern Hellene, then, and what identitary scheme does one acknowledge and subscribe to in order to claim that, indeed, one is a Hellene? Is it really as simple as the bifid identity of Héllēnas/Rōmiós? If it is, then how can we account for the notion of *Graikós,* the term that the Romans used to refer to the inhabitants of ancient Hellas and eventually to the Byzantines (whence we arrived at *Greek*), and its transformation to the autosarcasm of *Graikýlos?* If we probe a little further we will encounter more indications of the segmentary perceptions of identity, which are not by any means limited to the realm of nationality or ethnicity. Much like peeling an onion, the peeling of the multiple, unfixed, and layered notions of identity (the Foucauldian "truth") crystallizes into the daily experience of being and folds into the notion of personhood. National, ethnic, regional, sexual, religious, intellectual, and political identities are summed in the point where they create a specific and unique *personal* identity. And much like peeling an onion, as we remove more layers we approach not truth but the void, nothingness.

The many dimensions of this particular personal identity cannot be questioned and answered here. I am not even sure there are definitive answers to many of these queries. What does concern me here, however, are the ramifications of multiple identities and how their experience invades, transgresses, and translates into both quotidian life (the Greek *kathēmeri-nótēta*) and moments of crisis (*anatarachê*).

## WHY DEATH, INDEED?

There is a bullet on the wall of our living room in Athens. House lore has it that the bullet was shot from across the street, traversed the balcony, and came into the living room through the windowpane in the closed balcony door. Then it lodged on the wall at the height of a short man.

At the time the apartment belonged to an architect. Was he or any member of his family sitting nearby? Maybe he had his desk underneath the spot. Maybe he was leaning over his blueprints and floor plans, the way all of us lean over our books and writings. Maybe no one was home at the time, and the family returned later to find their space thus violated. What might have caused it? Why is it there? Since the building was built in 1955, we can securely surmise that the bullet did not belong to the Second World War, or to the ensuing civil war. As the surrounding buildings belong to the junta era, we can almost as safely assume that the bullet did not belong to the Polytechnic uprising of 1973. Is it a pre-junta stray bullet? Is it a more recent one, one that has nothing to do with the political conditions in the country, but with the human condition? A disenchanted lover? A gangster? Perhaps both suggestions are improbable, given the sociopolitical fabric of the culture, but not impossible. The particulars of the existence of the bullet are absolutely lost in concealment or in oblivion. The only thing we know is that no one died on account of it. The bullet is left in place, framed in glass on the wall. Its presence is thus underlined, to remind everyone who sees it that we are never far away from death, never safe from its existence, even though both death and we can never be present simultaneously.

It is in this way that death forces itself on us and makes itself the perfect (the total) subject of existence but also the perfect object of study. The study of death (as death alone, also) posits the issue of the subject against its own self. And the study of death offers the unique opportunity for a self-reflexive anthropology, that is, the exploration of the anthropologist's duplicitous role as both analyst and subject, and the exploration of the realm of existence where human beings (our euphemistic "subjects") become parts of the conditions of intersubjectivity that unite them with the anthropologist.

In his 1967 treatise on the social organization of dying, David Sudnow expressed a complaint about the absence of an ethnography of death —a legitimate complaint, especially when viewed within the context of the dominant anthropological discourse of the time and its prerequisite of participant observation. This particular discursive circumscription of anthropological practice and experience—which Sudnow was not allowed, within the disciplinary limits of the time, to detect—was the inhibiting factor in the construction of an ethnographic discourse on death. In other words, if participation in and observation of the praxis at hand were the determining factors for the analysis of death, then it follows that death—which one can participate in and observe only through the singular, specific, horrifyingly unique position of one's own dying—can only be described from the outside, thus making its study, de facto, an issue of epistemology rather than of phenomenology. Thus anthropology remained locked into the description of death-related behavior, rather than acknowledging the intersubjectivity that should inform any attempt to treat the subject (no pun intended). Johannes Fabian argues that since the idea of a universal culture was challenged, anthropology had no theoretical plane from which to embark on an analysis of the experience of death that would not be folkloristic or behavioristic (1973:181–83).

Times have changed, though, even in anthropology, and with this change a pronounced shift has occurred from taxonomic descriptions to theoretical queries which posit the issue of the subject against its very self. As both Ruth Behar (1991b) and Johannes Fabian (1973) have mentioned, the study of death offers an exemplary opportunity for embarking on a self-reflexive anthropology. This text, then, is not an "ethnography of death" as Sudnow would have wanted it (perhaps he might not even agree with its theorizations), partly because such an ethnography might no longer be possible. This text, rather, is an exploration of the possibilities and the legitimacy of the position of the analyst who accepts the duplicity of her role both as analyst and as "subject" in the context of an anthropological study on human death. It is further an inquiry into the conceptual irreducibility of social reality and the specific subjective participation in it. In other words, my social reality is here also my analytical reality. What I attempt to do here is, as Fabian has suggested, to engage in a metainterpretation, "a social hermeneutic, an interpretation of social reality which conceives itself as part of the processes it attempts to understand" (1971:201).

This is not an ethnography describing an *ethnos,* the very substance and notion of which has repeatedly been questioned and challenged.[8] Rather, it is an exploration of the *ethos* that governs death as a social praxis and its discourse within the framework of modern Athens and her multitude of identities.

31

## PARERGA

1. The cutting of the trees precipitated and provided one of the reasons for the student uprising of the Athens Polytechnic, on 14–18 November 1973, when approximately a half million people joined the students who had barricaded themselves within the grounds of the school. In the night of 16–17 November, before dawn, one of the junta's tanks positioned outside the main gate forced its way into the school, killing a number of students and maiming others when it rolled over them. The polytechnic uprising, although followed immediately by a change in the junta leadership that produced a much more cruel and restrictive state than the one it replaced, was eventually largely responsible for the collapse of the junta in July 1974, since it brought forth the collapse of the facade of decency that the junta had tried to present to the outside world.

The groves of Mégara were not the only olive groves that the junta cut down. They also cut the extensive groves of the Attikan plain, northeast of Athens—as ancient as the groves in Mégara—in order to build a cluster of public service buildings, with the intent of decentralizing the state apparatus by moving it from the center of the city to its fringes. As Prevelakis (1989) astutely notes, however, gestures like this one can only be successful if the effort is comprehensive and involves the entire state apparatus. In this case, as in every other case in Greece where a coordinated effort is demanded, reality fell well short of expectations. The only public service moved to the deforested plain was the telephone company (its headquarters, to be precise), and that happened in 1984, ten years after the fall of the junta.

2. *Soï* means kindred, lineage. As Campbell notes on the Sarakatsánoi (a transhumant population in northwestern Greece), the term "applies, of course, to both maternal and paternal relations" (1964:42 n6). The usage is usually contextual. My parents meant both the patriline and the matriline.

The term also denotes quality in general, as in the expression "*Ti soï einai?*" "What soï is this?" which actually means "Is this any good?" or "Is she (or he) any good?"

3. This knowledge should retrospectively be viewed as the innocent opposition to Hayano's note that "within several years I had virtually become one of the people I wanted to study!" (1979:149). My fascination with the Athigganoi (or Tsiggánoi, as Gypsies prefer to be called in Greece), what drew me to the window of the car to look at them, was underlined by the realization of our differences as much as by my desire to decipher the points of affinity and resemblance that my family acknowledged between

me and them (the Athigganoi). Certainly the issue of my affinity with the Tsiggánoi is a never-ending point of reference in the family, falling within the context of the relationship of the wider Greek society to them. Let me elaborate.

In the summer of 1988 my sister, Lea, her (then) husband Kōstês, and I went out for dinner at a small taverna near their house in Glyfádha. We sat outside in the garden, where a small boy, about eight to ten years old, approached me and asked for a ten-drachma coin. I asked him what he would use it for, and he said he would keep it until he had enough to buy a bicycle. "At your age you don't have a bicycle?" I asked. "No," he responded. "I had one, but a Gypsy [*énas gýphtos*] stole it from me." "A Gypsy," I said. "But what are you? Are you not a Gypsy, also?" "No," he answered. "I am not Gypsy. I am Tsiggános. My father is Gypsy." I was totally perplexed, and I got into a discussion with him regarding the differences between the two, his claims to two different languages, and how his mother always acted as an interpreter between him and his father, when I realized that Lea and Kōstês were becoming uncomfortable. I got up, took the little boy for an ice cream, and gave him the hard-earned ten-drachma coin that he had asked for ("informant compensation," it was called in the olden days of anthropology). When I came back, Lea tactfully indeed, told me that as she was looking at the boy and me she was not really sure that we did not belong together. "We didn't want people to think that we are all Gypsies," she said, half jokingly, referring to Kōstês and herself.

The same summer I took Lea's eldest son, Oréstēs, swimming at my cousin Vangeliô's house in Ōrōpós, a resort in the northern parts of the Attikan Peninsula. Oréstēs was five years old at the time. Vangeliô's two daughters, Maria and Sofia, who were much older than Oréstēs, joined us, and we all went to the waterfront, where a large family of Tsiggánoi had camped. The children went into the water, playing and giggling, and I found myself surrounded by about ten children from the camp, boys and girls, ranging in age from five to thirteen. We started talking, and Oréstēs became interested and came to join us. After a while the other children left, and Oréstēs, the girls, and I continued swimming and frolicking in the water until Oréstēs started acting up. I reprimanded him (not severely, I assure you), and he turned around and, paddling as briskly as he could, headed to the shore. "Where are you going?" the girls and I yelled out to him. "I am leaving," he said. "I'm going to become a Gypsy" (Páō na ginō gýftos"). The girls and I laughed, but I had finally come full circle.

4. It must be remembered that at the time, Latin was the lingua franca of the West (west of the Byzantine Empire, that is) and Greek the lingua

franca of the East, extending into the state and ecclesiastical discourses. Furthermore, it seems that the term *Rōmaioi* was still (at least partially) used by the Byzantines as a term of self-reference. Interestingly enough, in the Latin translation of Attaliatēs' text, the term *Rōmaioi* is translated as *Graeci,* referring thus to the Byzantines.

5. After the text by Attaliatēs, we encounter the term in Anna Komnena's *Alexias* (ca. 1148), then a repetition of Attaliatēs' quote in the middle of the twelfth century, then in the *Chronikê Synopsis* of Yeôrgios Akropolitēs in the middle of the thirteenth century. Akropolitēs mentions the phrase "the nation of the Alvanites" and the city of Alvanon approximately twelve times. See Vranousē 1970 for further details.

6. See especially Kollias 1990 regarding the position of the Arvanites in the modern Greek state. See also Kaklamanis 1984 and 1986 on the role of the Arvanites in the War of Independence and their relationship with the Ottomans. It is only lately, with the claims by the Albanian prime minister Alexander Mexis that the Arvanites are Albanians, that the Arvanites have been engaged in an active discourse regarding their ethnicity. They claim that they consider themselves an integral part of Greek society and not Albanian at all.

7. The break at Fallmerayer is not arbitrary but deliberate, as he spawned in Greece a line of Greek responses from the folklorists and historians of the nineteenth century to Ion Dragoumis (appropriated by the Greek Neo-Nazis) and the historians of the twentieth century such as Diomedes-Petsalis (appropriated by the Left). The fallout of those debates is apparent in the Campbell and Sherrard (1965) essay on the duality of the modern Greek identity, to Herzfeld's (1987) much celebrated formulation of *disemia* and the ensuing plethora of writings on the issue by social scientists, literary critics, cultural critics, political scientists, and those involved in the production of literature. The issue has been treated by so many authors, and from so many angles, that even a bibliographic mention of each one of them would be prohibitively lengthy here. See, for example, Tziovas 1989 and Gourgouris in press.

8. One need only look at the usage of the term in the cases of Homer ("the nations of the dead"), the Nation of Islam, or Queer Nation, all of which employ the idea of the nation in ways that are far removed from those either of the ethnographers or of the nationalists. In these formulations the nation is conceived as an idea, much more than an entity, which transcends time and space. It becomes an abstraction that can accommodate and be appropriated by anyone who wishes to be counted among

its members and is willing to subscribe to its transcendental rules. The idea is not wasted on Greece, which, as a nation, acknowledges anyone who *is* Greek (by birth, adoption, or heritage) or *feels* Greek; on these is thus bestowed symbolic Greekness, crystallized in the issuance of a Greek passport. See also Gourgouris' formulation of a "dream nation" (in press).

# 3

# The City

"SO IF IT'S BEAUTY . . ."

*So, if it's beauty you want . . . don't come to Athens where something else might happen.*
—Kevin Andrews, *Athens*

Indeed, what could happen if you came to Athens? Or should I rather ask, what could not happen? What is it that Andrews tried to warn us against? One thing is sure not to happen: the discovery of a classical city, the unearthing of a splendid gem, untouched by time and history, the confirmation of the human need for an unbroken continuous past, the exposition of the bare roots of Europe. This is what we should not expect to find. What is usually found is attested in numerous markings by travelers, starting with Jacob Spon and George Wheler in the 1650s, proceeding with James Stuart and Nicholas Revett, sent to Greece in the 1750s by the Society of the Dilettanti, and continuing with travelers in our days.

Coming into Athens, the traveler of previous centuries usually entered from the west, from the Eleusinian plain, having followed the ancient Sacred Road (Ierá Odhós), which today is a long, dirty, dusty, smelly, treeless, industrialized entryway into Athens. Apparently in those old days, and as recently as the 1930s, the road itself was quiet and pretty, and the view of Athens at the end of the road was magnificent. Having passed the groves of the Academy of Plato, one would get the first full view of Athens, with the rock of the Acropolis in the middle of the Attikan plain, with the hill of Lycabettus on the left, against the purple mass of Hymettus (Hymēttós) flanked by Pentelicus and Parnes. The scale of this perception was not always accepted unanimously. Where some saw impressive mountains, others—such as John Addington Symonds in 1898—saw "air-empurpled" hills.

Whatever their classificatory perceptions of the surroundings were, whether they considered Hymettus and Parnes and Pentelicus as hills or mountains, large or small, all travelers seemed to agree on two issues. First they agreed on the beauty of Athens: "The specific quality of the Athenian landscape is light—not richness or sublimity, or romantic loveliness or grandeur of mountain outline, but luminous beauty, serene exposure to the airs of heaven," wrote Symonds (in Tsigakou 1981:128).[1] Athens, perceived by the travelers as a city of ancient splendor and beauty, of Attikan elegance, Byzantine austerity, and Turkish dilapidation, also drew their consent on a preference for ancient (pre-Roman and post-Geometric) over modern-day Athens (Venetian, Turkish, Greek, German). These travelers walked in the streets of the city as if drawn by the monuments, as if their vision had been impaired by the beauty of the marbles, as if little else reflected light: "The beauty of the temples I well knew from endless drawings—but the immense sweep of plain with exquisitely formed mountains down to the sea—& the manner that huge mass of rock—the Akropolis—stands above the modern town with its glittering white marble ruins against the deep blue sky is quite beyond my expectations. . . . Poor old scrubby Rome sinks into nothing by the side of such beautiful magnificence" (Lear 1848).

How Rome, with all her Renaissance splendor, could "sink into nothing" is quite a mystery, but it also indicates two things: that by the time Edward Lear took his trip in 1848 Athens was timidly challenging Rome as the ideal classical land, and that travelers were rather oblivious or indifferent to both cities in their modern states. By reading Christopher Wordsworth's account, one would believe that Athens was merely another Pompeii, devoid of inhabitants, existing only through its ruins. During approximately the same period that Beethoven was composing *The Ruins of Athens,* lamenting the occupation of the land of Socrates by the Turks, Wordsworth informed his readers that "the town of Athens is now [A.D. 1832] lying in ruins. There is but one church in which divine service is performed. A few new wooden houses, one or two of more solid structure, and the two lines of planked sheds which form the bazaar, are all the inhabited dwellings that Athens can now boast" (1855:43). Wordsworth gave this description despite the fact that by other accounts Athens was not lying in ruins in 1832. It still had approximately eighty houses standing even after the devastation of the war and a number of churches that held liturgies. In fact, 1832 was the year that Athenians who had abandoned the city in the late 1820s on account of the war started returning to their homes. Had Wordsworth lingered a little longer, he would have experienced what was the last manifestation of the almost nomadic nature of the city's inhabitants.[2] From his comments, however, it becomes obvious that he means ancient Athens rather the idea of ancient Athens, not the city itself but rather the Athens that Philip II of Macedon had called "a state of mind." Wordsworth continues his account of his experience of Athens by attributing value to this *"modern* desolation . . . [which] simplifies the pictures, and leaves us alone with Antiquity" (1855:43).

The conceptual distance that the West had placed between itself and ancient Greece, on the one hand, and ancient and modern Greece, on the other, was such that it prompted the same recorded statement by two people who lived almost concurrently in places apart, a man and a woman who were never to meet one another, a woman from England and a man from Austria-Hungary. Mrs. Russell Barrington, writing in 1912 about her visit to Athens, after having visited Hadrian's Arch and the Temple of Olympian Zeus, exclaimed in utter disbelief: "The strangeness of actually being here! To be really at last in Athens almost stuns the capacity for taking in her sights. . . . A place that was till now put so far off in the imagination" (1912:49). Sigmund Freud visited the Acropolis in 1904 with his brother, and he recounted the incident in an open letter to Romain Rolland in 1936, in a manner that is similar to Mrs. Barrington's. Wrote Freud, also in utter disbelief, "When, finally, on the afternoon after our arrival, I stood on the Acropolis and cast my eyes around upon the landscape, a surprising thought suddenly entered my mind: 'So all this really *does* exist, just as we learned in school!'" (1950:307).

In neither account is there any attempt to link the specific sight of antiquity with its corresponding sight of modernity. Mrs. Barrington saw modern Athens as a place totally divorced from its antiquities, and a very disturbing place at that. Freud was so preoccupied with the disturbance of his own perception of the Acropolis that, reading his analysis of it, one could safely assume that the good doctor had been placed on a strange planet occupied exclusively by the Acropolis or even that he had suddenly crossed the mirror and found himself in the wonderland that kept the secrets of history and the human psyche.[3]

But this is not at all insensitivity on the part of Mrs. Barrington or Freud. In travel accounts, generally speaking, rarely do we see any descriptions of the inhabitants. The accounts are primarily what Michel de Certeau has called "narratives of space" (1985a:68). When they do transgress into a text about people, they are either too flattering, exalting similarities (existent or fictitious) of modern Greeks to their ancestors, or they are so polemical (as in the case of J. C. Hobhouse) that one cannot but wonder about the accuracy of the rest of the description. Noteworthy is the case of Lord Byron, who, as Stathis Gourgouris notes, "had little use for the Ancients" (see Gourgouris in press; and Leontis in press). Byron's philhellenism was that of "modernity," looking for contemporary resurrection of ancient traces, lamenting the lost opportunities of modern Greeks and their exploitation by foreigners, an overall condition rendering them "a melancholy example of the near connection between moral degradation and natural decay" (in McGann 1986:100).

This is a point not far removed from that of Herzfeld, who notes that "like the early nineteenth-century philhellene, the present-day visitor may arrive in a haze of romantic expectations, only to be thwarted by the importunities of ordinary experience" (1982a:vii). Athens is indeed the product of the Romantic era, of the nineteenth century, the product of an ideology that sought to forge a homogeneous entity out of the heterogeneity that constituted Europe up to that point. At the core of this homogenizing process, indeed the necessary ingredient, was a common history. This common history was sought in antiquity, in particular in classical Athens.

Hence, when we talk about modern Athens we talk about nineteenth-century Athens. That was the time, after the War of Independence, when Athenians sought to place their city among the great European cities and reimagined it along the lines of the dominant European style of neoclassicism, thus reaffirming their political and civic subjecthood through the material objects that constituted the city, further forging an organic relationship between themselves and the object of their creation (see Preziosi 1990:261–62). The creation of the city forges the creation of the subject, the subject of the newfound state in this case, as they provide each other support and validity and echo each other's existence. Thus neoclassicism, the product of the Enlightenment that came to encapsulate the idea of the modern world, became in Greece the crystallization of Europeanism. In all this we need to keep in mind the fact that Athens was built between 1832 and 1890, never too far away—philosophically, politically, theoretically, aesthetically—from Europe, where decisions about artistic/political/philosophical production were being made.

Athens wanted to be a modern city, which meant a European city, along the lines of the cities that had encapsulated and materialized the Enlightenment.[4] "Athens," wrote Mrs. R. C. Bosanquet in 1914, "sees herself as the Paris of the East, 'le petit Paris' as Athenians affectionately call her" (1914:255). Indeed, Athens strove to become as splendid as Paris, embarking on an interminable, it must have seemed, endeavor of construction. Arcades made of steel and masonry housed the central markets, reaffirming Bötticher's dictate that "with regard to the artistic form of the new system, the formal principle of the Hellenic style" should be introduced (in Benjamin 1979:147; see Benjamin also 1989). And of course, the arcade is the Hellenic architectural style par excellence. It was thus that the arcade, absent from Greece for centuries, was reintroduced into Greek urban thought, not as a point of archaeolatry, but through the urbanity of Paris.

## "THE FUCKING FIFTIES"

If modern Athens is a modern European city, contemporary bourgeois Athens is a city that has as its aesthetic point of reference the American fifties and the Marshall Plan, as E. Stasinopoulos correctly points out in his monumental *History of Athens* (1973:509–12), and as Loukianós Kēlaēdhónēs, the quintessential Athenian musician of the past two generations, sings in his song entitled "The Fucking Fifties":

| | |
|---|---|
| Máska, kopána, Garrard, | *Máska,* hooky, Garrard, |
| Nat King Cole | Nat King Cole |
| mbánio sto Edem, hōristra, | swimming in Edem, parted hair, |
| rock & roll | rock & roll |
| Mambo, Hafteia, Nákē, Sineák | Mambo, Hafteia, Nakes, Sineák |
| Venus, mēchanáki, Magic City, | Venus, scooter, Magic City, |
| kai ta prôta mas koniak | and our very first cognac |
| | |
| [Refrain:] Sonnez les Matins | [Refrain:] Sonnez les Matins |
| ding-dang-dong-dang | ding-dang-dong-dang |
| sonnez les Matins | sonnez les Matins |
| ding-dang-dong | ding-dang-dong |
| | |
| EVGA, billiárda, élegchos, kavgás | EVGA, billiards, report cards, reprimands, |
| party, boukála ki autómatos souyiás | parties, bottle spin, spring knives |
| cherry, soumádha, póka, dhaneiká | cherry, soumadha, poker, borrowed money |
| grámmata hasápē, Love Me Tender, | grammata hasape, Love Me Tender, |
| kai ta prôta Aggliká | and our first English lessons |
| | |
| [Refrain] | [Refrain] |
| | |
| Roziclair, Alaska, Kotopoulē | Roziclair, Alaska, Kotopoulē |
| Okinawa, kai Kókkino Ohyró | Okinawa, and the Red Fortress |
| brilliantine kai kókkino fouró | brilliantine and a red petticoat |
| Western, Sinalco, Tsitas, Rōssikón | Western, Sinalco, Tsitas, The Russian Room |

| | |
|---|---|
| Flipper, Skoufitsa, mikré mou s' agapô | Pin-balls, Skoufitsa, my little one I love you |
| Tram, Koutsoyiánnēs, Cadillac, Chez Nous, | Tram, Koutsoyiánnēs, Cadillac, Chez Nous |
| Salem, kabartina, Fucking Fifties, kai ta prôta rendez-vous | Salem, trenchcoats, Fucking Fifties, and our very first dates |

In this small, seemingly innocuous song, Kēlaēdhónēs manages to fix all the spaces (actual and symbolic) that constituted middle-class Athens in the 1950s as a modern city, which engaged in the circular production, reproduction, and emulation of a global culture.

*Máska* was the name of a popular publication that appeared around the end of the forties and existed until the early seventies. It included translations of American action stories, with detectives, spies, stupid blonds, and vicious brunettes. *Kopána* (hooky), of course, refers to the self-granted leave of absence from school that became extremely popular among students of the last grades of high school during the fifties. It granted them the necessary time to devote themselves to their favorite vocations: playing pinball machines, swimming at the beaches of the southern suburbs, and watching American movies. Garrard was the first type of turntable that appeared in Greece after the gramophones of the war era; it could play both 78 and 45 rpm records. Nat King Cole was very popular at parties, as his music always provided the much-needed excuse for close and slow dancing.

Edem was the favorite beach. It is the closest one to Athens, and students could reach it, swim, and be back within the time normally allotted to school attendance, and it was also the traditionally chic place for Athenian families to go for a swim before the war. The first *bain-mixtes* appeared there. Hafteia is the area around the Omónoia Square and below the Acropolis, a place where people move throughout the night, as it has the highest concentration of restaurants and dairy and pastry shops in the city, is close to the train and bus stations (hence, easily accessible to out-of-town visitors), and had at that time the highest concentration of brothels. Right in the heart of Hafteia was Mambo, the famous record shop, with an extensive collection of foreign 45 rpm records. Nowadays the area is still very much alive throughout the night, with the added presence of the Albanian immigrants.

Sineák was a movie theater that played cartoons and children's films on Sunday mornings, standard entertainment for our generation. Venus was a brand of wristwatches, the first ones given to high school students. Scooters, particularly the Italian brand Garelli, rented by the children of the

My Greece—an anonymous artist's conception of Athens in the mid-1950s, from a record cover

upper classes and owned by the children of the lower classes, were the first means of private transportation widely available to high school and university students in the fifties. In the sixties Fiat started producing small cars with 600-cc engines, which eventually replaced the scooters. Some university students, however, were fortunate enough, primarily through their personal labor, to afford a "real" motorcycle.[5] Magic City, a precursor of the electronics arcade, with pre-electric pinball machines, was frequented by truants and unemployed youth.

EVGA is an acronym for the Greek Milk Industry, a private endeavor which first pasteurized milk and standardized its distribution on a large scale. Until then milk was distributed at home by various milkmen, who bought it from the shepherds on the slopes of the Attikan mountains. EVGA not only standardized the distribution of milk but also set distribution points, also called EVGA, in each neighborhood for dairy products (except cheese) and some pastries. The clerks made hot tea and milk for their customers, and later also made breakfast. These very small stores, franchised and operated by single families, were the only stores open until late at night, and at those hours they were frequented by people who stayed up playing all night. Many a dawn had found fathers and sons meeting at the EVGA of the neighborhood, the son coming from an outing (a party or the casino) and the father buying fresh milk for the family breakfast.

*Elegchos* (security check) was the term used for the random checks that the city police conducted in the streets of Athens on (young) people, especially at night. Those were years of political oppression and intense fear, the Communist Party was illegal, and the state enforced a dress code on its citizens. Long hair, miniskirts, or a profusion of red color (the symbol of the Communist Party) on a suspicious-looking young individual could constitute the grounds on which the person could receive a number of reprimands, from a simple verbal citation to being taken into custody and kept in jail overnight. *Kavgás,* the Turkish word for quarrel, became at that time (among a specific, unconventional part of the youth) a marker of youth culture. The fight was an accepted medium for asserting one's manhood, by emulating the representational aesthetic of the "American" and the cinematography of social critique (mainly the films by Ford, Houston, Godard, Fellini, and Pasolini: *Blackboard Jungle, The Wild One, On the Waterfront,* and *Breathless,* to name but a few). Fighting was facilitated by the presence of a *souyiá* (spring penknife), the new addition to the already existing arsenal of butcher knives.

This was the way that I had interpreted *élegchos* and *kavgás.* Kēlaēdhónēs was gracious enough to correct me when I showed him the manuscript. None of the political and sociocultural dimensions that I had identified had played a role. *Elegchos* was, indeed, the term for the police security check, but this particular *élegchos* refers to the term used for school report cards, the marks on which, in many a case and certainly in the case of Kēlaēdhónēs, resulted in a fight, a *kavgá,* with the parents. In essence a reprimand, the term *kavgás* in this case was certainly a euphemism of manhood, since it was an absolutely unilateral reprimand that had nothing of the bilateral engagement present in a bona fide neighborhood *kavgá* between opposing factions.

Dancing parties became popular again, after the economic and political depression of World War II and the Civil War, even more so since the 1950s was the time of rebuilding of the city after the heavy damages it had sustained. This was the opportune time, it seemed, to do away with the old single and double family homes and build apartment buildings that would give, once again, the patina of Europeanness to the city and house greater numbers of people than had been previously possible, especially in light of the great influx of people from the countryside, which had been devastated during the decade of the wars. Along with the apartment buildings came the much-coveted penthouses—two at most on each apartment building—

43

with enormous balconies that seemed to beckon to the youth for parties in the summer. A favorite game at such parties was the *boukála*, the bottle spin, where all would sit in a circle on the floor and the leader of the game would spin an empty bottle on its side. The spinner had the right and the obligation to kiss the person pointed to by the neck of the bottle when it stopped. Much of this was chaste; a lot was not. Many a time the game had already been set up, bribes had been paid to the spinner, and promises had been made in advance for the control of the bottle neck. A little tampering with fate was common.

Roziclair, Alaska, and Kotopoulē were cinemas in downtown Athens. *Okinawa* and *Red Fort* were the famous American films about the Korean War; brilliantine became popular again after its all but complete disappearance during the wars, and a red petticoat became the *petit objet a* of every fashionably minded young woman. Western films went together with Sinalco (a Greek cola); Flippers were the pinball machines played in arcades along with billiards; and the tram was still the mode of transportation in the fifties. Cadillac, Kēlaēdhónēs says, "was the dream," and that, indeed, says it all. Chez Nous was a very popular bar in the center of Athens, next to the Archaeological Museum, with a magnificent terrace where older teenagers would go for dancing, and Kēlaēdhónēs admits that he spent many a day and night of his school years there. (By a funny twist of events, Magic City is nowadays one of the best-equipped recording studios in the country, the one that Kēlaēdhónēs uses exclusively.) That was also the time when older students were allowed (not only culturally, but also financially) to have their first taste of cognac at pastry shops, vermouth being reserved for parties. Salem identifies the American cigarettes which for the first time appeared in Greece with the American military presence after the war, and trenchcoats made of gabardine were an aesthetic remnant from the war, especially dear to the young Greek men who still had fond memories of the British military men (who originally sported the coats) and liked the allusion to victory that came along with the coat.

This was, to an extent, the face of Athens in the fifties, and many of these markers remained as almost permanent fixtures of the city until recently, certainly present during the sixties and seventies, the time when my generation came of age. Along with the scene described by Kēlaēdhónēs came a whole new musical scene that appeared in Greece for the first time in the sixties. The rock music produced and replicated in Greece by young Greek rock musicians (the Olympians and the Formings, among others) included not only the sound of the British and American rock-and-roll and folk scene but also the sound of the Beat generation. Through this combi-

The cover of volume 213 of *Máska,* entitled "In the Whirlwind of Death, and Other Adventures"

nation a new musical genre—To Néo Kýma (The New Wave)—flourished in Athens. It had a decidedly political, antiwar, leftist position and restructured the sounds of the "West" with traditional Greek musical elements (the *bouzouki,* Balkan beat rhythm and melody, and the lute) in musical arrangements that produced the distinctive sound of the youth for the first time in Greece. These markers circumscribed the generation that came of age during the years of the junta, a generation with strong political, cultural, and social opinions, commitments, and determination. After the dictatorship, with the return of political normalcy, the character of Athens became much less structured, much more indeterminate and elusive, and more resistant to classification.

## CONCRETE

The aircraft approaches the airport from the southwestern side of the Attikan Peninsula. On the left is the Saronic Gulf, blue, sparkling, inviting, despite its choking plentitude of colobacteria and motor oil residue. On the right is elegant Mount Hymettus, barren but for junipers, full of ravines and caves, its crest curved and serene. In between them, in the plain, lie the self-contradictory projections of Greek identity. Right before landing, on the lefthand side, one can see the lavishly built and landscaped resorts, mansions, gardens, and tennis courts; on the righthand side one finds the immensity of the modern Greek concrete, the "forest of *polykatoikies*" (as the Greek press calls it), a conglomeration of glass, concrete, and iron that stretches as far as one can see. The airport itself is a low-ceiling concrete building that is reminiscent of the Middle East and North Africa—the resemblance with the airport at Casablanca is uncanny—rather than the European city that Athens wants to be.[6]

There is an instant immersion in noise, voices, confusion. There is no question that Kevin Andrews' observation will be put to the test here and now, and the answer will be just as immediate: "If it's beauty you want go to Rome . . . don't come to Athens where something else might happen" (1967:45). One really has no idea, no foreknowledge of what one might find. As I go through customs, the official might greet me in the polite plural, with a heartfelt and heartwarming "Welcome" that makes me wonder how it has been possible for me to have stayed away for so long; or he might not even turn and give me a glance, not a kind word, not a smile, as if I am an imposition on his existence, and at times like this I wonder why I did not stay away a little longer. But it is this sense of the unexpected, this knowledge of the unknown, the unpredictability of it all, that is the familiarizing element, the one which connects me to Athens and makes me call this place home, and this familiarity simultaneously shields me from the two common field problems, as they have been identified by Hayano: "the potentially devastating effects of environmental change and culture shock" (1979:102).

There is no room for shock on my part as far as Athens is concerned. I know Athens. Athens is a polyphonous (perhaps, even, cacophonous) city, the 170-year-old capital city of Greece, with 3.6 million people. It is a city that is noisy, dusty, replete with buildings made of cheap concrete that shoot to the skies shadowing the streets of the inner city, black with exhaust fallout and marked by the running of rainwater. Buses, taxi cabs, cars, pickup trucks, motorcycles of every shape and horsepower, pedestrians, three wheelers, and the ubiquitous peddlers join voices and forces, as if part of a plan from above to create the picture of a city on the brink of ecological collapse and social dissolution.

In Athens one cannot find the powerfully charged atmosphere of the Western "power streets"; there is no Wall Street or Fleet Street here. The hub of economic power in Athens, the Athens Stock Exchange, is situated in the old part of the city, close to the National Center for Social Research, across the street from Rivoli (the all-day movie theater that plays porn and karate films in the afternoon), next to the arcades that house the central food market, between the salami and the Turkish delight shops, where manual laborers (and until a few years ago maids) would flock every day for their provisions. And every night the area, instead of becoming dangerously abandoned in the manner of Wall Street, becomes an area of revelry, with young people roaming the streets as they return from the tavernas in Plaka or the downtown nightclubs.

Neither can one find in Athens the uniform serenity of the American suburbs. Athens is not an easy city to accept; it is not unconditionally inviting to the uninitiated, either in the hot, sunny summer or in the wet, smog-ridden winter. Hence, says Andrews: "So, if it's beauty you want, go to Italy, go to the Cotswolds, go to a museum: don't come to Athens, where something else might happen" (1967:45).

Athens is also a city of quiet neighborhoods, usually only a few blocks away from this polyphony, where sidewalks are swept clean by the concierges of the apartment buildings or by the residents of the houses, where the midafternoon silence ordinance is kept and enforced by decree of the police, where children play in the streets in the after-school hours, and where neighbors greet neighbors by name.

## SOCCER AND EXCURSIONS (FABLES OF IDENTITY)

Athens is a pastiche of identities, multifaceted and not always at ease with each other. From a small city of twenty-nine thousand inhabitants in the 1840s, comprising, primarily, Cycladeans, Vlachs, and Arvanites, the Athens of today has grown to embrace a population that comes from ever part of Greece and, in the summer, from every part of the world. We may perhaps not hear Vlach spoken in Athens today, nor Arvanitika, but the accents marking the assortment of regional and class identities are easily discernible. The diversity of Athens results partly from the fact that a majority of its inhabitants (those living in the city between 1956 and 1976) were born and raised in other regions.[7] With the influx of refugees from Asia Minor in 1922, Athens acquired an added element of multiculturalism and urbanism, since most of these refugees came from urban centers and maintained their urban identity (see Hirschon 1989). A multiplicity of identities in Athens and its neighborhoods encompasses not only the variety of regional origins but the added elements of social class and heritage (see Sutton 1983; Hirschon 1983, 1989).

A number of things, places, and ideas serve as markers of Athenicity, but here I will mention only three, as they are pertinent to the understanding of identity in the cluster of families that figure in my text. They are the Athenian soccer team Panathenaïkós, the Byzantine monastery of Kaisarianê, and the Coalition of Old Zográphou Residents (Sýndhesmos Palaiôn Zōgraphiōtôn), which acts as the opposite of the regional associations of immigrants to the city.

## Soccer

The name of Panathenaïkós, the Athenian soccer team, actually means "All Athenian." The team was the first established in the city at the turn of the century, and the Panourgiás family has been closely and organically connected with it, not only as *philathloi* (fans) but also as active members. Kōnstantinos, my father, played for the team in his youth, long before the team became professional in 1978, and another Panourgiás (from a different branch of the family) was the president of the team for a long period of time. Panathenaïkós (PAO to its friends, *vaséles*—from Vaseline—to its foes) is not simply taken as the team of the city (as a point of identification) but also as a point of distinction between bourgeois Athens and proletarian Piraeus and its team Olympiakós (*Thrýlos*—legend—to its friends, *gávroi*—smelts—to its foes). This, of course, does not mean that there is a monolithic devotion of the citizens of the two cities to their respective

48

teams. The devotion of an individual to a team many times is superseded by an alliance of a different order, always ad hoc and largely unclassifiable. Yiôrgos Panourgiás, my grandfather, who fought in the Greco-Turkish war of 1921, always supported the Athletic Association of Constantinopolitans (AEK) because he felt an affinity with the refugees from Asia Minor. His son Nikólaos Panourgiás is a fan of Olympiakós because the man who taught him soccer, when he was still a boy, was a member of that team. But these cases are rather the exception, or were the exception in the world of soccer alliances in the preprofessional era. Now all teams are professional, and alliances—not among the older but among the younger philathloi— are determined by factors such as the winning record of a team. Hence, the relationship of Athenians to soccer should be understood as a joined point of identification and differentiation, as signifying what "Athenian" is and what it is not.

Soccer in Greece, in general, is no laughing matter and is certainly not governed by rules of social standing and class, as James Faubion (1993) has tried to establish. Faubion seeks a dialectical relationship between high social status and high culture on the one hand, and low social status and popular culture on the other, when he says that those Athenians with "the appropriate interests and social credentials" belong to historical or garden clubs, whereas those lacking the appropriate requisites support the local soccer team (1993:45). Although this analysis has a certain appeal, it completely misses the point in the case of Greek soccer. First of all, since all Athenians do not support Panathenaïkós and all Peireôtes do not support Olympiakós, the allegiance to the "local team" is not deterministically guaranteed. Furthermore, the president of the most prestigious country club in Athens, the Ekálē Club, is Marianna Látsē, the daughter of one of the most powerful and influential Greek shipowners. The colorful character that her father is, he never misses the opportunity to point out that he is financially self-made, has worked for every drachma he has received, and has tried not to allow his daughter to forget that. The owner of Panathenaïkós is Yiôrgos Vardinoyiánnēs, a member of the most powerful oil industrial family in Greece, which controls most oil refining, circulation, and distribution in the country, in addition to a television station and a major daily newspaper. He comes from an old, rather well-off Cretan family that has produced oil magnates and politicians. The Latsēs and the Vardinoyiánnises are often spotted both at the Ekale Club *and* at the soccer games without their suffering any class identity crisis.[8]

A considerable number of people, however, were ideologically opposed to soccer for a long time, until the restoration of a normal political life

49

in the mid-1980s. The reason for this aversion can be traced to the junta years and the development of the left-wing movement in Greece. Especially during the junta years (1967–74), soccer was used by the government as a means of distraction of public attention from political, economic, and national issues. Members of the Left quickly recognized the strategy—after all, it had already been used by dictators in Latin America—and denounced soccer as the disorientation, *apoprosanatolismós,* of the masses.

Nowadays the soccer teams are a major source of revenue for the country in general and their owners in particular. As their financial importance cannot be overestimated, neither can their symbolic and political power. Panathenaïkós was exploited by the junta, since its team color—green— is symbolically opposed to the red color of communism, also the color of Olympiakós. Thus the junta was able to capitalize on and further contribute to the traditional antagonism between the two teams and cities. After the restoration of political power in 1974 came the professionalization of athletics in Greece in 1978, roughly coinciding with the waning of political enthusiasm that had swept the country in the previous four years. More young people and many more women started going to the soccer matches, and by the mid-1980s the soccer field, not the political rally and demonstration, was the only place where youth fervor could be found concentrated. Even the music from the old Theodorakis song "It's Two of Us, It's Three of Us, It's a Thousand Thirteen of Us," previously sung during demonstrations accompanied by police beatings and smoke bombs to combat political disobedience, is now the greeting anthem of philathloi (as "Thrýlos Olé" or "PAO Olé") and hooligans alike of all teams, again accompanied by police beatings and sometimes smoke bombs to quell civic disobedience. Some philathloi (the more politically minded ones) know the source of the music, can sing the original lyrics, and can identify the song's origins in the political past of Greece. Most, however, ignore that. Thus this vital part of political resistance has been reimagined along the lines of challenging of the civic order. One could perhaps argue that in the long run—much longer than the junta had envisioned or expected—the disorientation plan worked. Now it is certainly true what Umberto Eco said in 1978 about soccer on account of that year's World Cup: you can launch an attack against all public places except the soccer field.

More recently soccer, through the power, money, and political clout that come along with its ownership and management, and because of the fact that soccer constitutes a multimillion-dollar, multifaceted industry, has been implicated in the demise of not one but two political administrations. In 1989, through the scandal of the Bank of Crete and its major international money-laundering apparatus in which the administration of Olympiakós (through its then owner and Bank of Crete president George Koskotas) was involved, the PASOK administration was brought down. In 1993 the Nea Demokratia government was toppled partly because its administration became involved in negotiations regarding the collection of taxes that Olympiakós owed the state. Although the tax revenue issue was not the decisive factor in the demise of the government, it did manage to set in motion a set of chain reactions in the soccer world (which is also the main business world) that helped bring PASOK back into power. It is not, perhaps, coincidental that the main reason for the change in the electoral outcome was a combination of the government's decision to privatize the telephone company (primarily through foreign investment) and the scandal of selling the large public company Hēraklês Cements to the bankrupt Italian Casterlucci, thus implicating the Italian business world in what seems to be the largest scandal that has ever connected the two countries. The outcome in Italy has been much more tragic than in Greece, since a number of Italian politicians and businessmen have committed suicide on account of these dealings. The main contender for the purchasing of the Cellular Phone Division of the telephone company was the president of Olympiakós, who played both political parties against each other, helped in the election of PASOK, and finally won the bid for cellular technology.

Panathenaïkós has been spared such scandalous expositions in recent politics, not because it has not been involved in scandals (which it has) but because the team that carries the most symbolic (and hence also political and financial) power throughout Greece now is Olympiakós, not Panathenaïkós. Finally, it is not by accident that the heavier the involvement of the soccer teams in political scandals, the more rumors arise about arranged, rigged (*siké*, in Greek soccer lingo) matches, something which is often compared with what is perceived as the arranged, rigged, siké political life of the country.[9]

## Excursions

The monastery of Kaisarianê, now an archaeological site, has been frequented by Athenians as long as it has existed as a monastery (see Gennadeios 1935). The area is visible from downtown Athens, right on the southeastern slope of Mount Hymettus. It is beautifully forested, with pine and plane trees. The monastery contains one church and two chapels, and it has two springs of its own, Panayiá and Kalopoula. A long list of legends is

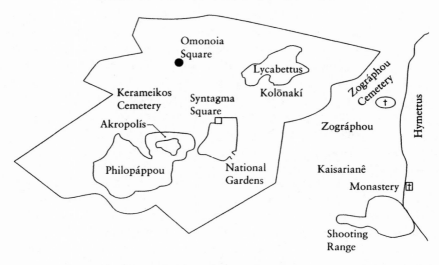

Map of the municipality of Athens

associated with the place, still remembered by old Athenians, and the cemetery is mentioned many times in the literature of Ioannis Kambouroglous and Alexandros Papadiamantis.

The monastery (later turned into a convent, although there is no terminological differentiation in Greek) was built in the eleventh or twelfth century on the site of an ancient shrine to Aphrodite. The monastery was dedicated to the Néa Kyrá (New Lady), the Virgin Mary, in juxtaposition to the Paliá Kyrá (Old Lady), the goddess Athena (Gennadeios 1935). At a short distance from the stone wall of the monastery, another two churches were built later: the Taxiarch, which served as the cemetery for the monks, and Saint Markos, which was used for some time by the Venetian rulers of Athens.

Kalopoula, the spring above Kaisarianê, has been believed since ancient times to possess powers of fecundity, and women, in ancient times under the protection of Aphrodite and in modern times under the protection of Panayia, the Virgin Mary, have gone to the spring so as to ensure fertility, easy delivery, and beautiful children. In cases of infertility women would even spend the night in the church—a very old practice called *enkoimēsis*—sleeping underneath the icon of Panayia, and would drink water from the spring at regular intervals. It seems that these practices ceased to exist by the turn of the century, but they have survived as memories in the narratives of old Athenians.

The monastery had served as a major learning center for the area, with great collections of books, particularly on ancient and Christian philosophy, and an extensive collection of manuscripts. Unfortunately the library is all but gone, initially plundered by the Venetians when they ruled Athens in the fifteenth century and Catholic monks took over the administration of the monastery (see Gennadeios 1935; Stasinopoulos 1973; Benizelos 1986). The final destruction of the library occurred when the paper from the books was used for the manufacturing of bullets during the War of Independence (1821–29). Despite the fact that the real estate value of the property that belonged to the monastery was of mythic proportions, the *hēgoumenoi* (abbots) of the monastery had always managed to persuade the sultans to exempt it from taxation. Eventually the monastery fell into abandonment, its buildings starting crumbling for lack of maintenance, it lost its income, and the number of monks and nuns dwindled considerably. After the Second World War one of the old Athenian families, the Argyropouloi, initiated the reforestation of the area that surrounds the monastery and also the restoration of its grounds and buildings. I remember two remaining nuns and an old priest who lived there in the 1960s. Now they are all dead.

The Panourgiás family house was in Zográphou, the borough downwind from the cemetery, within walking distance of it. Often, in the years before the war, the family, usually led by Evangelia Panourgiá's mother, Katina, would pack a lunch and take it to the monastery for a picnic. Kōnstantinos remembers that without warning, his grandmother would prepare a skewer of entrails (a *kokorétsi*) early in the morning, pack it with some bread, take the children and walk the distance between the house and the monastery, and be back at dusk. The whole distance traversed a forest, and the monastery could only be reached by walking or by taking the dirt path on cart or carriage. Now the path has become a paved loop around the monastery, and it borders the heavily used loop that goes around the city. The forest has been cut down and burned many times, once to expose the hideouts of the partisans in the Civil War, repeatedly by arson, other times by negligence. With the influx of the refugees from Asia Minor after the Greco-Turkish war of 1919–22, the area below the monastery, previously inhabited only by a family of shepherds, was targeted as a relocation point for the refugees. A whole community was created there (much like the one described by Renée Hirschon [1989] in Gerani). In time, it developed its own identity and left-wing politics. On the imaginary level, however, it remained outside the realm of the communities that surrounded it, the major one of which is Zográphou, the municipality where the Panourgiádhes have their property. The identification of the Zographiôtes still is with the monastery, not with the muncipality of Kaisarianê.

Kaisarianê, however, has another, much darker connection with the city of Athens in general, and Zográphou in particular. During the German occupation, the shooting range of Kaisarianê, a place of sportsmanship before the war, became the place of execution for members of the Resistance. One of the most gruesome instances came at the end of the war, when the people captured at the uprising in Kokkinia (Piraeus) were brought there by the tens, on trucks, and were executed in shifts. I was told of that particular execution by both Kōnstantinos Panourgiás and Hara Tzavella-Evjen, who did not know each other then, although they lived rather close together and are of the same generation (although Hara is younger than Kōnstantinos). They both watched the trucks go by with their cargo, and although they really did not know who the people were and where they had been gathered from, "it was obvious that they were being taken to be executed—just like when the shepherds drove their sheep through the streets of Maroussi, to slaughter them for Easter," Hara said. The terror was grafted so deeply in the psyches of people who watched the constant hauling of humans into this space of cruelly instant death that for years Kaisarianê was considered a most undesirable place of residence and was left to its original refugees. With the influx of people into the city in the seventies, however, some entrepreneurial contractors started building large, modern, expensive apartment buildings all around the area, especially around the shooting range. We all wondered who would buy them and why. "There are enough villagers with money who will think they are Athenians if they buy a flat there. They'll hear the cries of the dead better too," Kōnstantinos said sarcastically.

## Fables of Identity

The Coalition of Old Zográphou Residents was established in 1988 as a private club to which membership could be attained only by those who were among the first to have inhabited Zográphou. The only other native (as opposed to immigrant) organization that had preceded it was the Club of the Athenians, established in 1895, which later acquired satellites in the United States and in Australia. Not new as an idea by any means, this construction of autochthony is but another heterology which seeks to create an identity of exclusiveness.[10] What makes it interesting as an idea, however, is the fact that the coalition is not intended as a commemoration of an exotopic, originary topographic ascription, but rather as the redefinition of the specific *same* topography as such, that is, as the same over time. In other words, whereas the regional organizations in Susan Sutton's study define themselves through the absence of their originary topos from the specific time and space (their referential topos is always removed from the topos of their organization, which inevitably removes it temporally as well), the Sýndhesmos Palaiôn Zōgraphiôtôn defines itself through the *presence* of the originary topos at the point of identification with the specific and present time and space.

Zográphou, on the slopes of Mount Hymettus, is a municipality of Athens established at the turn of the century, situated five kilometers northeast of the center of Athens. It was incorporated as a municipality in 1929. Although the area is naturally heavily forested, during the Civil War a battalion of guerrillas was positioned in the forests above Zográphou, and the Ministry of War decided to cut down the trees in order to expose the guerrilla hideouts.[11] After the trees were cut, the Third Mountain Brigade (Tritē Oreinê Taxiarcheia, the group after which, in the 1950s, the municipal government renamed the street on which our house was built in the late 1800s) moved into the mountain and exterminated the guerrilla forces. Or so legend has it. The end result remains the same: until lately Hymettus was barren, with a few patches of pine forests trying to gain foothold. In the summer of 1988 a fire at the Kaisarianê monastery left the mountain charred and barren once again.

In the 1960s almost all the buildings in Zográphou were still houses. In a circle with a radius of two kilometers around the Drakos-Panourgiás house, there were three apartment buildings: the "new one," built in the late 1960s; the "old one," built ten years earlier; and one other large structure, the Kambylafkás Clinic, built at the turn of the century, burned down in the 1930s, and rebuilt as an apartment building shortly afterward to be used first as police headquarters and subsequently as apartments. It was replaced by an architectural monstrosity of concrete in the 1970s. The old river Ilissos flowed freely and, at many places, was uncovered. The area was originally inhabited by big landowners and stock breeders. The initial landowners started selling their land at the turn of the century, and the area acquired an identity representative of the different social classes and places of origin of the new residents. According to the 1981 census, Zográphou then had eighty-six thousand inhabitants, in an area of four square kilometers. The municipal Department of Statistics estimates that the population now is over 150,000. Zográphou has been exploding in size since the 1960s, with the wave of internal migration that was one of the results of the military junta of 1967–1974 (Woodhouse 1984). Before its establishment as a municipality, it had a few scattered houses (the old Drakos house was there, along with property that Evangelia Panourgiá's stepfather owned and eventually sold), and the area primarily comprised fields, beehives, and, at the foot of Hymettus, piggeries kept by Vlachs.[12] My grandfather (a now-on, now-off Arvanitēs) said: "The only non-Arvanites Athenians are the Anafiôtes. They are the ones who were here long before anyone else came; they must have come the same time we [Arvanites] did." "What are the rest?" "The rest came with the revolution [of 1821]. That's when everyone flocked to Athens. We [the family] had all that area of Papagou; we owned it. Then after they started coming in, we started selling it. And now, look around you. How many Athenians, real Athenians [*gágaroi*, the Arvanitika term], are there?"

The point he was trying to make was even better illustrated in an exchange that took place when his eldest son, Tássos, was being treated for cancer at the Anti-Cancer Institute of Athens. Tássos was in a room with three other patients, their beds separated with curtains. His was next to the window. One day his daughter, Vangeliô, with her husband, Dēmê-trēs, and I went to visit him. Vangeliô started telling her father that the previous week she and Dēmêtrēs had been the *koumbároi* at a Vlach wedding.[13] She said, "You know last week we went to a wedding of the Vlachs [*Stous Vláchous*]."[14] Tássos, mistaking the Vlach identity for the "Athenian" term *vláchos* (hillbilly) and worried that some of the people around him might be offended, responded: "Shhh. They are all *vláchoi* here."

A story recounted to me by Aristides Baltas offers another illustration: "I was driving along the loop on Lycabettus, and from the opposite direction was coming a guy on a scooter, a black guy, really dark, from Africa. It seems that somehow I cut in front of him, and he turned around, yelled at me, and threw a slur to my face: 'Ante re vlácho!' [You vlach you, get out of here!] In perfect Greek he said it. That's what this guy from Africa called me. I stopped dead in my tracks, speechless."[15]

The point is that in this context, "real Athenians" means autochthonous Athenians, a condition which is by itself limited temporally and is manipulable for inclusion or exclusion, at will. The Athenian discourse of self-origins, however, only dates back to the first travelers of the seventeenth century. The issue of the identity of Athenian residents might not be of any importance to anyone other than the residents themselves, but it lends itself to the extremely interesting discussion of autochthony and the rights it warrants. Naturally, the question that begs to be asked is: To what and whom is this autochthony related? Furthermore, is there a temporal dimension to it? All this is further encompassed in the overarching question of why autochthony is discussed at all in a land where there is no exercise of apartheid (whence prosecution, if any exists, is not couched upon origin) and where there has been a constant occupation since neolithic times. Obviously no one claims (any longer, that is) that present-day residents of Athens are the "same" people as those of antiquity (whatever this "sameness" might imply and whichever way it might be construed, but, analytically, always within the context of opposition to de Certeau's heterological discourse).

A discourse on autochthony in Greece, however, developed at the time of the political and constitutional unrest of the 1840s and eventually resulted in a clause in the constitution of 1843. Under this clause, those subjects of the Greek kingdom born outside the boundaries of modern Greece were deemed *heteróchthones* and were relieved from their positions in the public and civic sectors. The only exception made was in the educational system, where these heteróchthones retained their positions, presumably for lack of enough educated "autochthonous Greeks" to satisfy the country's educational needs. Interestingly enough, a victim of this clause was Greece's first national historian, K. D. Paparrigopoulos, who lost his position at the Ministry of Justice and was rehired as a secondary school teacher (Dimaras 1986:122, 442n). Although the clause was later retracted, an active discourse on autochthony still exists, which seeks to separate the center (any given center, always changing and redefining itself as such) from its peripheries (always circumscribed by the changes of the center). The opposition is not a binary one between one center and one Other but a multidimensional one between the autochthonous center and the ever-elusive multiplicity of the nonautochthonous center. The relationship between center and periphery, then, becomes rather autoscopic and explicitly self-referential (see Vergopoulos 1985; Wallerstein 1991; and Leontis 1995). Hence the development of Athenicity as an issue, as a contrasting point, not to the rest of the Greeks but to the non-Athenians, was lucidly (and caustically, I would add) verbalized by Michael Defner in 1923, when he wrote of the Athenian character: "Athenians will perpetually be the same, unstable [*ástatoi*] like their skies; they will love discussions about the air and the water, for they have a plentitude of the former and a scarcity of the latter; and they will always ask, 'What news?' because news quickly becomes old to them" (27).

Anyone who has been to modern Athens can attest to the fact that the city lacks a sense of direction, to put it euphemistically. A feel of anarchy is palpable in its architecture, in the way public services operate, in the constant appropriations of public space for private profit, and also in the spot that private businesses occupy in the structure of the city. Two separate theories seek to explain the factors that have contributed to this state of affairs in Athens. The first is by George Prevelakis (1989), who, in a convincing argument in which he traces the development of Athens from the Greek Revolution to modern times, concludes that Athens has been transformed into the city it is today largely on account of the migrants who moved there from other parts of Greece during the seventies and eighties, through an intricate combination of partisan politics, economic prospectorship, and personal ideology. This new group of immigrants, Prevelakis argues, was much more detached from the idea of the city than all previous groups together. Despite moving to the city, the new migrants maintained very close and intimate contacts with their places of origin, visiting there almost every weekend, now that better and more abundant means of transportation have made the Greek countryside more accessible than ever before. So it's the immigrants who don't love the city, who don't see it as one of their concerns, who have contributed to its degradation and the lack of a sense of community that has permeated the relationships of its inhabitants in the last decade.

This brings me to the other point that I want to make regarding the state of affairs in Athens today; it is informed by Baltas' theory of "deep communism" (1993). Deep communism, Baltas explains, is the final stage in socialism, whose working principle is not "From everyone according to his capacities, to everyone according to his work" (the operating principle of the first stage of socialism and a developing communist society). Neither is it the second, more developed principle, which governs the second stage of socialism and a developed communist society: "From everyone according to his capacities, to everyone according to his needs." The third stage, which is not governed by need, is the stage of deep communism, whose operative principle is "From everyone according to his fancy, to everyone according to his pleasure." This last stage reflects the driving force behind people's actions in Athens.

Thus, in a city that is inhabited by people who, in their majority, do not love it and are given to a struggle for the fulfillment of their personal pleasure move and live the people portrayed in this study. And it is for this reason, in the writing of a text about these people, these *anthropoi,* that this is an *anthropography.*

PARERGA

1. The "special Attikan light," beyond being simply constructed, constitutes also a point of reference for later Greek writers, whose position was clearly informed by this philattikan rhetoric. The first point of reference lies precisely at the "splendor that was Greece," whose topos was decisively Attika. The similarities between the turn-of-the-century writer Periklis Yiannopoulos and Symonds in his description of the Attikan landscape are striking. In "The Hellenic Line, the Hellenic Color," Yiannopoulos circumscribes Hellenicity by the physical attributes of its topos through the specificity of its aesthetics. He notes that "the aesthetic building-blocks of Hellas are the curved line [kambylē] and transparent light [fôs] which is reflected everywhere in the color of deep blue [kyanós]" (in Leontis 1995). This passage, Leontis argues, defines the fundamental function of the aesthetic sphere as a determining and regulating force of Neo-Hellenism's national individuality. And it does so, I would add, at the point where Greece and this same Greek national individuality are reduced and contained within not only the geographic but also the conceptual and aesthetic boundaries of the Attikan landscape. This discourse on light should be read within Tziovas' framework for analyzing nationism (1989) or, as Terzakis would have it, "atmospheric nationalism" (in Tziovas 1989:67), which is couched in terms of the interplay between the environment and its effects on society.

2. According to many accounts, primarily those of Benizelos, Gennadeios, Sathas, Sourmelis, and Stasinopoulos, Athenians left for the nearby island of Salamis when they needed protection of any sort, such as during plunder by invaders or outbreaks of diseases like cholera and plague. They returned to the city when they felt secure enough to do so. During those times Athens would, indeed, have given the impression of a deserted city. In all this, however, what should not escape our attention is the hidden agenda of the commentator. If one wishes to make a case against the validity of Athens as a modern city, the argument that Athens was deserted in 1832, when Otto chose it as the capital of his kingdom, would serve rather well. If one looks carefully at the accounts of travelers over a period of time, and if one also pays attention to the Greek historiography of the period 1600–1830, one can see this almost transitory relationship of the Athenians to their city.

3. There is no reason for us to believe that Mrs. Barrington had any knowledge of Freud's experience on the Acropolis, since Freud published his letter for the first time in January 1936. See Freud 1950.

4. The idea of Athens as a European city has been amply demonstrated by Tsiomis, in his various articles. Tsiomis and I, independent of each other, have been thinking along similar lines in regard to the nature and conceptualization of Athens as a nineteenth-century city. Elsewhere I have expanded on this idea of a need for the development of a historiography that would draw on the intellectual, stylistic, and aesthetic connections among the new European nations of the nineteenth century and particularly on the role that architectural neoclassicism played in this process [see Panourgiá 1994].

5. The reasons for the replacement can be found first in the fact that a car—even one as small as a 600–cc Fiat—could transport more people than a scooter. Also, these were the cars favored by the young anticonformist characters created by Fellini, Antonioni, Godard, and Truffaut that had become the cultural icons of Greek youths of the fifties and sixties. The car came to encapsulate the spirit of the youth culture of the times—modernity, sophistication, political awareness, and involvement. The refrain is a well-known French nursery song, one of the first songs we learned as children, which Kēlaēdhónēs included as a tribute to the two years he spent at the Lycée Française in Athens. Kēlaēdhónēs acknowledges that "The Fucking Fifties" contains the "Rosenlaube" from the Osten book of piano études in its entirety; he mentioned to me that this was the first melodic piece he learned, since most of the other exercises in the book were scales.

6. On the quality of the Attikan landscape, consider the latest comments by Tzannis Tzanetakis (a minister in the previous right-wing government of Nea Demokratia). Plans were made for the building of a new airport in the Spata area, in the Mesogeia plain, one of the oldest continuously cultivated areas of Athens. Since preclassical times, the area has produced figs, olives and olive oil, pistachios, and resinated wine. After being attacked for the choice of the area, the former minister proudly answered, "It will change the face of Mesogeia," not realizing that this is precisely the fear of all of us who have known and loved Mesogeia the way it is now.

7. Commenting on this pattern of internal migration, Safilios-Rothchild proposes that "the analysis of the families residing in Athens by regions of origins can, in fact, represent a regional analysis of family structure and dynamics" (1976:410).

8. Similarly, now that the political exigencies of Greece are of a more negotiable order, many intellectuals (*dhianooúmenoi*) and literary people (poets and novelists, *logotéchnes*) exhibit their fondness for soccer openly and without any compromises to their intellectualism, left-wing political orientation, or human sensitivities. On a number of occasions I have wit-

nessed such intellectuals and *logotéchnes* at matches, accompanied by their wives, girlfriends, lovers, male and female cousins, and friends, reaching a frenzy during the match. At particularly moving moments, men and women, swaying rhythmically on the bleachers, yell to the opposite team: "That's the way, Peir-aus-fucks" ("Etsi gamáei ho Peiraiás"). They admit that when they see the colors of their team, their hearts flutter and they lose their minds. Their cheer prompted the public literary reply by the poet and composer Orphéas Peridēs: "This is the way the Avenue fucks / this is the way poets love" ("Etsi gamei he Leōphóros, / étsi agapoún hoi poiētés"). Leōphóros refers to Alexándras Avenue, where the original Panathenaïkós soccer field and headquarters were, directly across from the Anti-Cancer Institute.

The behavior of the fans during the match does not in any way contradict or undermine the serious discussions in which they might engage in the same evening, or the commentary, in the form of cultural critique, on which they might embark immediately after the match, on the metro on the way home.

9. This is not an exclusively Greek state of affairs. In Italy, which has been rife with scandals over the past years, the latest elections brought to power an extreme right-wing government, led by S. Berlusconi, owner of the Italian soccer champion team Milan and also owner of the largest mass media conglomerate in the country.

10. In his radio address "On the Question: What Is German?" Adorno tackles the problematic of the discontinuity between an imaginary articulation of the *existence* of identity and the articulation of its imaginary *notion:* "The question itself is burdened by those . . . definitions which assume as the specifically German not what actually *is* German but rather what one wishes it were" (1985:121). Even if we accept as a mere working hypothesis the existence of an identitary *actuality* (that is, an entity, reified or idealized, existing outside, in spite of, and beside any ideologemes of identity), the basic premise of Adorno's problematic still underlines the issue that has determined Greek political culture for the past 170 years: namely, the issue of compromising the ideal of Greece (what one wishes Greece were) and what it actually is. But what Greece actually is cannot be taken for granted or at face value now, after Anderson's development of the theory of "imagined communities" (1983); Anderson's formulation implies that community does not exist actually, although it imagines itself to be many things. See also Gourgouris in press for the elaboration of this point in reference to the case of Greece.

This compromise brings into focus the issue of Attikan and Athenian identities, which are so intimately connected that one cannot consider one-self an Athenian without also considering oneself an Attikan. More important and revealing, Athenians do not count non-Attikans as belonging among them. Of course, the reality is very different. Defying canon and order, people define themselves in whatever way is most profitable, in whatever way accords them the greatest degree of inclusion in any given group. And finally, we should always bear in mind the fact that the expressed identification of any group or community—what is being understood as identity politics—is largely nurtured by a culture that circulates capital (symbolic or financial) through the segmentation of old identities and the creation and support of new ones. It seems that the field of cultural studies has found a way of understanding the economic and symbolic ramifications of this process. For an encapsulation of the discussions that are currently taking place on the issue, see Ross 1993.

11. Attika in general was much more thickly forested in the nineteenth century than it is now. In the first years after the 1821 war, Attika was 70 percent forested. Shortly before the German occupation in 1941, the percentage had dropped to 30. See Schizas 1991 on the history and environmental conditions of Attika in general and Hymettus in particular.

12. Piggeries were kept until the 1960s, despite government resolutions adopted as early as 1934 and 1936 declaring Hymettus an area of reforestation and strictly prohibiting logging and animal husbandry. The only area on Hymettus open to pasturing was Karapánou, around the airport, where until 1977 approximately nine hundred goats grazed freely.

13. A *koumbáros* (pl. *koumbároi*) is the ritual sponsor of a wedding (the person who exchanges the wedding crowns) or a baptism (the one who applies the ritual oil on the infant, thus sanctioning the name) (Dimitrakos 1959). The term is a medieval Venetian word from *compare* (Andriotis 1983), etymologically akin to the Spanish and Italian *compadre*, which in Greece is used catachrestically in the case of weddings. Crete is the only place in Greece where the medieval Greek term *sýnteknos*, instead of *koumbáros*, is used exclusively in the case of baptisms. It has also acquired a generic usage in the context of social greetings. Thus, a *sýnteknos* can be either the sponsor at the baptism of one's child or the strange man one encounters and greets in the street. For detailed analyses of the issue, see Friedl 1962; Campbell 1964; du Boulay 1984; Herzfeld 1985; Velioti 1987; and D'Onofrio 1991.

14. A Vláchos is a member of the Vlachs, an ethnic group living primarily in northwestern Greece. The term has become, in the vernacular, an equivalent of *hillbilly*. See "Vlach Men and Women" 1852; Bérard 1893;

Wace and Thompson 1914; Campbell 1964; Schein 1975; Papazisis 1976; Herzfeld 1980a; and Balamaci 1991.

15. Lycabettus (Lycavēttós in Greek) is one of the three main hills of Athens, the other two being the Acropolis and (across from it) Philopappou. On the crest of the hill of Lycabettus is a small, late Byzantine chapel dedicated to St. George Lycabettus (the wolf-chasing one), because legend has it that the hill was full of wolves (*lýkous*) preying on the Athenians below until Saint George appeared and drove them away. The road on the hill is a shortcut that connects the downtown with the arteries that lead out of the city, bypassing quite a bit of the downtown traffic. The fashionable neighborhood Kolonaki is on the southwestern flank of the hill, and the hill in its entirety has been built up over the past sixty years, with exclusive apartment buildings occupied nowadays primarily by members of the foreign community of Athens (journalists, visiting foreign scholars, itinerant anthropologists, and members of the diplomatic corps), some old Athenians who have refused to flee the city for the suburbs, and a generous number of nouveaux riches (see Faubion 1993). The hill has a thick pine forest, one of the few concentrated green spaces in Athens, which has been a point of attraction for the inhabitants. Below the chapel the Greek Tourist Organization erected an open-air theater that serves as the alternative point to the Roman Herod Atticus theater below the Acropolis, for (alternative) cultural performances, such as concerts by the Lounge Lizards, Diamanda Galás, Nina Simone, or the Greek composer Loukianós Kēlaēdhónēs.

# 4

# The Self

## THE FAMILY

"There was no plot," William said, "and I discovered it by mistake."
—Umberto Eco, *The Name of the Rose*

And so I decided to conduct my fieldwork among my family. This is a family which calls itself not only urban but also decidedly Athenian. Family legend has it that our history can be traced back to the Phanar, where some ancestor was a dragoman to the Sublime Porte. Sometime in the late 1600s the family moved to mainland Greece and established themselves in the Roumeli region, in what is now Amfissa (old Sálōna). The family name then was *Xērós*. In 1754 the first Panourgiás was born, acquiring the name by a fluke: As was the custom at the time, during the baptism the parents presented the baby—dressed in a long lace dress—to the godfather, and when the time came for the name to be pronounced, they stepped out of the church. The godfather, who had no knowledge of the gender of the child, looked at him and decided that this was a beautiful little girl who deserved the name Panōraia ("The All-Beautiful One"). But the child was a boy, not a girl, and since in the Greek Orthodox Church the baptismal name can never be changed for any reason, the only recourse the parents had was to concoct a masculine gender for this feminine name. Hence the name Panourgiás was born, originally as a first name. When this first Panourgiás became a renowned leader in the Greek War of Independence (1821–29), his son Nákos (Iōánnis) adopted the name as a surname. Since then, one branch of the family developed the practice of naming the first male child

64

of a family Panourgiás (so that the first name is the same as the last) and his son Nákos.

After independence in 1829, our branch of the family moved to the Mesogeia area, specifically to Keratéa, subsequently moving to Markó-poulo, where the family property still is. Through a compensatory program for the fighters of the War of Independence, instituted by the Greek government, the family acquired land in Athens. This land was later, through intermarriage between the Panourgiás and the yet older Attikan Hassiôtēs family, incorporated into the Hassiôtēs property. Thus an expanse of land was consolidated which started in the southern parts of Mesogeia and ended at the northern edge of Athens. Although the land was largely deemed noncultivable and was sold or given away piecemeal as wedding gifts to members of the extended family and to godchildren, nonetheless it was through the ownership of this property that a conceptual corridor linking Athens to Mesogeia was established, providing a foundation for a specific identity. As we will see, this was hardly an exceptional situation among the Arvanites of Markópoulo.

Evangelia Panourgiá (born Tsalapátēs and later adopted by the Drakos family) was born in Paeania—called Liópesi by its Arvanites residents—to a family with holdings in Zográphou. The family house in Zográphou, given to Evangelia Panourgiá by her stepfather, was built in the late 1800s. (It was demolished to make way for an apartment building in 1978.) After Drakos' death, Evangelia inherited the house and the surrounding land. Evangelia Drákou (1902–1975) married Yiôrgos Panourgiás (1901–1986) in 1925. By that time Yiôrgos had already fought in the Greco-Turkish War in Asia Minor in 1919–22. He and Evangelia had four sons: Anastásios (affectionately called Tássos), Kōnstantinos (Kōstēs), Nikólaos (Nikos), and Christóforos. Evangelia was employed as an embroiderer at the palace, and Yiôrgos worked as a middle-level administrator, initially for the Department of Public Transportation and eventually for the British Water Company (OULEN), from which he retired. Both graduates of the scholarchion (the equivalent of American junior high school), they insisted on further education for their children.

Anastásios studied at the Panteios School of Social and Economic Sciences and worked until the dictatorship (1967) for the Commercial Bank of Greece. Kōnstantinos studied mechanical engineering at the Lower Polytechnic School and eventually acquired his fame and wealth as a chemical engineer specializing in plastics. Nikólaos is the only one without a degree in higher education. After trying his hand at starting various businesses

Evangelia Tsalapátē, on the left, with her two sisters Athanasia (seated) and Sofia in the 1920s. Athanasia is wearing their great-grandmother's wedding dress.

in Athens, he migrated to South Africa, where, after a short spell in the plastics business, he opened a chain of restaurants for an integrated clientele. Christóforos, a graduate of the School of Business of Piraeus, after an ill-fated attempt at a business of his own in Athens, followed his brother to Johannesburg, where he started his own business in the plastics industry. During the dictatorship and after his dismissal (as a leftist) from the bank, Anastásios joined his two brothers in Johannesburg. He returned to Greece within a year, however, and eventually worked for his brother Kōnstantinos as a supervisor at one of the company plants.

Anastásios, Kōnstantinos, and Nikólaos married women who, although born outside Athens, had been brought up in Athens, had property there, and considered themselves Athenians. Christóforos married a young woman from the island of Cefallonia who had lived in Athens as a college student. The difference between the first three women and the last is that the former had acquired their Athenian identity before World War II, a point most crucial, as Constantina Safilios-Rothchild (1976) points out. Anastásios' wife, Sofia, born in Ōrōpós, on the Attikan Peninsula, and a high school graduate, was the only housewife. Kōnstantinos' wife, Dêmētra, born in the northern Peloponnese and a graduate of the University of Athens, is a retired educator. Nikólaos' wife, Chryssoula, born on the island of Euboea, northeast of Athens, and a high school graduate, had her own dry cleaning and tailoring business. Christóforos' wife, Angelikê, graduated from a private school of accounting and worked for the National Bank of Greece in Athens and in Johannesburg until, a few years ago, she resigned her position at the bank and joined her husband in the administration of the plastics business. In 1962, when their daughter was nine years old, Anastásios and Sofia divorced, and Sofia moved to Ōrōpós, where she remarried and had another daughter with her second husband. She had custody of her elder daughter, Vangeliô, for a while. When Anastásios gained custody, he brought Vangeliô back to Athens, where he raised her with help from his parents. Vangeliô married her high-school sweetheart (from Ōrōpós) after she graduated as a graphics artist from the Doxiadis School. They had two daughters, and in 1983 the four of them moved back to Ōrōpós and built a house on land that her mother provided for them. Anastásios remaried in 1971. His second wife, Garyfaliá (also called Litsa), a woman fourteen years his junior, was born in Crete and raised in Athens by parents who were both refugees from Asia Minor. Garyfaliá, a graduate of grammar school, had her own hairdressing salon in Athens. They did not have any children.

Kōnstantinos and Dêmētra lived apart for the first five years of their

Nikólaos and Chryssoula at their wedding in Athens in 1958. On the right is Léngō Sidérē, Yiôrgos Panourgiás' eldest sister, who is dressed in black because of mourning for her husband.

Dêmētra on an excursion with her students in 1956

marriage, since Dêmētra, a public educator, was given posts away from Athens (Macedonia and the Peloponnese), whereas Kōnstantinos, whose work was based in Athens, traveled abroad almost constantly for business purposes, spending long periods of time in Cyprus, Beirut, and Spain. They had two daughters, Eléni (affectionately called Neni), who has a doctorate in anthropology from a university in the United States, and Stélla-Evangelia (Lea), who, after studies at the Vakalo School for the Visual and Plastic Arts, worked as a freelance artist before opening her own bookstore. They are both divorced. Lea has two sons, Orêstēs and Iásōn.

Nikólaos' son, Yiôrgos (named after his grandfather), was born in Athens but raised in Johannesburg. After an automobile accident in his late adolescence left him partly disabled and cut short his dreams for a career as a jet pilot, he joined his father's business. His mother, Chryssoula, opened a tailor's atelier in Johannesburg but also helps with her husband's business.

Christóforos and Angelikê had three children: Evangelia, Yiôrgos, and Kôstas. Evangelia is a student at the Medical School at the University of Athens, and Yiôrgos and Kôstas are students at the School of Engineering at the University of Witwatersrand, in Johannesburg. Politically speaking, the whole family adheres to the left of the center (from Venize-

69

los, to George Papandreou, to Andreas Papandreou) with the exception of Nikólaos, who was the only one aligned with the Communist Party, and Evangelia (wife of Yiôrgos Panourgiás), who, through her affiliation with the palace, counted herself among the royalists. Evangelia's politics has been the standing family joke: "*Oi Vasileis*—the royal couple—Mom used to say," her sons said when mention of her politics was made. This remark was usually accompanied by the characteristic sideways movement of the head indicating indignation for those who would allow their professional alliances to interfere with their politics. All female children admit an adherence to the Marxist left, either through party lines (the Communist Party of Greece and the Ecological Party) or through a nonpartisan leftist ideology (for a good discussion of the notion of class in the study of modern Greek society, see Mouzelis 1976; Tsoucalas 1975; and Tsaoussis 1976).

This is the core group of people that I had decided to "study," my family. Although well-grounded in kinship and descent theory, I did not yet have a clear idea of what exactly I would study, how I would apply this experimental/experiential/ethnographic theory to such a study, but I had faith in Tyche, the protectress of ethnographers. Unfortunately the opportunity came, a very bitter and painful one. Halfway through my fieldwork, after I had collected, unwillingly and unknowingly, notes upon notes on family relations, complaints about the in-laws, and gossip about siblings and distant kindred, my paternal grandfather, Yiôrgos Panourgiás, took ill and died. The shock was tremendous, first of all because, as a granddaughter, I had the secret hope that my grandfather would never die, and since he was in excellent health (despite his eighty-five years of age), nothing warned me of his imminent death. Second, I had a special relationship with my grandfather, a very close relationship. His death affected me deeply. I was angry, outraged at life, at biological evolution, at death, at the world. I did not want to accept it, although logically I conceded that his death was not a tragic loss, that he had lived his life to its fullest, that he died at home, on his bed, with all his children, grandchildren, and great-grandchildren around him. He did not suffer much or for too long, and he had all his faculties until a few hours before his death. He died a good death (*kaló thánato*), one that many people envied, because it was relatively quick and painless, and it had come at the end of a full and satisfying life.

I looked back to the other deaths that had occurred between 1984, when I conducted my first summer fieldwork, and 1986. The comparison was unfavorable. Those previous deaths were so much worse; they were all untimely, far too early. They had happened to young people, after long

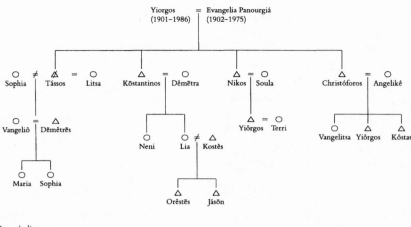

Key: ≠ divorce
  ⚰ death of a male
  ⊘ death of a female

Kinship chart of the Panourgiás family

illnesses or freak accidents. They were unfair. Such thoughts, however, did not make my grandfather's death any more tolerable. I decided to explore death in general and the constructions of its understanding in my circle of relatives and friends. Along with the deaths came disruption, discord, and rancor among the members of the families: old disputes were brought back to life, thirty-year-old debts were remembered, and bad words, spoken long before I was even born, were given, once more, their original sting. It was obvious that for some reason the unitive elements of the family had weakened in favor of the antagonism brought forth by the dialectics of totality, of universality, of particularity, and of individuality (the requisites for the smooth operations of the bourgeois family). I was not even sure, at that point, that what I had understood as the unitive elements of the family had always been there. Suddenly I was not sure that the family had *ever* been one cohesive unit, immune to strife and antagonism. I was angry and hurt, and I wanted to expose all this.

Three more deaths, following my grandfather's death and the beginning of the writing of this text, intensified these feelings. I would emply my analytical skills, I decided, to expose this face of the family, to tell the world about it. And then, after I had decided this, as if cathartically, it occurred to me that there is no mystique, no interest, no value, in the knowledge of this discord. Only pain. And I would be perpetuating this pain if I wrote about these intimate moments of the family. Dispute, discord, and unrest are parts, faces, realities, of every family, just as are love, protection, and affection. I finally saw "family" for what it really is: a group of people forced into relationships which, most of the time, they have not initiated themselves, who are involved in interminable daily negotiations about everyday matters that affect their lives, shifting their alliances and loyalties as a means of ensuring their emotional survival. I looked at my relationship to "family," my struggle for individuality through the acceptance of my need for it for emotional support, a relationship that is not static but rather "a dynamic process of tensions and oppositions which are always in precarious equilibrium" (Lévi-Strauss 1985:61).

Suddenly there was no mystery, there was no intrigue, there was no plot, there were no intended contrivances. Things were really much simpler than I had first thought. My grandfather chose my grandmother as his partner in life and got four sons as part of the deal. He did not have to like them as people, although he loved them dearly as his children. He had not chosen his in-laws, and his alliances with them were based strictly on his personal feelings toward them, not on a sense of obligation among kindred. And the same was true of his in-laws in their dealings with him. When his father-in-law decided to sell the plot of land on which a house stood that my grandmother had been given as a dowry, my grandfather offered to buy it. The sum was fifteen gold sovereigns, the incident in the 1920s. Drakos (my great-grandfather, whose name, incidentally, means "dragon") gave my grandfather a week's time to procure the money. On the eve of the expiration date, my grandfather had fourteen of the fifteen pieces of gold. The land was sold to someone else, who appeared with all fifteen sovereigns in hand early the next morning. "You see, Drakos couldn't wait another day," my grandfather recounted. He shook his head in disapproval. "Did that hurt you?" I asked. "He wanted his money. I can understand that. But after all, I had been a good son-in-law to him. He could have waited until I got all the money together."

My fury about families was gone. After all, essentially we all love each other, and our aberrations in behavior can, most of the time, be attributed to this "love," which can be viewed as the collaborative, if metaphorical, effort of the relationship.[1] As Robert Murphy pointed out, "Life and love stand opposed to death and alienation" (1985:223), and this "love" that binds us is what has kept us together against death and the alienation it brings.[2]

Could then, I thought, an analytical (and self-analytical) approach help me (and my readers) to understand death? Or if not to understand death, then at least to look at it, to look for "signs" that anticipate the confrontation, not with our own death, but with the deaths of those we love? Does the cause of death play any role in our acceptance of it? How different would my understanding/acceptance/experience of my grandfather's death have been had he not died of cancer of the liver but, let's say, of senile dementia, of a narcotics overdose, of cardiac arrest, or in an automobile accident? What was the impact on us, the family, of the short period, nine and a half weeks to be exact, of his illness? I wondered if a longer illness would have produced different feelings and interactions. Finally, how would my professional identity, as an ethnographer, interact with my identity as a daughter/granddaughter/niece/sister/cousin? Would the combination of these multiple identities and multiple levels of inclusion accord me a different view of the situation? Through all this, however, I was certain that there was one thing I did not want to produce through this endeavor, and that was a programmatic socialization of death (as Fabian termed it [1973:188]), in which I would be dispensing recipes for coping with its existence.

The questions were all put to the test when my father's brother Tássos, at sixty years of age, took ill with a rare cancer (the second rarest in Greece, and second in fatalities after melanomas), a myosarcoma in his knee. His illness lasted a complete year, from Christmas of 1987 to Christmas of 1988. In three days his cousin Tassoulēs died of a heart attack at the age of forty-eight. Forty days later Tassoulēs' mother, Léngō (my grandfather's eldest sister), crushed by her son's death, died at the age of ninety-two. I looked back at "my" other deaths. For some reason, for some time, superstition overcame me.[3] In the beginning of 1984, a leap year, my childhood friend Panayês (at age twenty-six) died in a car accident.[4] In midyear (in July) my friend Télēs (at thirty) died of a heroin overdose (although his family are still not entirely convinced that it was not forcibly given to him). At Christmastime another childhood friend, Katerina (twenty-six), and a cousin-in-law, Thékle (forty), died of cancer—Katerina of a brain tumor, Thékle of complications after a metastasized breast cancer.

The intellectual and emotional connections I made with superstition, however, did not stop at the leap year. I noticed that every time I visited Greece someone either took ill or died. I worried that others might make the same connections and consider me the bearer of bad luck. As much as discourses on superstition and luck can be taken as simply points of everyday rhetoric, I realized that I needed to start writing about this, not for the reputed therapeutic but rather for the cathartic value of the writing process. And so the writing of this text, concerning the deaths of dear family members, close friends, an unattained love, began.

## THE SUBJECT

Καί ψυχή
εἰ μέλλει γνώσεσθαι αὐτήν
εἰς ψυχήν αὐτήν βλεπτέον:

τόν ξένο καί τόν ἐχθρό τόν εἴδαμε στόν καθρέφτη

And psyche
if she is to know herself
she ought to look
into psyche

the stranger and the enemy we saw them in the mirror
—George Seferis, "Argonauts"

Or on the monitor in the operating room, I might add. That was where I first saw my own stranger and enemy, in myself, and it was myself. There I was, lying on one of the operating tables at the hospital of the University of Pennsylvania, with the teams of an oncologist and an infertility expert leaning over me, half listening to their discussion and half discussing with my anaesthesiologist the clear advantages of an epidural over total anaesthesia. With the corner of my eye I was watching the monitor, my insides being moved around, searched, poked, and cut, when the chief surgeon leaned over my head and said: "Ms Panourgiá, I am afraid we will have to remove your fallopian tube after all." I asked if there was an alternative. "I am afraid not" was the answer. "Then let's do it," I replied, including myself not only in the decision-making process but also, somehow, in the procedure.

I also was puzzled at my surgeon's insistence on clarifying, in the most absolute terms, that I did want that piece of useless equipment out of my body that I did not insist on keeping it. "It is part of yourself, just like your cysts and your tumor," was my doctor's explanation. "It was not a different body, did not belong to anyone else. And if you wanted to keep it there, I would have left it, although I would have advised you differently." Therefore, my tumor (its benign nature notwithstanding) and my cysts were as much part of myself as my reproductive organs were. This was a rather enlightened view, first of all coming from a physician, second because that discourse did not yet exist in the biomedical environment in 1985, when I had my operation, but was introduced, rather belatedly, in the later years of the decade.

74

This is a point exceptionally elaborated by Michael Taussig, who contends that "in denying the human relations embodied in signs, symptoms, and therapy, we mystify those relations and also reproduce a political ideology in the guise of a science of physical things" (1980:3). He positions this scientification within a framework of reification leading to the development of a "biological and physical thinghood," an objectification of illness whose theorization fits so nicely into the discourse of otherness. The issue of otherness in relationship to disease and illness is hardly new, but still infinitely perplexing, because for one thing its directional point has not been made clear to us.

In reading Panos Apostolides' poem "Cancer," we see this becoming painfully apparent, since we cannot decipher whether it is he or his cancer that is being called a monster:

> Κέντησαν καί πῆραν δείγμα ἀπό τά σπλάγχνα μου
> καί μέ φωνάξαν "τέρας" κι εἴπαν ψέμματα
> πώς τάχα τῆς ὑφῆς μου τά κύτταρα δέν εἶναι κακοήθη

> They pricked and got samples from my viscera
> and they called me a "monster" and they lied
> that the cells of my texture are not malignant.
>
> (1983:36)

We do not have a fixed *topos,* a locus, a landmarking of this Other; it is unclear if it is within the body of the diseased, if it is outside the body, or if it is the ill person himself who has been accorded this condition of otherness. But this issue is also perplexing because it institutes a set of conceptual contradictions, the first of which has been situated in the mind of the patient. How can a patient think of the self if components of this self are considered other? (This point is especially crucial for the discourse of selfhood in the case of artificial limbs.) Murphy has pointed out that for four years he was unable to write about his personal bout with a tumor because of his inability to look upon himself as both "subject and object of [his] observations, to act simultaneously as author and chief protagonist, to be both ethnographer and informant" (1987:3).

This conceptual antithesis might be totally fictitious, a dichotomy construed from the inability of subjectivists and objectivists to look at the world in any combination of relationships other than binary. Such a dichotomy, scientistically, has created the need for a conceptual Other. Through our inability to look at ourselves as both the subject and the object, we are denying ourselves the possibility of being the *same* during our health and our illness, paradoxical as this might appear, as Durand would have pointed out. Ascribing to illness an otherness which is not necessarily existent, we deny our involvement in it while simultaneously embodying this otherness, creating an object in us where none exists. Furthermore, by relegating illness to the land of otherness we build a wall between the ill person and the point in that person's life that creates this different position. We divorce the cause from its effect, and consequently, "this wall, which hides reality from us, keeps us from knowing it and facing it, while it does not prevent this very reality from existing" (Rigatos 1985:148).

This reality is deeply felt and experienced not only by the patient but also by the patient's family and loved ones. The oncologist is also positioned in a precarious situation vis-à-vis the otherness of the patients. Through this objectification, this distancing of the cancer patient from the realm of the self to the realm of the Other, a paradoxical situation is created whereby this position of the cancerous person might soon enough be occupied by the physician. In this case the very ontology of the person will be challenged: Will he be himself, or will he be an Other?

Susan Sontag, after her own painful ordeal with cancer, angrily challenged the use of military metaphors in the discourse of illness, where metaphors acted as the agents of the Other, thus constructing the dominant discourse on cancer. "As TB was the disease of the sick self, cancer is the disease of the Other . . . it proceeds by a science-fiction scenario: an invasion of 'alien' or 'mutant' cells" (1979:66). The point is well taken, but it does raise a question: If medical knowledge changes in regard to the "invading" character of cancer (as in many cases it has) and considers cancer as something that anyone can *develop* rather than *contract,* would then cancer become the disease of the self instead of the Other? In other words, is cancer considered the disease of the Other because of its malevolence (a conscious personification on my part here) or because of its point of origin? And even if it is because of its point of origin, then how do we ascribe/categorize/classify otherness? How other is something from the outside, and how, really, is self something from within? What are our criteria of inclusiveness and exclusiveness, and how do we interrogate these categories? The answers can literally be a matter of life and death, as the psychosocial oncologists rightly point out.

There is nothing wrong with the idea of the Other, at least on the surface. Intrinsically it seems that the Other has replaced the exotic, the different, the alien, the evil, as an analytical and classificatory device, and here

I am concerned with how appropriate this application of otherness onto cancer might be. First of all, what is the Other, philosophically? As Gourgouris aptly points out (albeit in a different context—military discourse), the Other "is an existentialist term which very often excuses an autochthonous precautionary/preemptive expansionism" (1989:44). Therefore, by objectifying illness, by classifying it as the Other of the self and of the same, by placing it outside the embodiment of the self, the various claimants of autochthony (which, by definition, is closer to the self than is the Other), can legitimate their expansionism onto the body of the ill person.[5] In other words, the Other becomes an imaginary, a classificatory topos, where autochthony is the conceptual equal to authority and warrants natural, ethical, and territorial rights. This involves a hierarchy where the pathologist ranks above the radiologist but below the surgeon, where motherhood ranks above siblingship but below matrimony, where institutionalization of care ranks above privatization but below home care.[6] Once introduced, this heterological discourse simultaneously begs and delegitimates the complementary, relevant question of a homological discourse.

If otherness marks cancer, then does sameness mark something else, especially now that tuberculosis has generally ceased claiming lives?[7] By insisting on these binary conceptual constructions regarding illness, the locus between them is left unaccounted for and unclaimed. As Murphy has pointed out, all paraplegics and quadriplegics, all cancer and tumor patients, do not consider themselves as members of the same group. And no one could claim, by far, that all the rest of us, the "healthy" ones, belong to yet another group. Seen from a different viewpoint, this marks an "orientalist" approach to health and disease, where all those suffering from cancer are segregated to "another existence," where "interiority" is the result of the aggression of cancer that negates illness as part of human existence. In addition, it becomes also the apparent manifestation of the frustration over understanding illness—in this case a particular and individualized illness, cancer.

As an answer to this frustration, various local theories of oncogenesis have developed, each of them equally dominant within its own discourse. I will not concern myself here with biomedical explications of oncogenesis, a dominant discourse both within and outside its own locality. The theories that interest me here are the various minor ones (read: nonscientific/nonscientist) and the newly reformulated theory of psychosocial oncology, which, beyond the fact that it acknowledges possible carcinogenic agents within the realm of the psyche, also operates quite consciously as an agent of self-criticism within biomedical discourse by removing cancer and cancer patients from the topos of the Other and returning them to the sphere of humanity.

I was sitting in the lounge of the Third Surgical Clinic at the Anti-Cancer Institute of Athens, more commonly known as Aghios Savvas (Saint Sabas), keeping company with my uncle Tássos' wife, Litsa, the wife and daughter-in-law of another cancer patient, and a relatively young male patient and his wife. My uncle, who had recently undergone surgery for the extraction of a sarcoma from his leg, was being visited by his doctor. Tired, emotionally exhausted, and, because of my close relationship with my uncle, interminably frightened for his life, I was trying to catch a quick nap while politely paying some sort of attention to Litsa's murmur. "I know who did this to him," she said. I did not quite understand, and frankly, I did not want to talk to her. You see, creating my own heterologies, I was holding her responsible for my uncle's position, because she had not taken the proper steps in obtaining a diagnosis. Instead of insisting that he go to a specialist, she took him to a series of practitioners (*praktikous;* read: healers), operating under her own intellectual bias and from a traditional mistrust of Greeks toward their physicians (see Badone 1990a; and Skiffington 1990).[8]

"She did it. Iōánna did it," she continued. Iōánna is my uncle's first cousin, a spinster living with her mother who is still very attractive in her late forties. I asked what exactly Iōánna had done. "Máyia," Litsa said, a term which could loosely be rendered as "magic," or "witchcraft."[9] I was stunned and outraged. I felt the urge to tell her to go to hell. After all, who was she, an outsider to the family, accusing my cousin of having inflicted cancer upon my uncle?

Then the wife of another patient (who had been listening to the conversation, not terribly discreetly) said in a reassuring manner: "Máyia, eh?" My anthropological training dominated me, along with an unabashed curiosity about this sudden outbreak of the belief in magic. I asked Litsa how she knew this. What were the signs that signified to her that this was, indeed, an act of magic and not an act of nature? "First of all, your uncle never smoked, and second, I found a bundle in the yard made of a piece of fabric, some twigs, and hair. Underneath the pistachio trees I found it," she said.[10] I suggested that she might be wrong, that this bundle might have been formed by the wind hurling heterogeneous garbage together. Of course her answer was no. Iōánna had wanted my uncle sexually, and since she could not have him to herself she would not leave him to another woman, Litsa thought. "They are all *máyisses* [witches]," said Litsa. "You should call on a priest," said the other woman. "He will be able to tell you if it was really *máyia*. It might be only a *mountza*." (A *mountza* is the act of open palm that, properly done, addressed, and decoded is the invocation for misfortune and disaster, as well as a practical curse.) "Máyia, mountzes, kai prásina áloga" ("*Máyia, mountzes,* and green horses—rubbish"), responded the wife of the third patient, Katerina. "These things are given by God. He can inflict illness, the same way he can take it away." It seems that everyone was in agreement, that God really did have a lot to do with it all, except for me (and I was not about to say differently) and Eléni, the daughter-in-law, who became outraged and cried out: "What are you all talking about—magic, and luck, and God, and everything? Had my father-in-law not been the sensitive person he is and felt all this depression [*stenohôries*], he would never have gotten cancer."

There they were, major and minor, dominant and subordinate, lay and scientistic exegeses of oncogenesis, from the deeply religious, to the deeply satanological, to the affirmed psychosocial. There I had the development not of one truth, but of the multiplicity of "truths," explaining, understanding, perplexing, challenging their beholders, reaching for an explanation that would render the one truth, the real cause, the single answer to the question "Why?" epiphanous. This was a conscious attempt to bring their ill persons, to bring *our* ill persons, closer to us, not to send them away to a domain that we cannot reach, conceptually, emotionally, or spiritually. Such a domain does exist, and it is the ultimate unsame, the final nonself, indeed the "Other world," *ho állos kósmos.* In Deborah Gordon's words, these were theorizations aiming at "keeping the 'condemned' in this social world, and keeping death, decay, and suffering in the 'other' " (1990:276).

Tássos felt this threat later, during the last days of his life. His cancer metastasized to his lungs, and he was kept in bed strapped on an oxygen pump for a few weeks. Dêmêtra, Angelikê, and Lea went to see him. Litsa was there. Dêmêtra told me later, "We were sitting there, in his room, and we were talking very softly. We didn't want to disturb him. And he turned to us—you know, your uncle couldn't enunciate very well toward the end—and he turned to us and said, 'Speak up *paidhiá* [guys], so that I can hear too.' " That was a cry for incorporation, resulting from a fear of exclusion (even if the exclusion was the result of thoughtful discretion). Tássos asked not to be kept out, as he had not yet joined the ranks of the unsame, the unnameable, the absent, and the speechless. "Oh, we immediately complied. After all, he was still alive, with us, even though cancer had almost eaten him up. And after all, who knew? He could have made a comeback," Dêmêtra said afterward.

It may be, however, that the relegation of cancer to the realm of otherness is not a universal phenomenon. Or, said differently, maybe the Anglo-Saxon preoccupation with what Milan Kundera has called "the beautification of the world" results in a refusal to accept the ugliness of illness as part of life, thus transferring it to a land other than its own. Thus, as Father Philotheos Pharos argues (1988:65), death is accepted as the natural ending of life, it is incorporated into everyday discourse (so as to neutralize its potency?), and public conscience has been steered into a collective imagery of death as sleep, where dying has been smoothed into "resting in the hands of the Lord." Death has become Max Horkheimer and Theodor Adorno's conceptual delineation of the self, with its "prescribed beautified behavior which seeks to clothe the nakedness of death with a cloak of opulence," and "the beautified corpse [is] a formality for the hardened survivors," placed in its coffin as it is, made-up and with its watch keeping perfect time (1972:215–16).

After we returned to Tássos' room that afternoon at the hospital, we found him in good spirits, reading the newspaper. I had just spoken with his doctor, who was enthusiastic about Tássos' progress. I was happy. I stood at the foot of his bed, and he looked out of the window, from where he had a full view of Mount Hymettus and the area of Kaisarianê. Thick smoke was coming from there. He asked what was happening. I said that the whole area was burning; it had been burning since the previous evening, and firefighters did not know whether they would be able to stop the spread of the fire before it reached the monastery, because of the high winds. He turned to me, stunned: "Who would want to burn down Kaisarianê?" I didn't know. "There are all these people who have no connections with the place. Probably they want to burn it down so they can build a hotel or something there," he continued. "They have no feelings for the place," he said again. Then he asked about my conference with the doctor. I told him that the news seemed very good. "When am I going home?" he asked. I said probably in the middle of the summer, at the end of August, something like that. "Will we have time to pick the pistachios?" he asked again. I nodded. He nodded back. What did I nod? What did he nod? I am not sure. I didn't think at the time that he would be able to pick the pistachios. I was wrong. He lived almost three months past the harvest.

That night Oréstēs, then age five, and I were alone at home. It was a sweet Athenian night, most people were gone, so the air was clean, there was no smog, and we could actually smell the honeysuckle and the jasmine. We sat down to a game of Scrabble. "Tássos," Oréstēs started saying. "Uncle Tássos," I corrected him. "Yes, Uncle Tássos—he is grandfather's

Orêstēs at the time of Tássos' death

brother, eh?" Oréstēs tried his hand at kinship identification. "Indeed he is," I said. "You know, it's not *that* bad that he is dying, because he is not dying alone," he continued. "What do you mean?" I asked. "I mean, it's very bad that he is dying, but he is not dying alone. He has Vangeliô [his daughter], and Maria and Sofia [his granddaughters], and all of us, and we love him, so it's not so bad. Think if he didn't have anybody. He would just be sitting in that hospital all alone. But now he has all of us, and we love him so much." I agreed and thought of my grandfather's death two summers earlier. That night Oréstēs beat me at Scrabble with the word *óstrako* (shell).

### PARERGA

1. As Lakoff and Johnson have suggested, human experience can and should be considered under the scheme of a constructed metaphor. Metaphors, they argue, "have the power to create a new reality." Conversely, the

metaphor of love can create the reality of love in an experiential situation where love is expected to exist but is not always "objectively" attainable. But we can make love attainable, they further argue, "when we start to comprehend our experience in terms of a metaphor, and it becomes a deeper reality when we begin to act in terms of it" (1980:145). Of course, it is virtually impossible to produce a definition of *love* that would be a priori acceptable by all bound to it. Therefore, conceptual and emotional negotiations are in order for the creation of a commonly accepted metaphor of love.

2. This operation of love in family relations is something that du Boulay has also pointed out in the case of rural Greece, where "according to people's own categories it is love and affection and trust which are the true states in which humans should live" (1974:211). Of course, people's lives are not always organized according to the principles of love.

3. I use the notion of superstition as proposed by Loukatos, who writes that "superstitions are the remnants of old psychic fears of people . . . and conditions of social life" (1977:240), although it is highly debatable whether the term itself should be used to refer to the conceptualizations which organize the cosmological point of reference. The classifications of "superstition" and "superstitious" objects have a wide range, as is evident from Hobhouse's remark, in which the totality of the Greek Church falls in that category: "You may be aware that the Christian religion, if the degrading superstition of the Greek church can deserve such a title . . ." ([1817] 1971:130). My fear of the leap year was, certainly, embedded in my upbringing by a nanny from the island of Corfu, who still talked about the fairies (*neráidhes*) in the woods, although as she herself allowed, she "did not believe it, but it was beautiful to talk about it." As Stewart points out, from Levy-Bruhl's work through that of Evans-Pritchard to the more recent discussions on the "supernatural," the issue has "been treated by anthropologists (and philosophers) as a question of rationality. . . . By formulating the problem as one of 'rationality,' many of these works seem to miss the degree to which individual cognition is socially influenced, if not determined" (1989:87; see also Stewart 1991). In other words, rationality (or lack thereof), has little to do with a "belief" in the supernatural, which is rather determined or influenced by the particular social environment and the uses of it by the individual. Furthermore, Stewart argues, in present-day Greece there is a resurgence of interest in the supernatural by the upper socio-educational classes which corresponds to a parallel relative decline in belief in this same supernatural by the lower and nonurban classes, as the former have appropriated the cosmology of the latter as a medium

for "social distinction" (1989:96). Perhaps it is in this category that my connections with superstition fall. Also, having "logically" decided and theoretically accepted that any belief in the supernatural is constructed and predetermined, I have retained some feeling of it as a point of connection with my particular ethnic and social identity. See Stewart 1991 for an excellent discussion of the issue of belief, a critical inquiry into the classifications of the supernatural, and a sophisticated analysis of the preemptive role of cultural appropriations in the hegemonic relationship of the classes. See also de Certeau 1985b for a commentary on the contractual relationship between the believer and the subject.

4. Leap years were created as a result of Pope Gregory XIII's decision in 1582 to revise the Julian calendar in order to correct its inconsistencies regarding solstices and equinoxes. The new calendar was marked by the suppression of ten days (eleven after A.D. 1700) and the restriction that only years divisible by 4 would be leap years, with the exception of centesimal years, which must be divisible by 400 to be leap years. A leap year is considered particularly ominous; some people, even in present-day Athens, prefer to abstain from any significant and important actions during such a year (especially marriage and baptisms). The fear is not readily explainable, in local terms, although the prevailing explication offered is that in every leap year, February (a personification of the month, endowed and empowered with human qualities and feelings) is reminded of the injustice done to him through the robbing of his twenty-ninth day, so he retaliates by injuring those who defy him by being happy. The notion is centered around death and personal injury, and it has permeated modern Greek literature, not only at the folk level, as can be seen in the "Paralogê of the Dead Brother"—"and a leap year came along with angry months / and death came, and the nine brothers died" (in Politis 1978:140)—but also metaphorically, at the learned level, as expressed by George Seferis in "The House by the Sea": "It so happened that the years were leap; / wars destruction migration" (1964:223).

As with anything different, the fear about a leap year is based on its exclusion from order and canon, through the process of its own creation. Such a fear, Douglas argues, is created by the creation or existence of the disorderly situation, which "spoils pattern." The orderly pattern gets disrupted, becomes unrestricted, and "by implication is unlimited . . . but its potential for patterning is indefinite. This is why, though we seek to create order, we do not simply condemn disorder" (Douglas 1966:94). This idea is further reinforced by the recognition of the fabrication of that order and canon by an agent: the consecutive calendar makers—Thoth, the

Babylonians, Julius Caesar, Octavius Augustus, and Pope Gregory XIII—introduced disorder (the leap year) through their invention of order (the amendments of the calendar). Thus, a whole new cosmological discourse was created through the need for synchronization of real time with business time, and the desire of a pope for modernization and scientification of timekeeping—although it is not at all out of the question that there was an ulterior motive in operation, that of the complete and final eradication of the last institutionalized reminder of paganism (Bickerman 1974). Two facts are noteworthy: first, Greece did not adopt the new calendar until 1923, nearly 350 years after its initial introduction; and second, the fear of the leap year has permeated even the discourse on organization of life among the Greeks, despite the recent introduction of the leap year. The Old Calendrists (*Palaeoēmerologites*) have rejected this amendment of the calendar and are still keeping time according to the Julian. Almost half of the Panourgiás family are Old Calendrists.

5. *Autochthony* here can be taken in its broadest sense, that of residence, of prioritized rights, of a construction with the purpose of justifying aggression (see Leontis 1990).

6. This is a point which further informs Gourgouris' marking of the "precautionary/preemptive expansionism" of the autochthonous onto the Other, and it is especially crucial in the discussion of the hegemonic relationship between physician and patient.

7. During the past decade tuberculosis (and eventually, death by it) has returned as a serious threat, primarily in the inner-city ghettos and barrios, as a result of AIDS complications, deteriorating socioeconomic conditions, and lack of primary health care.

8. The issue of mistrust among patients, families, and physicians is well recognized within the modern Greek biomedical environment, and it is more a projection of the general mistrust experienced by the occupants of diverse positions than a personal feeling toward physicians. It also reflects a subordination of the patient to the hegemonic knowledge of the physician, especially if viewed within the context of the historical defeat of Enlightenment thought in Greece with the consequent development of a set of values that would have otherwise created a discourse of humanism and medical altruism. For an assessment of the problematic of the Englightenment in the logic of domination, see Horkheimer and Adorno 1972. For a discussion of the Enlightenment in Greece, see Dimaras 1985; Kondylis 1988; and Gourgouris in press. For a study of the specific relationship between the Greek Enlightenment and medical discourse, see Nikolaou 1984.

9. There hardly exists an analytical discourse among Greeks on urban

witchcraft and magic in or on Greece. Local exegeses are rare and range from "I don't believe in it" (which Iōánna said when I told her what Litsa had said), through "I don't believe in it but the Church accepts it," to Litsa's original position. Such a discursive absence, however, might be explained by the still dominant position of E. E. Evans-Pritchard that "systematically denied the very existence of rural witchcraft in present day Europe" (Favret-Saada 1990:191). In itself, this position reflects a European self-delineation of identity which positions Europe beyond the intellectual realm of witchcraft, further underlining the distinction between "the others"—who still discuss witchcraft—and "us"—who have liberated ourselves from the otherness of witchcraft and have thus acquired an analytical autonomy. Greece, being on the conceptual and geographic fringes of the idea of Europe (and even perhaps of European thought) and relegated to that liminal space between fatherhood of Western culture and "the looking glass" of its imaginary (Herzfeld 1987), has been tangled in the temporal dimensions of this homological-heterological discourse. The study of rural, not urban, witchcraft and magic by turn-of-the-century folklorists—primarily Politis and Lawson, in search of classical projections of modern Greek culture—constructed a temporal and spatial distance of magic from the analytical center—in this case, Athens and Europe. This separation, in turn, became the point of according modern Greece a place among "us," the intellectually and politically hegemonic "Europe," away from the even more temporally and spatially removed Other (Africa, Asia, the Americas), where witchcraft was still not only observable but also acceptable and allowable.

10. Her statement about smoking was totally irrelevant, medically, since sarcomas of the soft tissues are not associated with smoking (Konstantinidis 1982:549), but the remark is extremely valuable to the discussion of the acquisition, dissemination, and misappropriation of knowledge.

# Part II

# FRAGMENTS
# OF THE SELF

The large side of the *prósforo* seal

# List of Characters

(The names are not invented but have been recirculated through the family.)

| | |
|---|---|
| YiôrgoPanourgiás | The grandfather |
| Vangeliô | His late wife |
| | |
| Pétros | |
| Nákos | His sons |
| Aléxēs | |
| Frangiskos | |
| | |
| Violétta | |
| Chrysánthē | His daughters-in-law |
| Marina | |
| Vétta | |
| | |
| Vangeliô | |
| Myrtô | His granddaughters |
| Vangeliô-Sofia | |
| Vangeliô-Léngō | |
| | |
| Yiôrgos | Granddaughter Vangeliô's husband |
| | |
| Kyrilos | Vangeliô-Léngō's husband |
| | |
| Loukianós | His great-grandson |
| | |
| Militsa | |
| Katina | His sisters |
| Sosô | |
| Marô | |
| | |
| Ismênē | Militsa's daughter |

| | |
|---|---|
| Yiánnēs | His brother |
| Tsikō | Yiánnēs' wife |
| Achilléas | Yiánnēs and Tsikō's son |
| | |
| Nikólas | The doctor |
| | |
| Kassimēs | The undertaker |
| Yerássimos | Kassimēs' assistant |
| | |
| Iōánna | |
| Hará | Friends |
| Panōraia | |
| Nikē | |

This chapter is divided into two narratives that complement each other: "Thanatos" and "Parerga." The first provides the description, the second the analysis. Because the two chapters are so tightly connected and the analysis corresponds almost organically with the narration, I have placed them parallel to each other, "Thanatos" on top, "Parerga" underneath it. You might read them separately, or you might read them alternately, or you might glance at "Parerga" while reading "Thanatos." The parerga are placed here to act as your guide, to let you know that the questions raised in the narrative will be answered. "Parerga" is meant as a companion, a reassurance that I, the author, am with you in the endeavor of reading my narrative.

# 5

# Breath and Pulse

Ἄλυπός ἐστίν ὁ ἐν τῷ γήρᾳ θάνατος

The death of the old is without sorrow.
—Aristotle, *Micra physica*

*[handwritten margin note: means death]*

## NARRATIVE ONE: THANATOS

My grandfather YiôrgoPanourgiás took ill the summer of my fieldwork and perished, of cancer, within two and a half months. Since it was summer,

▲▲▲▲▲▲▲▲▲▲▲▲▲▲▲▲▲▲▲▲▲▲▲▲▲▲▲▲▲▲

## NARRATIVE TWO: PARERGA

### To Name

Primarily in deference to Yiôrgos Panourgiás, I use here the Arvanitikē mode of calling, whereby the first and last names are combined into a single utterance, thus indicating not only the patriline but also the ordinal number of the person in the family. In other words, given the usual Greek naming pattern of alternating the names of the children between the two sets of grandparents, where the firstborn is named after the paternal father or mother (according to gender), the second child after a maternal grandparent, and the next ones alternating, my father's name (Kōnstantinos) could only be had by the second child, since it was the name of his maternal grandfather. However, I, a first child, was named after my maternal grandmother (Eléni), since when I was born my paternal grandmother (Evangelia) informed my parents that she did not wish me named after her (since my elder cousin had already been named after her) and she preferred that I be named after her own mother, Katina. Allegedly my mother, Dêmētra, said, "You must be crazy if you think I am going to name my daughter *that*," and decided to name me after her own mother. My sister, three years younger than I, was given a triple name which included my paternal grandmother's name: Stélla-Evangelia-Vassilikê.

most of the family was in Greece, visiting from the various areas around the globe where they live permanently. A brother was here, a *nýphē* there, a grandchild vacationing at an island.[1] As his health worsened, the rest of the members of the family appeared, creating the perfect setting for what would follow—an almost complete disruption of the family and its eventual restructuring. But this was hardly a novel development in the relationships of the family. In the past, at any given time, any one of the brothers—four of them all together—would not be on speaking terms with any one of the others. The usual explanation for this was financial, that someone gave someone else money for which the first was never reimbursed. The "real" reason for this lies outside the consanguineous family, according to one of the brothers: "It's all the fault of the in-laws. When we are only family, just the siblings alone, we can make it. When the wives get in the way, that's when we can't stand the sight of each other. You know that from your experience with your brother-in-law. You know that with my brother, before we both married, we never exchanged a bitter word. Our friends were envious. One day something happened—it was the day that

▲▲▲▲▲▲▲▲▲▲▲▲▲▲▲▲▲▲▲▲▲▲▲▲▲▲▲▲▲▲▲▲

The triple naming of Stélla offers an illuminating example of the factors and prescriptions that inform the selection and bestowing of a name. Stélla was born dangerously premature and was kept in a special unit at the Children's Hospital for almost five months. Several times a week the nurses would phone to tell us that her death was imminent and to ask what name my mother wanted to call her so that the nurses could "air-baptize" her, so that she would be named when she arrived in heaven. Dêmētra had decided that she would name the baby after Saint Stylianos, the patron saint of newborns. When Stélla was released from the hospital and all danger had passed, new discussions started about her naming. Dêmētra thought that it was only fair to keep her promise to the saint but also to honor her mother-in-law, Evangelia, by giving the baby both names. When time came for the baptism and the priest asked in church, in front of all the guests, what the name of the baby would be, Dêmētra answered, "Stylianê-Evangelia." The priest countered that a double name was not an option and that Dêmētra would have to pick one of the two. Both insisted on their position, and a heated argument ensued, during which Dêmētra grabbed the baby from the hands of the priest, headed toward the door, and told him, as she now says, "Fine. I'll take her to the Catholics, who will give her twenty-two names if I so wish." At that point the other priest of the *enoria,* the elderly and sweet Patêr Vassileios, snatched the baby from

92

our grandfather died—we started arguing, one word led to another, and we started fighting. It was a spectacle new in the neighborhood. Our friends gathered around, telling each other, 'The Panourgiádhes are fighting,' and eventually they tried to break us up. The moment they moved in we forgot all about our fight, and we turned against them. That's how close we were. And now look at us, we are fighting like dogs."

Another reason, however, has contributed to the rancor among these four brothers. When Frangiskos ended his love affair with Violétta after he met Vétta (whom he eventually married), his brother Pétros (already divorced and with a teenage daughter from his previous marriage), thought that Violétta had suffered an injustice and took it upon himself to repair it by marrying her. What followed was a physical and emotional separation of the two brothers and, furthermore, a separation of the family, which has not met as a complete unit for twenty-two years except at the funerals of the parents and, eventually, the funeral of Pétros himself.

The setting is in Athens, in the summer of 1986. Three of YiôrgoPanourgiás' four sons are there. All his daughters-in-law, all his grandchildren and

▲▲▲▲▲▲▲▲▲▲▲▲▲▲▲▲▲▲▲▲▲▲▲▲▲▲▲▲

Dêmētra's hands, plunged her into the baptismal basin (the *kolymbêthra*), and named her Styliané-Evangelia-Vassilikê (Vassilikê being the feminine of his own name). No one ever understood why that happened. When the official papers were produced, Styliané had been changed to Stélla. We all call her Lea as a combination of the three names.

As Herzfeld has observed, one should avoid "simplistic formulations about the existence of *a* [naming] system" (1982b:289), a note of warning which alludes to the complexity of naming practices throughout Greece. Herzfeld also notes that "the transmission of property never absolutely follows that of names, even in the formal norms" (291), a point which liberates the discussion on the connections between *onomatothesia* (naming) and inheritance from the strictness of social norms and forms and allows for individual and identitary strategic movements on the part of the actors. Simply put, Herzfeld's formulation on the lack of an exact and strictly canonized correlation between naming patterns and inheritance rights allows actors some choice of names (other than those belonging to either set of grandparents) without constant fear or concern of repercussions in inheritance. Thus viewed, Stélla-Evangelia's naming of her two sons Oréstēs and Iásōn (when her father's name is Kōnstantinos and her former father-in-law's Dēmêtrēs) should be interpreted not simply as a "strategic" movement toward a liberation from tradition but also as a

great-grandchildren, are there. He is ill and he knows it, but he still prefers to live alone in his apartment, accepting the visits of his son Pétros and his daughter-in-law Violétta. They come around about once a week, they take him for a ride, and they have lunch with him, which he has cooked for them. Occasionally his granddaughter Myrtô comes to see him; he tells her stories and off-color jokes and complains about his children. They don't visit him enough, "although they live so close"; they don't help each other out, "though they can afford it. What can I say, my child? I dread the time I close my eyes, because I fear that they will never talk to each other again." The days pass, and he is put in the hospital for tests. His health is deteriorating rapidly, and only Myrtô (who has nothing else to do) is there all the time. Some of his sons go to see him every other day; some of his daughters-in-law go every three or four days. Some never do. When he returns home, his son Aléxēs—just landed from abroad expressly to be with his father in his illness—and Myrtô stay with him. Time passes as they watch him wither away. One day his sisters come to see him. They come once, a short journey of forty kilometers. It bothers him that this was the only time they came. Another day his brother comes. They sit, reminiscing, talking about the fields.

YiôrgoPanourgiás ninety days before his death

Within a couple of weeks he confined himself to bed. He only brought himself to the table to have lunch with Aléxēs and Myrtô. One day I was having lunch with them, and YiôrgoPanourgiás felt sick at the table. Aléxēs—out of a sense of decency, as he explained later to me—left the table and moved to the veranda, where his nýphē (his brother Nákos' wife), Kyria Chrysánthē, was sitting. Myrtô followed her grandfather to the bathroom to help him. When they came back to the table he pointed at his son, still on the veranda, and said to her, "When I talk to you, you should listen. Do you see them? They all turn their backs on me when they see my ugliness." Later, recounting the story, Myrtô could not help but cry, because, she said, "it really was not right what Grandpa said, Neni. Aléxēs was not disgusted. But Grandpa could not see it that way. He wanted to feel rejected, so that he would reject himself easier when the time came."

Not long thereafter we saw another sign of this. It was the beginning of the fifteen-day lent for the Dormition of the Virgin, the Dhekapentaúgoustos, and Myrtô knew that her grandfather would not live until another Dormition. She discussed it with Aléxēs, and they decided that Yiôrgo-

▲▲▲▲▲▲▲▲▲▲▲▲▲▲▲▲▲▲▲▲▲▲▲▲▲▲▲▲▲▲

consciously and equally strategic movement to distance herself from her parents and former in-laws. (For a more detailed analysis of the issue of naming, self-identification, and inheritance, see Herzfeld 1985 and Vernier 1984. On the development of dowry and property transfers in Athens, see Sant Cassia and Bada 1992.)

## Exoterics

Certainly the argument of an antagonistic relationship among in-laws is not new in anthropological theory, as the early anthropological analyses of Greece attest, especially the work done by Friedl (1962), Campbell (1964), and du Boulay (1974). What is apparent from Aléxēs' statement, however, is that the argument exhibits its falsehood by its own utterance. The statement that "it's all the fault of the in-laws" directly disagrees with the recounting of the fighting story, since when the fight occurred there were no in-laws yet present. Hence the statement (and its mendacity) manifests the discordance between the hegemony of the ideal in family relations ("We never exchanged a bitter word") and the acceptance of an unwanted reality ("We fought, and they tried to break us up").

The problem seems to be accentuated with the marriage of sons, who bring home *nýphēs* (brides) who become daughters-in-law and sisters-in-

Panourgiás would probably like to go to church and take Communion. Myrtô started coaxing him to go. His evasions were only too obvious to be taken for legitimate excuses. "We will see how I feel . . . if I am feeling better . . . I can't make any plans . . . the church is too far away . . . it's so hot out." Finally, when Myrtô went on the eve of the holiday to discuss the particulars of the churchgoing, YiôrgoPanourgiás exclaimed, pointing at his protruding bones: "Look at me. Look at my *katándia* [sorry state]. How can I show my face in church like this? What will my friends think, eh? They will say: 'Look at Panourgiás, how he was and what he looks like now [*pos échei katandêsei*]. Let it pass. We'll go together next year." Thirteen days later he died.

"He didn't care as much as to take Communion, Neni," Myrtô told me some time later, "although what Communion did my grandfather need? He was as clean in heart as a Paschal Lamb. But his dignity, his self-esteem, his whole cosmology, were shattered. His illness did not bother him as much as his protruding bones, the ugliness of his body."

"Homer has said it all," our friend Hará said. "Look at the passage

▲▲▲▲▲▲▲▲▲▲▲▲▲▲▲▲▲▲▲▲▲▲▲▲▲▲▲▲▲▲

law (also *nýphēs*). Since these women come to the families as classificatory daughters, they are expected to exhibit a heightened emotional involvement with the affairs of the family, since women are understood to be emotionally both more sensitive and stronger than men. Emotional involvement, however, also means a greater degree of participation, and this situation inevitably involves disagreements as well as agreements. There the game of alliances and inclusion is played. When everyone agrees, everyone is part of the same family. When the newcomers disagree, then their allegiance to the family unit is questioned, and they are considered outsiders, *exōterikoi*, of the family (even if momentarily). All the daughters-in-law in a family are, to each other, *synyphádhes* (*syn-nýphēs*, brides together), a relationship which positions each woman in an antithetical and antagonistic relationship with the rest, for the attainment of the favors of her in-laws. In this scheme, what actually figures prominently are the allowances that parents make for their children and a certain favoritism, which is perpetuated and transferred to the new family of the favored child and in turn to that child's spouse.

## An Other Death

The Dhekapentaúgoustos is the third major celebration of the Orthodox Church. The beginning of August marks the beginning of the fifteen-day

where Priam loathes death because his ugly, aged body would be displayed for all to see."

A few days after the church incident, Myrtô (a self-proclaimed Christian atheist, it should be noted in passing) arranged for an *efhélaio,* the ritual of Holy Unction which takes place every Holy Wednesday or whenever a Christian feels the need to have the house blessed. I went with her to call on the priest of the *enoria* (parish) who comes to perform the ritual at the house. Myrtô had wanted to ask Patêr Theofánēs, her grandfather's confessor (*pneumatikós*), but he was away on vacation. We talked to a new priest. He agreed to come for the efhélaio. Then he informed her that any members of the family who were not Greek Orthodox, or had had a civil rather than a religious wedding were not allowed to attend. Myrtô answered that a Roman Catholic in-law was away at the moment. Then they set the day and the time for the *efhélaio.* She arranged for a small group of kin and nonkin family to be there: her sister, Léngō; her mother, Kyria Chrysánthē; two of her aunts, Violétta and Marina; her cousin Sofia; and two friends, Iōánna and Panōraia. No members of her mother's side of the

▲▲▲▲▲▲▲▲▲▲▲▲▲▲▲▲▲▲▲▲▲▲▲▲▲▲▲▲▲▲

lent, the shortest of the three long-term lenten periods (the other two being the forty-day periods preceding Christmas and Easter). As Megas notes (1963:146), this is an easy lent to keep, since August is a month abundant in fresh fruits and vegetables. Thus abstention from meat is not difficult, nor is it experienced as deprivation. There is only one break in the lent that allows for the consumption of fish—but not of meat or dairy products— and that is the celebration of the Transfiguration of Christ. This is actually a self-referential circle to Christ through the consumption of fish (*ichthys*), which is also the attribute of Christ (*ICHTHYS—Iēsous CHristós THeou Yiós Sōtêr,* Jesus Christ Son of God Savior).

Each evening of the fifteen-day period, vespers are sung in church to Mary. The day of the Dormition, which is the end of lent, commemorates the death of Mary. The importance of the religious celebration has been augmented by the added fact of the bombing of the submarine *Héllē* at the port of the island of Tenos, site of the largest church and most important shrine dedicated to Mary, on 15 August 1940, which opened the way for Greece's involvement in the Second World War (see Dubisch 1990).

## Negotiations

The *efhélaio* was suggested by various friends of the family, and by Iōánna, Myrtô's good friend, to ward off a curse that might have been placed on

family appeared at the house before the funeral, since there has not been much interaction between the two families over the years, and relationships and courtesy calls have been kept to a level of social politeness. I was there helping Myrtô arrange everything. We filled one bowl with flour, another one with water, and a third one with oil. In the flour we stuck seven yellow candles. When the priest arrived he spread his cloth on the table and blessed the flour, the oil, and the water. He read the liturgy, anointed us all with the blessed oil, and sprinkled the room with *ayiasmó* (blessed water), using a sprig of fresh basil. Then he asked where the invalid was so that he could anoint and bless him. Myrtô told him that her grandfather did not want to be disturbed; he was feeling very weak. The priest read, sotto voce, so as not to be heard by the ailing old gentleman, a prayer for his soul. Myrtô cleared the table, kept the flour to make a *prósforo* (offering bread), and took some ayiasmó to her grandfather. "Tomorrow," he said, "before breakfast." He never took it. He only looked at his wife's picture on the wall and sighed. "Ah, Kyrá Vangeliô," he said. Nothing else.

▲▲▲▲▲▲▲▲▲▲▲▲▲▲▲▲▲▲▲▲▲▲▲▲▲▲▲▲▲▲

the family. Iōánna, a fellow "atheist" and a member of the Greek Communist Party—unknowingly echoing Pascal's famous bet—had an answer ready for Myrtô when the latter insisted that she believed neither in curses nor in the efhélaio. "Have it," Iōánna said. "If there is a God, he will be pleased, and if there isn't, you have nothing to lose." This statement is the encapsulation of the personal, almost casual, relationship of Greeks to religion and the organized church, in contrast to their intimate, almost organic, relationship with ritual.

If the efhélaio is the supplication on behalf of the ill, the Thrice Holy Prayer (the Trisáyio) is the supplication on behalf of the dead. It is said not only as a means of intervention for the salvation of the soul of the departed but also as an evocation for the intervention of the departed on behalf of the bereaved. "If the dead are honored, known, and recognized, they win differentially, and in terms of structural differences, bestow blessings," notes Victor Turner (1992:34). In other words, the equation is more or less as follows: I, the living, will say a Trisáyio for your salvation, since you are dead, because I remember you and want to ensure that your soul is resting peacefully, and because I expect you in turn to intervene for my well-being while I am alive and my salvation when I die. This practice, however, in a religion that does not have an official notion of Purgatory, does raise a few questions, which I will address later.

For the following few days he spoke little. He mostly kept to himself. He complained about his inability to eat anything. "I am like a baby. Only what comes in a spoon can I eat," he said. Once, two days before he died, he looked up and sighed, "Ah, Christ, why don't you take me?" He was progressively worried about Myrtô, and in his precomatose condition, having lost the sense of time, mistaking day for night, he would reprimand her because she was still up at four o'clock—at night, he thought. The evening before he died he came to a moment of clarity. He could not utter his words very clearly, and the only one able to communicate with him was Myrtô. He woke up and realized that the telephone had been removed from his side into the living room. He asked for it, but since Myrtô was not there at the moment, no one could understand what he was saying. They sent for Myrtô, who asked him what he wanted. "The telephone," he replied with as much authority as his condition would allow him. "The telephone will stay here." Myrtô took the telephone to him, and he lapsed back into his coma. His son Frangiskos asked, "What does he want the telephone for?"

▲▲▲▲▲▲▲▲▲▲▲▲▲▲▲▲▲▲▲▲▲▲▲▲▲▲▲▲▲

A number of nonkin members of the family participate in these rituals, namely friends who have gained status as family members through the love, support, and affiliation they have exhibited toward the family throughout the years. Iōánna (Myrtô's friend) and Nikē (Kyria Chrysánthē's fellow teacher) are the two women here accorded by Myrtô and her sister, Léngō, this privileged status. The two missing from this are Katerina and her husband, Sōtêrēs, who were away on vacation. The family-member status of these people is manifested in Katerina's frequent jocular comment about our relationships until now having been utterly incestuous (*aimo-meiktikés*).

## Seals and Signs

*Prósforo* is the offering bread, usually made by women of the parish, which is used at Holy Eucharist. One can make the bread and bring it to church as a supplication for a special favor by a saint or the Virgin Mary. Whenever the sacrament of the Holy Unction is performed privately, at home, the flour used has to be made into a prósforo (also known as *litouryiá,* a term akin to *litouryía,* or liturgy).

The bread is made without any oil—simply with flour, salt, and water— and it is shaped into a perfect round. After the first rising a seal bearing the sign of the Cross and the inscription "Jesus Christ Conquers All" is

Everybody laughed. The next day YiôrgoPanourgiás got up once to use the bathroom. He asked Myrtô to trim his fingernails and comb his hair. He fell back into his coma, and later that day, at 3:40 P.M., he died.

The day he died Myrtô had been with him constantly. The family had been expecting him to die that day. "He is much worse [*váryne*]," everyone said. Friends and distant relatives started dropping by, concerned and worried. Myrtô had a book she was reading while waiting with him, James Mitchener's *Centennial*. I stayed with her. Our little nephew, Loukianós, three years of age, was with us. I tried to get him out of the room, telling him that his grandpa needed quiet. "I'll be quiet. I'll sit right here, on the bed next to you, and you won't hear a peep from me," he said. He sat on the bed next to me, and for a very long time he watched, saying nothing. He just sat there. Then he said, "What does it mean to die, Neni?" I tried to explain to him that death is the cessation of life. "Is it because everything has an end?" he continued. I agreed. "If we loved Great-Grandpa more, would he still have died?" I said, "Yes, he would still have died." He seemed perplexed and interested, but not upset. He asked about the heavy

▲▲▲▲▲▲▲▲▲▲▲▲▲▲▲▲▲▲▲▲▲▲▲▲▲▲▲▲▲▲▲▲

pressed on the top, and the bread is allowed to rise for the second time. The seal is removed before baking, and when the bread is taken to church to be used in the liturgy, the priest cuts first around the sign of the seal, saves that part, and then proceeds with the cutting of the rest of the bread. The part that bears the seal is the part that goes into the chalice and is mixed with the wine to produce the Eucharist. The rest of the bread is distributed, after the liturgy, to the members of the congregation who did not partake in Communion. Certainly the symbolism of the bread cannot be overstressed in the southern and eastern Mediterranean cultural environment. As Piña-Cabral notes about Portugal, "The bread is used as a symbol of community created through the unity of commensality" (1986:42). Doubly so is bread which has been blessed. Inherent in the symbolism of the bread is the Christian parable of the grain of wheat that has to die in order to sprout again and give forth life. Hence at funerals and memorial liturgies a small round sweetened loaf of bread is given away along with the *kóllyva*.

As far as the official church is concerned, the prósforo cannot be touched by a woman during her menstrual period. If the time to offer it coincides with that, then she must have someone purchase it at the bakery and deliver it to the priest. As with everything else, however, this is simply the prescription and not always the praxis. When Myrtô wanted to make the prósforo after the efhélaio at her grandfather's apartment, she

breathing sound that was coming from YiôrgoPanourgiás. I took him to the living room, where I tried to tell him that even a comatose person might still be able to listen to things around him, and it might not be easy for him to listen to people talking about his death. Loukianós looked at me with incredulity at my stupidity. "But he is dying," he said. "Don't you think he knows it?"

I realized that I was falling into the same trap that Michel de Certeau had warned me against, the presumption of the need of the dying man to remain calm and rested. I was unable to utter the anguish and the pain, much like the staff of the hospital in de Certeau's example. I too could not *say* it, although I was refusing, with all my strength, to treat my grandfather as already dead.[2] Loukianós' questioning brought all these thoughts and feelings to the forefront again, and I had no answers to give him.

Iôánna came in with some coffee and saved me from further embarrassment. "I thought you could use some," she said. She left almost immediately, taking Loukianós with her, despite his protests that he wanted to watch his great-grandfather die. Myrtô turned to me: "See? How can I

▲▲▲▲▲▲▲▲▲▲▲▲▲▲▲▲▲▲▲▲▲▲▲▲▲▲▲▲▲▲▲▲▲▲

was menstruating and told her mother, Chrysánthē, about her hesitations over baking it. Chrysánthē became furious "Are you out of your mind? Of course you will make it, and you will proudly [*perêfana*] take it to that billygoat (*ston trágo* [the priest])," she said. (On the ambiguous and, more often than not, antithetical relationship between priest and congregation, especially the women, see Seremetakis 1991.)

The symbolism of wine is as strongly associated with death as that of oil and bread (see Hatzisotiriou 1980:138–41). Long before Christianity and the equation of wine with the wasted blood of Christ, wine and oil were the two substances used in the libation rituals of ancient Greece. Wine is used in the last washing of the dead body, before it is taken away and interred, and oil is used in the oil lamp that is kept lit in front of the icons (at home and in the church), as well as on the grave. Great controversy erupted a few years ago, when churches started using electric instead of oil lamps in front of their icons. Church officials contend that this is a much safer practice, as it minimizes the possibilities of accidental fires. Many *enorites* (parishioners) counter that it does not have much to do with safety but rather with modernity, which they feel should not be part of the official church.

Handling of the prósforo by women during their menstruation is not the only prohibition concerning the relationship of women with the Church.

not consider Iōánna closer than most of my family? Who else thought to bring us anything all these hours that we have been here?"

The doctor, an old family friend who had been summoned a few hours earlier, and Chrysánthē came in. The doctor confirmed Myrtô's diagnosis: her grandfather was in a coma. He did not respond to any stimuli. Probably his lungs had collapsed, since he was breathing very heavily, making a sound like a reed flute. Myrtô waited. Kyria Chrysánthē came in and tried to feed some milk to her father-in-law. He mechanically swallowed it. Myrtô became impatient with her: Why was she torturing him? He was ready to die in a few hours. Why was she doing it? Kyria Chrysánthē kept at it: "He is burning inside from the cancer. I remember from Grandmother too. I know. We have to give him liquids continually," she said. Myrtô chased her and the doctor out of the room, but they soon returned. There was still no sign of relief, so they left. Myrtô moved over, sat at the edge of his bed, and stroked his hand, but he tried to pull it away. "Pappou," she said, "Pappou, do you hear me? Do something, Pappoulē."[3] Yiôrgo-Panourgiás took four long, deep breaths, turned his eyes, and died. It was

▲▲▲▲▲▲▲▲▲▲▲▲▲▲▲▲▲▲▲▲▲▲▲▲▲▲▲▲▲▲▲

Even greater is the prohibition regarding the altar and the sanctum, the *hierón*. The hierón, behind the templum, is the area where the altar is placed. The templum, the altar screen, is a part of the church structure exclusive to the Eastern Orthodox Church. It separates and conceals the area of the altar from the rest of the church. Made of wood, marble, or a combination of marble and wood, very intricately carved, it carries on it in predesignated places the icons of Christ, the Virgin Mary, Saint John the Baptist, Saint Nikólaos, the Archangels Michael and Gabriel, and the icon of the patron saint of the specific church.

## Tactful Words

We expect someone to die rather than expect it (death) to happen. Hatzisotiriou, a medical doctor and folklorist extraordinaire, has collected a number of different expressions which seem to be in standard use. He has, further, reported on expressions used by the dying themselves, the commonest being "Please let me die so that I will get to rest and not exhaust my family [*tous dhikous mou*], for they might regret me [*tha me varyngō-máne*]" (1980:137). The expression, if taken apart etymologically, alludes to the weight an ailing person might impose on his or her family; the term has two components: weight (*város*) and opinion (*gnômē*). It is indeed

almost four o'clock in the afternoon. I stood there looking at this person who in a split second was transformed from alive to dead, from a personality to a corpse, from a name to a body, this person whom I had dearly loved all my life, who had marked me as a person, who had placed me in a separate category from the rest of his grandchildren. I stood there, stunned, unable to move, to do anything, even to cry or close his eyes. Then I remembered Nikólas, the doctor, waiting with Kyria Chrysánthē in her apartment. I had to summon him. He had to sign the death certificate. I wanted Myrtô with me, but we did not want to leave our grandfather alone—as if it really mattered. We went for the doctor together. He came in, soon followed by Kyria Chrysánthē. He checked for vital signs and found none. Then he asked me to do the same, which I did. It was a strange feeling, feeling for a pulse in a warm body that has none. The incongruity of it startled me. Nikólas confirmed the death. He looked at me and said, "You are very composed." I could not explain to him at the moment that had I not assumed this anthropologically informed "composure" I would have broken down with grief, anger, and despair, something which, inevi-

▲▲▲▲▲▲▲▲▲▲▲▲▲▲▲▲▲▲▲▲▲▲▲▲▲▲▲▲▲▲

understood as a courtesy to the dying for people to possess tact, good manners. Or as Freud has put it, in regard to the death of the Other, the civilized man avoids mentioning the possibility of death, if there is a chance that the dying one might be listening. Only children violate this restriction (1991:341). The emphasis here is not on the "civilized man" but rather on the violation of the restriction by the yet uncivilized (that is, unsocialized) children.

## The Price of the Rite

The cost and the "class" (grade) of the funeral are two points of primary importance. There are three classes of funerals available in urban centers— C, B, and A—and they are progressively more expensive. The basic service is the same. In all cases the funeral home is responsible for the removal of the body from the place of death and its transportation to the funeral parlor and, eventually, to the cemetery. The undertakers also make all the arrangements for the funeral: they contact the cemetery and arrange the day and the time of the funeral, arrange for the kóllyva to be prepared, and arrange for the preparation of the grave. All funerals have at least one priest, assisted by a deacon and a cantor. A class B funeral has an additional priest, three cantors, and cut flowers placed in vases around the coffin.

tably, happened later. To this day Kyria Chrysánthē insists that she and Nikólas were present when YiôrgoPanourgiás died, that the rest is simply a figment of Myrtô's and my imagination, shaken and disturbed by our grandfather's death.

Kyria Chrysánthē, then, in an almost narrational twist, started taking charge in matters pertaining to the funeral. She called the funeral parlor and had the manager, Kassimēs, come to the house and arrange the particulars. I marveled at her ability to negotiate the best possible price for a class A funeral. She reminded Kassimēs that they had been doing business together for almost twenty years, that his father had been a friend of YiôrgoPanourgiás and his wife since the war, and that Kassimēs should get his profit through other people, not through the Panourgiás family. It was a little speech that aimed directly at his self-worth (*filótimo*) and challenged his loyalty to a family who had patronized his business for a long time. It worked like a charm. Kassimēs promised that Zográphou had not yet seen a funeral as resplendent as this one would be. Myrtô said she would like the funeral to take place at the old chapel of Saint Nikólaos, where

▲▲▲▲▲▲▲▲▲▲▲▲▲▲▲▲▲▲▲▲▲▲▲▲▲▲▲▲▲▲▲

Class A is the most expensive funeral, and it involves the presence of three priests and a bishop, a choir in addition to the three cantors, and potted plants in addition to the cut flowers. This was a first-class funeral based on the number of priests officiating (three), the rank (a bishop), the choir, and the number of flowers.

The funeral is certainly the most important, public, and staged drama of the whole process of death. As Prior points out, the director of this staged drama, where the dead body is the main prop, is the undertaker (1989:155). In this drama the performance addresses the society of the living, not the society of the dead. As Firth has noted, "It is a social rite *par excellence*. Its ostensible object is the dead person, but it benefits not the dead, but the living" (1951:63).

## Not to Name

References to the "dead" by all the survivors (not only the bereaved but also the undertakers) indicate a relationship among people that goes beyond the professional categorizations into identitary groups, such as the physicians' reference to the "patient." After all, being a patient is a potentially reversible condition. Being a "dead" is not. Being a "dead" (instead of a patient, a person, or a woman) is rather a characterization that sepa-

her grandmother's funeral had been held eleven years before. Kassimēs appeared reluctant, saying that the chapel was too small, it would be too hot and crowded, they were expecting a lot of people to attend, and all of them could not be accommodated comfortably there. "We'll do it in the new church. We'll put nice flowers, we'll have the choir, the bishop. There will be space for people to move around. It will be really pretty. Don't you worry, we'll take very good care of your grandfather. You'll like it. I want to do something proper [*sōstó*] for him," he told Myrtô. She was still reluctant to give in. Then her mother intervened feebly: "Let him do it where he wants. Don't you see he wants to do something really nice? It won't matter to your grandfather anyhow," she said. Myrtô finally agreed, and they made the arrangements for the funeral to take place in the new church, Saints Kōnstantinos and Eléni.

Within one hour the closest relatives had been informed by telephone, called by the close friends, relatives, and neighbors who came as soon as the death occurred. The message was short and clear: "Aunt Militsa, life to us" ("Theia Militsa, zoë s'emás"). Vangeliô-Sophia, who was making the

▲▲▲▲▲▲▲▲▲▲▲▲▲▲▲▲▲▲▲▲▲▲▲▲▲▲▲▲▲▲

rates life from death, persons from objects, souls from flesh, much like the police or the coroner's category of "the body" or "the cadaver." Papayiorgis (1991) argues that the traumatic point of the deceased ceasing to be familiar lies in the fact that the exit from life is experienced through the definitive and ultimate exit from the house. Thus the term *dead* (*ho nekrós*) becomes the official term, the announcement, marking the space of death as separate from life, straddled only by the engraving of the name of the "dead" on the tombstone, labeling the new and permanent home.

## Beheadings and Displacements

It is understood that children should visit their dead parents as soon as the death occurs. Not all children can bear do that; not all of us can, either. Nákos could not. That was not how Nákos' reluctance, indeed refusal, to cross the small corridor and go into his father's apartment to see him dead was read, however. The general feeling conveyed was that Nákos was simply untouched by his father's death but was hiding it behind a facade of aversion toward death. It should be noted, however, that a few days before his father's death Nákos had a violent disagreement with his daughter Léngō and her husband, Kyrilos, over their son, Loukianós. Léngō had been in bed with the flu at Nákos' house, and her son and husband were

telephone call, did not have the chance to say anything else. The response was immediate at the other end: "*Au, móy dialyith,* he is gone, he left us [*éfyghe*]." "What can we do, *theia mou?* Grandpa left us." "When did it happen, *móy dialyith?*" "Fifteen minutes ago. We called Kassimēs, to arrange for the funeral. I will call you to tell you when it is, *theia mou.* We are hoping tomorrow, so that he doesn't have to stay too long in refrigeration. Do you think you can call the rest of the relatives there and tell them?" "Tell them? What can I tell them, *móy koitçi mou?* How can I tell them our brother died? I'll have Ismēnē call them."[4]

In a similar manner the rest of the relatives and friends were informed, and the first mourners started arriving. Myrtô's sister, Léngō, had been on the way to visit her grandfather, but stuck in traffic, she did not get to the house until after he died. The undertaker was there and had already displayed the cover of the coffin at the entrance of the building, to inform the neighbors that a death had occurred. Léngō immediately guessed that the cover signaled her grandfather's death and nobody else's. On the doorstep she met the undertaker. She came upstairs, drenched in tears and shaking.

▲▲▲▲▲▲▲▲▲▲▲▲▲▲▲▲▲▲▲▲▲▲▲▲▲▲▲▲▲▲

there visiting. Kyrilos reprimanded Loukianós for something he had done and spanked him. Nákos became furious over the spanking of his grandchild and reprimanded Kyrilos, who defended his position. Léngō became involved in the argument, and at this point her father kicked all three of them out of his house. Myrtô intervened in a rather moralistic manner, trying to remind Nákos that Léngō was his daughter and that she was ill. "Ill people go to hospitals," answered Nákos. "You are all driving me mad," he said, and slapped Myrtô across the face. As Myrtô said later, she knew that the slap was not intended for her but rather for everyone who had been, in various ways, pressuring him. The incident would not have any more significance other than as a marker of some family relationships had it occurred outside the context of death. Nákos is a very reserved man, who prides himself on being in control of his emotions, on being logical, methodical, objective, and well organized. His behavior could be described as erratic, except that it happened a few days before his father's death and thus should be viewed through the general framework of grieving and mourning. And grieving and mourning can indeed have a tremendous impact on people's behavior toward their surroundings, even bringing to the surface feelings that are, on a superficial level, incongruous with the specific person but perfectly human and understandable nevertheless.

Rosaldo (1984) has argued that head-hunting among the Ilongot should

"I had been expecting it, Neni, all this time," she said as I held her. "But I didn't want to find out about it in such a way—seeing that crow [*to koráki*] downstairs! And the coffin cover! He didn't say anything, but he had that smile on his face, that peevish goatlegged man [*o katsikopódharos*]."

Meanwhile Yerássimos, Kassimēs' assistant, came in and asked where the "dead one" (*ho nekrós*) was. I realized that from then on my grandfather did not have a name. No one would refer to him as YiôrgoPanourgiás, but as *ho nekrós*. His identity did not coincide with that of persons any longer but belonged to the ranks of nonpersons. He was indeed part of death, the unnameable itself.[5] I resolved to notice who would and who would not refer to him by his name.

Yerássimos started preparing the body. Myrtô and I, along with Kyria Chrysánthē, an accomplished mourner who was capable at preparing dead bodies for burial herself, remained in the bedroom. Myrtô took out the shroud that her grandfather had purchased from the Church of the Dormition in Jerusalem and laid it out for Yerássimos to use. Yerássimos undressed the body and washed it with the red wine that Kyria Chrysán-

▲▲▲▲▲▲▲▲▲▲▲▲▲▲▲▲▲▲▲▲▲▲▲▲▲▲▲▲▲▲

also be viewed within the context of grief and mourning. By beheading an unsuspecting victim and tossing the head away, the headhunter releases part of his grief and pain and vents his anger toward death. I position Nákos' behavior within this conceptual framework, and his suggestion that his (unsuspecting, ill) daughter go to a hospital constitutes a symbolic beheading, which is a reaction to his sense of grief and bereavement. Within this context, his encounter with Myrtô later at the cemetery takes on a hue of apology, an acceptance of the death of his father, and the formation of a unity between him and his daughter which excluded others.

## Conspirators in Noise

Very confidentially, Chrysánthē told Myrtô and me to break the plate, in the usual manner, inside the house, as the body was carried through the threshold. Nothing was strange about that; after all, it was something she and I had done before. There are some inconsistencies, though. Papayiorgis (1991) mentions the breaking as taking place *outside* the house. Politis (1894), in addition to the breaking of the plate, mentions the practice of breaking a jug full of water. In Cyprus, Cypriot friends tell me, the jug is full of oil, and it is broken at the gravesite. On the island of Kalymnos, in the village of Emborios, the jug is broken at the grave and then used as a

A grave on the island of Kalymnos marked by a broken jug instead of a cross

marker on the head of the grave instead of a cross. Aristides Baltas told me of an even further abstraction of the symbolic use of the jug on the island of Corfu, where jugs full of water are hurled into the streets from the windows of the houses on Good Saturday morning, still a time of mourning for Christ's death, before the liturgy of the Resurrection. Politis (1893, 1894) mentions that the practice was in extensive use in the Peloponnese, parts of Macedonia, the Cyclades, Crete, and the island of Chios, where people believe that the vessels are broken to frighten Cháro (Charon, Death, the Reaper) and avert his attention. Hence, this instance of the breaking of the plate is only a variant. What does it mean then? Or does it really matter?

108

thē had provided, using a large piece of cotton. "What can we do, Kyria Panourgiá?" he said to her. "People loathe our profession, but who would do this if we didn't? Someone has to do it. You see, people like yourself, who know how to prepare a dead person properly, are becoming very scarce. And people don't want their own to be buried unprepared. Nevertheless, they go on calling us crows."

After washing the body with the wine, he patted it dry and asked for a razor and foam in order to shave YiôrgoPanourgiás. These procured, he shaved him, applied cologne, and asked for the shroud, which he had to wrap around the body, against the skin. He started at the neck, wrapped it around the clavicle, then underneath the arms and around the thorax, so that Christ's face, which is imprinted on the shroud, would rest on the deceased's heart. He wrapped it once more around the loins, underneath the right leg, up over the pelvis, and under the left leg, so that the shroud would resemble Christ's loincloth on the Cross. Then he put clean undergarments on the dead body, as well as the clothes that Myrtô and I had picked out for Grandfather's last journey. Since it was summer, we chose

▲▲▲▲▲▲▲▲▲▲▲▲▲▲▲▲▲▲▲▲▲▲▲▲▲▲▲▲▲▲

The analysis posits certain problems, for not only is the practice not widespread, but it seems that the few people who know about it (and either perform it or do not) have very strong feelings about it. Those who keep it as a practice do it because they consider it an integral part of the funeral, without considerations as to its theological or religious sanctity. Those who oppose it do so because they consider it pagan. Although the pagan roots of the practice are not particularly clear, and all answers on the matter have been at best evasive, supporters of this view hold it as a truth. The vessel is broken by a close relative or friend of the deceased, most often an older woman, over fifty years of age; a young person is not permitted to perform the rite, because young people are unable to face Cháro, or rather, because people fear Cháro's revenge, they prefer to expose an older person to it rather than a younger one (Politis 1894:280).

These points, however, raise two issues. First, if young people are prohibited from the practice, the request that I break the plate becomes problematic. Since I doubt that there was malicious intent on the part of Kyria Chrysánthē when she asked us to break the plate, I am led to conclude that the practice has fallen into that gray area that Greeks call, condescendingly, "folklore," not in reference to the discipline of folklore but rather to the construction of a body of knowledge, devoid of meaning or significance, which organizes someone's life based on a principle of habituation. Hence

a light blue shirt, a dark blue necktie with a miniature depiction of the Parthenon woven in white on it, and a light gray pin-striped suit. Kyria Chrysánthē suggested that we put on him a pair of black wing tips that his eldest grandson, Yiôrgos, had given him some time before, which Yiôrgo-Panourgiás never wore because they were too big for him. "They are too big for anyone. Let's put these on—they do come from Yiôrgos anyway—and we'll keep his other pairs of shoes and give them to the poor who need them, so someone will say a prayer for his soul," Kyria Chrysánthē said. So we picked a pair of dark blue socks to go with the shoes, and we put a small white handkerchief in the pocket of his jacket. We combed his hair and crossed his hands on his chest, and thus he was ready to receive the last kiss from his loved ones. Yerássimos asked Kyria Chrysánthē if she wanted him to remove the gold teeth and the wedding band. She replied that he did not have any gold teeth, he had all his original teeth, and as for the wedding band, he was going to meet his wife, and how could he do that without his wedding band? During the whole period of the death, the funeral, and the ensuing memorials, this was the only reference I heard to a personal and

▲▲▲▲▲▲▲▲▲▲▲▲▲▲▲▲▲▲▲▲▲▲▲▲▲▲▲▲▲▲

the term *folklór* is used in opposition to *laografía,* the scholarly term for folklore. The second issue, retrospectively, is that of the belief in the efficacy of the practice in actually frightening Cháro. Politis leaves readers in the dark as to the possible reasons for the association of the noise made by a breaking plate during an obsequy with death, although he comments, "No one would ever dare imagine that Cháros would flee at the noise of a breaking vessel" (1894:282). As Huntington and Metcalf note, "Use [of] noise production in funerals achieves the same kind of universality as the emotion of grief" (1985:50). Although they refrain from exploring the possible uses of noise other than percussion in a funerary context, they do establish that a variety of cultures associate noise with death.

This was not the first time that I had been asked to break a plate at a funeral. The last time, a few years before, it was at the funeral of Marika, Elenitsa's mother. Elenitsa is my classificatory sister. She is a woman in her midthirties who lives in Aigeion, a city of twenty-five thousand in the northern rim of the Peloponnese. Her parents divorced when she was barely one year old, and her father moved to Connecticut, leaving Marika, Elenitsa, and Marika's elderly father alone in Aigeion. Marika took boarders into the house to supplement the family income, and Elenitsa, upon graduation from high school, started working as a clerk, first at a paper mill and eventually at city hall. Kyria Chrysánthē's brother, Yiánnēs, and Marika's

social existence and activity beyond the grave. I asked Yerássimos why he had suggested that. "A lot of people consider it a waste," he replied. "What good is gold in the grave? But your family does not need that gold, so we will leave it right where it is."

Yerássimos went out to the living room, where the mourners were sitting, and announced that they could pay their respects to YiôrgoPanourgiás. Myrtô, Kyria Chrysánthē, and I had stayed in the bedroom. First two of his sons entered the room, at which point Myrtô left, but her mother remained. Kyria Chrysánthē hugged both of her brothers-in-law, muttering the two stylized phrases of comfort: "Condolences" (*syllypētêria*). "May life be unto us" (*Zoë s'emás*). Then came Léngō, Vangeliô, Marina, and Vétta. "How could you be here when they were washing him? How could you stand it?" Vangeliô asked. "I was shaking," I wanted to say. "I wanted to watch," I said instead. Myrtô did not answer. The rest of the relatives followed, except for Myrtô's father, Nákos, who under no circumstances would see his father dead. Each of his daughters and his wife tried to coax him into entering his father's apartment, but he repeatedly refused. Then

▲▲▲▲▲▲▲▲▲▲▲▲▲▲▲▲▲▲▲▲▲▲▲▲▲▲▲▲▲▲▲

brother Nikos worked together during the years of the Metaxas dictatorship in the 1930s. Later, during the German occupation, Marika's other brother, Charálambos, was being sought by the Gestapo (as a member of the Resistance), and Kyria Chrysánthē's father kept him and his family hidden in the cellar of the family house in Akráta for several months. Through that connection Kyria Chrysánthē went first to Charálambos' house when she was stationed in Aigeion as a high school teacher in 1961, while her husband was first in Beirut and then in Famagusta, Cyprus, as a chemical engineer. Through that family she met Marika, and the two women lived together with their children for almost five years.

Most of Marika's relatives live in Athens, and after her father died, she and Elenitsa were left alone in the house. When Marika died in the early eighties, at the age of sixty-three, from complications of a metastasized breast cancer, all her relatives flooded in from Athens, occupied every room in the house, and took over the affairs of the funeral, from covering the expenses to preparing the funeral meal and buying black clothing for Elenitsa. A day before Marika died Myrtô and I went to Aigeion to be with Elenitsa. Although we had been expecting the death, when it came we both collapsed, and all we could do was sit by the coffin in the living room, caressing Marika and crying in each other's embrace. All night long we stayed up for the wake, keeping company with the body of the dead

his brothers and close friends encouraged him, but to no avail. Finally all agreed that it was probably better to allow him to mourn in his own way, although everyone present considered it odd that he did not wish to have a last view of his father.

Coffee was served, accompanied by cold water. The coffee was not made to everyone's taste but was slightly bitter, befitting of the bitterness of sentiments. The close female relatives left to change into black clothes, taking turns leaving the apartment, so that at any given moment one of them would be there tending to the needs of the more distant mourners. More people came in as they found out about the death. Condolences were offered: "He is resting now. You should be happy he did not suffer." Advice was given: "He was an old man. You shouldn't mourn too long, especially you, girls, who have young children." Questions were asked: "Did he leave a will? Had he divided the property among his sons before he died?"

During all this time the children of the friends and the family, obviously in awe over the event of death, had free access to the apartment and the bedroom. None of them had previously encountered death at such proximity.

▲▲▲▲▲▲▲▲▲▲▲▲▲▲▲▲▲▲▲▲▲▲▲▲▲▲▲▲▲▲

woman. In the morning, when the undertaker came to take Marika away, my mother came up to Myrtô and me and asked me to break a plate by striking it to the floor, "as the coffin is carried through the threshold." I agreed, and she gave me the plate. Not too long after that, Elenitsa's elder cousin, Katerina, approached us with a conflicting request. "I heard that they asked you to break a plate," she said, "but I am asking you not to do it. These things are not Christian. They are pagan [eidōlolatriká]." Katerina was at the time in her late fifties, a plump and short spinster who, for reasons that have much to do with her individual psychology and personal history, had become involved with one of the Greek Orthodox fundamentalist groups. (The truth is that these groups are not taken seriously by anyone outside their ranks, and it is rather ridiculous to talk about a fundamentalist movement in Greece.)

There are two such groups: He Zōê (The Life) and Ho Sōtêr (The Savior). Until the end of the 1970s both groups existed almost on the margins of the official Church and preoccupied themselves with group readings of the Bible, weekly gatherings to discuss the life of Christ and the saints, visits to monasteries and faraway churches, and (in the case of The Savior) visits to schools and hospitals for the distribution of literature. The Life is an organization that could be described as a social club loosely held together by a common favorite book (the New Testament) and a rather

The next day, the day of the funeral, these children would bear the responsibility of caring for the youngest ones, of setting the tables for the funerary meal, of answering telephones and directing people to the cemetery. The eldest was thirteen years of age, the youngest three.

Approximately ninety minutes had passed since the time of death, and the body had to be transported to the mortuary before rigor mortis set in. Yerássimos and Kassimēs came back into the house (they had been waiting at a coffee shop), bringing a large sheet in which to put the body. YiôrgoPanourgiás lived in an apartment building where any attempt for an obsequy (*ekforá*) in a coffin would have involved negotiating a winding staircase.[6] The body was placed into the sheet and lifted from the bed, and Yerássimos carried it across the apartment to the door, where Kassimēs was waiting, holding the door of the elevator for the three of them to descend. Yerássimos crossed the threshold, a few people said "God forgive him," his sons cried, Violétta made the sign of the Cross over the threshold, and Myrtô and I were instructed by Kyria Chrysánthē to break a plate in the kitchen by striking it on the floor. Thus he was cried for, he was prayed

▲▲▲▲▲▲▲▲▲▲▲▲▲▲▲▲▲▲▲▲▲▲▲▲▲▲▲▲▲▲▲▲

liberal approach to religion, with no clothing prohibitions or rigid law of social conduct. Evangelia Panourgiá belonged to it. She had her own "circle" (she was a *cyclárhis*) and every Thursday held weekly meetings at home, where she met with her friends and sometimes a priest or a nun. They read some passages from the New Testament, restored and reconditioned Byzantine icons, mended the garments of the priests, exchanged recipes, and planned excursions to various churches and monasteries in the countryside. Sometimes she took one of her grandchildren on these trips.

The Savior is by far the more militant of the two groups, and the organizations are at great odds with each other—The Savior drawing the scorn of The Life for being hypocritically pious, austere, and religious, and The Life drawing the scorn of The Savior for being not pious and austere enough. It should be noted that The Savior has been accused of having collaborated with the military junta of 1967–74 in running Christian indoctrination programs in schools, political prisons, and army camps. The members of the group are easily recognizable in the streets. When a few years ago the group staged a demonstration outside a movie theater in Athens to protest the showing of *The Last Temptation of Christ*, my friend Evē wrote to me: "We went yesterday to look at all the Christians protesting the film. There were about 150 of them, some men, but most of them women, and you know what? It's not that I'm prejudiced against them, but I looked and

for, and noise was made for him. He was ready to go. This was his last time through his door, his last time in a familiar and personal environment. What lay ahead was unknown and impersonal—a common mortuary, a common church, a common funerary service. The only personal, familiar, and familial space now would be his common grave with his wife.

I realize that at this point I should have followed the undertaker to the funeral parlor and should have observed—even perhaps participated in— the preparations for the funeral that involve the placement of the body in the casket, the transfer to refrigeration, and the final transportation to the funeral and then the cemetery. I did not. I found it far more comforting to stay at home helping with the preparations for the substitute, body-less wake and tomorrow's funeral. Nor did I ever feel guilty for having left him alone, unaccompanied but for the undertakers.

After the removal of the body, some people (both family and friends) left for a while to tend to their affairs. It was now close to six o'clock, the time when shops opened for the afternoon shift. Groceries had to be bought, fish had to be procured, arrangements had to be made with the

▲▲▲▲▲▲▲▲▲▲▲▲▲▲▲▲▲▲▲▲▲▲▲▲▲▲▲▲▲▲

looked in the crowd and didn't find even one, not one, beautiful woman. They were all dressed in those long skirts, and those glasses, and their hair pulled back! I was frightened. I had never thought before that we could be so ugly as a people."

As prejudiced as Evē's account might appear, the truth is that the women of The Savior are, as I said, easily discernible in a crowd. They invariably wear long-sleeved long dresses or skirts (they did so even in the eras of the miniskirts and hot pants that flooded Athens), with their collars and cuffs buttoned even in the heat of the Athenian summer. Their hair is always put in a chignon at the base of the nape, and they sport horn-and-gold-rimmed glasses. They are meticulously clean, and no trace of makeup can be found on their faces. As children we were resolutely terrified by them, as they had absolutely no reservations about stopping us in the middle of the street—stranger women stopping stranger children— and reprimanding us over the length of our skirts, our conduct in the street, our occasional makeup, or our proximity to the other sex. This terror was further augmented by the comments of the grown-ups as they discussed the new recruits: they wouldn't say, "She was recruited by The Savior" ("Pêge me ton Sōtêra") or even "She was picked up by The Savior" ("Tên père ho Sōtêras"); they would say, "She fell in the talons of The Savior" ("Epese sta nýchia tou Sōtêros").

114

bakery for the next day's funeral meal. The women of the family had to buy or borrow black clothing and accessories for the funeral, so they took turns leaving the apartment and went in search of shoes, handbags, and stockings for themselves, for shirts and neckties for the men of the family. Iōánna stayed at the apartment, tending to small chores as they arose, making coffee for the more distant visitors and the elderly relatives, washing cups and *brikia,* serving brandy, answering the telephone, and assigning tasks to the children, who were responsible for watering the plants, feeding the birds, and informing Iōánna about the needs and desires of the visitors.[7] Kyria Chrysánthē, Myrtô, Léngō, and Violétta returned from shopping, having found fillets of fresh cod, which they would bake with quartered potatoes in a lemon and olive oil sauce. For the moment they put the fish away, changed into house clothes that were cooler than the long-sleeved, long-skirted apparel they had worn to the market, and joined the visitors.

A couple of hours of daylight still remained, as it was at the end of August, so they sat in the living room, while others were on the veranda, and passed the time making small talk. By then it was time for people

▲▲▲▲▲▲▲▲▲▲▲▲▲▲▲▲▲▲▲▲▲▲▲▲▲▲▲▲

Katerina belonged to The Savior, which in addition to the activities mentioned above, seeks to eradicate all pre-Christian, Greek, and pagan elements from Orthodoxy. In this case, however, Katerina tried, unsuccessfully, to appeal to our Christian logic and sentiment. The moment the coffin was carried over the threshold, I broke the plate on the kitchen floor. Later I recounted the incident to my mother, Elenitsa, and Marika's cousins. Elenitsa said with mirth, "Didn't you tell her that we are all saved here and she can take her salvation someplace else?"

## Ichthyology

Nothing red should appear at the table, because red is the color of blood. Fish should be eaten because fish (*ichthys*) is symbolic of Christ. Since in Greece protein is always accompanied by starch, and rice and pasta are not considered appropriate accompaniments for fish (except in the case of soup and crustaceans), the only other choice is potatoes. Since tomatoes are not allowed in the sauce, lemon juice is the only other culturally accepted option. The wine consumed is also white. Papadiamantis in his short story "A Soul" gives us a lovely description of this meal:

The old woman, who had retained many of her teeth, dined on fried fish and eggs (because the habit is for people, among those households who hold to the old

in the neighborhood, more distant than the earlier visitors, to ask about the specifics of the death. Since the area had been family property given to YiôrgoPanourgiás' wife, Vangeliô, as an inheritance after her father's death, many members of her extended family live there. The buildings around the *polykatoikia* (apartment building) are, at least partly, owned and inhabited by relatives. Conversations started with people in neighboring buildings as far as fifty meters away. The usual condolences ensued, the same questions were repeated about the particulars of the funeral, and shadows began to fall as the sun set.

A small lamp was switched on inside the apartment, where nine people were still sitting. The conversation had turned to politics, examining the role of the bureaucrats in supporting the government. As usual, the mention of bureaucracy sparked a feeling of mirth mixed with outrage, which led to strong statements about the issue followed by caustic, ridiculing remarks that led to laughter. At one of these moments Léngō's husband, Kyrilos, walked in, having just returned from work. With an exclamation of incredulity, he said to Léngō, "Isn't anyone crying in this house?" He

▲▲▲▲▲▲▲▲▲▲▲▲▲▲▲▲▲▲▲▲▲▲▲▲▲▲▲▲▲▲

customs, to abstain from meat for many days after the death of a member of the family) . . . and since there was no wine available, but some *mastich* left over from the pareyoryiá [the consolation] (the funerary meal after the funeral) of the previous evening, there was, as we said, some *mastich* left over, the old woman asked to drink some as if to wash off her mouth. (1988:83)

Karp has also commented, briefly, on mortuary food prohibitions in Nilotic symbolism. Among the Iteso of Kenya, familial segmentation is marked by the exclusivity of the consumption of the thigh bone of a cow, in a mortuary context, only by "lineage or exogamous sub-clan" (1988:45). However, as William Robertson-Smith noted in 1889, "the essence of the thing lies in the physical act of eating together," interpreted by Mintz as "a bond, created simply by partaking of food, linking human beings with one another" (1985:4). This is an idea also elaborated by Herzog (1983), in that the partaking of the meal further strengthens the sense of the imagined communion of the dead among them and with the living. Although an affirmation of death, it is also an acceptance of the fact that human existence extends beyond itself.

The symbolism of the fish in this case not only bonds human beings with one another through the physical act of eating together but also links the partaking human beings with their spiritual cosmos (which incorporates

was overheard by his mother-in-law, Kyria Chrysánthē, and her answer came sharp and quick: "There is no tearless wedding or laughless funeral." Around half past ten some of the neighbors left for dinner, and the family members were fed whatever was at hand, supplemented by tidbits supplied by Iōánna.

After midnight everyone left but Myrtô, me, and our uncle Aléxēs, who had been sharing the care of his father for the past month. That night I slept on my grandfather's bed, the one on which he had died, much to everyone's horror the next morning. I checked, as I had been instructed to do, that his *kandêli*—his oil lamp, set among the icons—was lit and lay down. For the first time I had the same view of the room that YiôrgoPanourgiás had all those weeks of his illness. The bed was directly across from the bedroom door; to its right was the balcony door, to its left the wall where Vangeliô's picture hung. Against the wall to my right was the bed that I had used for the past three weeks, and directly in front was the closet and the *iconostási,* the shrine where icons and the kandêli are kept. I started thinking what it would have been like to view the world from that angle, day in

▲▲▲▲▲▲▲▲▲▲▲▲▲▲▲▲▲▲▲▲▲▲▲▲▲▲▲▲▲

their dead ones) through the incorporation of a symbol of Christ into their ritual consumption of it, as it further suggests an abstracted performance of the Eucharist.

In most cases nothing would be cooked in the mourning house for three days, and the family would be fed by friends and kin. The assumption is that grief is so intense during the first three days of mourning that the bereaved cannot take care of themselves. Also implicit is the assumption that grief *should* be so intense as to interfere with the bodily desires of the bereaved, so that they will not think about food as their loved one is being interred. The following two opposite examples will illustrate both the acceptance and the rejection of this supposition.

The day of Marika's funeral in Aigeion I got up and went to the kitchen to offer my services to Elenitsa's cousins, who had started preparing the meal. I was chased out of the kitchen, being told that my place was in the living room, next to the coffin, that they were doing fine without me, and that I would have a chance to help out after the third-day memorial. It was not because I was not a member of the family that I was not being allowed to participate in the preparations; it was precisely because I *was* a member of the family that I was escorted back to my place, by the coffin. The next day, however, Elenitsa and I started making the kóllyva that we would take

and day out, an angle that led only to death and nowhere else. I thought of all these faces leaning over to kiss his face, stroke his hair, feed him, with me watching, playing at being the anthropologist-granddaughter. I thought of all the times that I myself had lain down after one operation or another, with physicians, nurses, parents, friends, lovers, leaning over me to offer comfort. I thought of the one time that I really feared I would die and the exhilaration after the results came back negative: I was not going to die. Did my grandfather really believe that we would take Communion together the next summer? Did he really think that he would get better? Did he really believe that all that was wrong with him was loss of appetite due to a minor ulcer? Did he want us in there, all this time he was ill? Could he see me now, lying down on his bed that until a few hours ago was warmed by his body, which now was forever cold?

There was nothing to light the darkness except for the flickering of the kandêli. Strange shadows were created by this trembling light, as if everything were alive. Monsters and angels exchanged places on the walls, frightening and soothing me as they went by. Finally a moth came and

▲▲▲▲▲▲▲▲▲▲▲▲▲▲▲▲▲▲▲▲▲▲▲▲▲▲▲▲▲▲▲▲

to the grave for the third-day memorial. It was the only cooking we were allowed to do until then.

The complete opposite happened at the death of Kyrios Demópoulos, a retired schoolteacher, who had moved to Athens from the city of Pyrgos in the western Peloponnese in the 1930s. Kos Demópoulos lived with his wife, Dêmētra, his daughter Lila, his granddaughter, and his son-in-law in a bilevel apartment next to my parents and to YiôrgoPanourgiás. His wife had been a casual friend of my mother's, and they usually got together for their morning coffee. The day of the funeral (which took place in the afternoon) my mother went to Dêmētra's apartment to let her and Lila know that she would be cooking the funeral meal for them. I went along, not only because I wanted to "record" the encounter, but also because I wanted to prevent my mother from pressing her case too firmly. We went across the corridor and found Dêmētra and Lila, and my mother, who had already purchased the fish for the meal, told them of her plan. Lila said politely: "Thank you, Kyria Panourgiá, but we will not have a meal after the funeral. If anyone comes around we will order something from the grill downstairs." My mother insisted: "But why, dear child, go to all the expense, and the trouble of ordering and everything, since I've already bought the fish?" Lila was firm. She declined once more. I whispered to my mother that we should go and then gently pulled her out of there. She looked at

118

swirled around the light. I started crying. I remembered the belief that the soul, in the form of a moth, comes back to its beloved environs for forty days after the death, and that if the kandêli is not lit the soul will never come back, for that means that the living have forgotten their dead. Hence I had been admonished to light the kandêli. It would not be allowed to go out for the next forty days. "For forty days lasts the wandering of the psyche, led by the guardian angel; for forty days it will burn, the sleepless and memorial lamp."[8] I remembered Papadiamantis' words in his fin de siècle story of Anghelikoúla, the young girl who died of tuberculosis when she was barely sixteen years old. Her mother was lucky enough to witness the return of her daughter's soul in the form of a moth above the kandêli, but she lost it when she attempted to speak to it and share the sighting with her sister. I remembered the feeling of desolation that permeated the story by the double loss felt by that mother. I fell asleep listening to Aléxēs' snoring in the next room.

We were awakened by Iōánna the next morning. The funeral had been set for half past eleven, so we needed to get ready, go to the viewing room

▲▲▲▲▲▲▲▲▲▲▲▲▲▲▲▲▲▲▲▲▲▲▲▲▲▲▲▲

me, astounded. "How can they not have a meal after the funeral?" she said. I tried to explain to her that probably they would have a meal, but they simply did not want her to prepare it. They looked pretty composed to me anyhow, I said, and perfectly capable of handling their own meal. "But they are friends, and neighbors, and what are friends for, if not at a time of need?" It took some time and some energy for both me and my father to convince her that help was good when it was needed and desired and at no other time.

The sugar prohibition extends a full year as far as sweetmeats and confections are concerned, although tea and coffee with sugar are acceptable. The sugar prohibition, however, does not apply to a new bride (within a year of the wedding) except when the deceased is her husband.

The fact that the food in all these instances was sent to the neighborhood bakery to be baked should not strike us as unusual. *Foúrnos,* the bakery, is an interesting phenomenon of Greek culture. It not only provides bread for the neighborhood but also offers facilities for the baking of meals. No doubt it is a handy remnant from the times that ovens were not commonly available for homes, and all baking had to be done either as a favor by a neighbor who did have an oven or at the neighborhood bakery. Since all homes now have their own stoves, and given the importance of a distinct, separate stove and cooking area even in communal

of the church to spend some time with Grandfather before the service, and follow the procession. The close family gathered at YiôrgoPanourgiás' once more, and from there they left for the cemetery, leaving the children behind to peel the potatoes for the fish, wash and cut the salad, set the tables, prepare the dishes, take the food to the baker's. Places were found in the cars to accommodate everyone, making certain that adversaries would not be made to sit together, and all left for the funeral. I walked down the stairs with Léngō, Myrtô, and Violétta. At the entrance Violétta came face to face with Vétta. They did not acknowledge each other's presence. Violétta, however, noticed some eyeliner on Vétta's face. She turned bitterly to Léngō and said, "Don't you say anything if *I* put makeup on in a few days. All right? Remember this." "And who cares if she does?" Léngō said to me a little later. "Does she mean that if she does not wear makeup she will be more sad about Grandfather? We know she hated him."

As we sat in the car on the way to the church, Kyria Chrysánthē started a monologue: "We will have a funeral that will give people something to talk about for years. Like Grandma's, do you remember? Everybody

▲▲▲▲▲▲▲▲▲▲▲▲▲▲▲▲▲▲▲▲▲▲▲▲▲▲▲▲▲▲

living arrangements (Hirschon 1983, 1989), the continued significance of the neighborhood bakery as a baking facility is puzzling; it can perhaps be attributed to a sense of habituation and added leisure. Especially during the summer vacation, when most families go to the beach twice a day, the bakery provides immense help by cooking the meal, thus freeing women of the responsibility and allowing them to tan themselves at ease. It has become such a trademark of Greek Sunday life that the publications of the National Tourist Organization of Greece often contain pictures of men carrying pans with food to and from the bakery. (Hatzisotiriou [1980] provides a good discussion on the symbolism of the foods offered at the funerary meal, which concurs with my observations.)

## Klausigelos: *(To Laugh and to Cry)*

Sometimes we laugh at funerals and cry at weddings. Manners tell us that we should do neither, but nevertheless we falter. Not only do we falter, but we have verbalized the commonality of this behavior as well. Both Alexiou (1974) and Hirschon (1989) mention the expression en passant, and Karp (1988:35–52) has reported on a parallel but inverted (since it concerns marriage ceremonies rather than funerary rites) action among the Iteso of Kenya. Karp based his analysis on the theory of performance, regarding as simplistic the usual exegesis (supported by Pharos [1988], among others)

120

came then, half the district followed the procession, Mimēs [then mayor of Athens] was there, half the faculty from school came, and the church, eh? Though it was Aghios Nikólaos, and that's a small church, do you remember? Packed, people were standing outside, in the cold. Beautiful hyacinths we had, white. The whole church smelled. But that was in the winter. He could find them. Kassimēs said he has the church full of white gladioli and gardenias. Let's see how many wreaths will be sent. He arranged for the choir, also, and the bishop. Full regalia. No one will dare say that we didn't take care of your grandpa's funeral, that we didn't do everything that could be done. Do you think I would have allowed those magpies [*káryies*] to say a word?"

Kyria Chrysánthē recounted the events of the last funeral in the family, eleven years before. Everyone had assumed that her mother-in-law had not left a will, until it was discovered that her father-in-law had found and kept it. He never explained to anyone why he had done so, since when the time came for the property to be divided among the children everything was done according to her will. Why did he keep it secret from everyone?

▲▲▲▲▲▲▲▲▲▲▲▲▲▲▲▲▲▲▲▲▲▲▲▲▲▲▲▲▲▲▲▲▲▲

that inversions of behavior are tools for the release of tension. As Karp notes, "The analysis of ritual requires a greater appreciation of contradictions internal to the process" (36), and he proposes that a performance-centered approach to laughter at marriage (a serious and somber ceremony of the Iteso) explicates this behavior by positioning it within the wider context of official ideology and its subversion. Iteso women, who lead in this gaiety, "celebrate their resistance to control through laughter" (50). Through this culturally sanctioned disorderly conduct, the unofficial is transformed into the official, thus empowering the actor.

In analyzing the expression "There is no tearless wedding or laughless funeral," I would attempt to take Karp's analysis a step further, by noting the main two divergences of the expression from his account. The first one concerns the rituals themselves. In the Athenian context weddings are considered festive occasions, where the prescribed mood is indeed that of gaiety and laughter. The opposite holds true for funerals, where grief, mourning, and despair are expected to be felt, or at least exhibited. The second difference is that, unlike the situation of the Iteso, where this digression is ritualized (thus institutionalized), canonized (at least in regard to its expectancy and its operations), and structured in its brevity and nonverbalization, the Athenian expression is a post-hoc explication of behavior which is outside the realm of ritual. It is digressive, provocative, and un-

She could not explain that, nor could anyone else, as far as she could tell: "Probably it was because he didn't want the will to fall into the hands of their daughters-in-law. [She, of course, was one of them.] Who knows what those women could have done with it? All and all, it was a good idea to keep it from everyone. But you see, now, we haven't found his will. I don't think he wanted to be responsible for the distribution of the property. He left it to us to pluck each other's eyes out."

By this time we were at the church. We were first shown into the *krýptē*, on the ground floor of the church, where the dead are laid out in coffins so that relatives and friends can spend time with them before the funeral. A very modest, confined room, where the dead await their turns to be brought out and greeted by their loved ones, it is long and narrow, with bare, stark white walls and a low ceiling. The entrance is hardly able to accommodate anyone larger than average size. In the front was a small patio with irises and gladioli, a long bench, and a few chairs. Léngō and I went outside and sat on the bench. Looking at the floor, I saw a pair of feet, beautifully naked in their black leather sandals, despite the prescription for black at-

▲▲▲▲▲▲▲▲▲▲▲▲▲▲▲▲▲▲▲▲▲▲▲▲▲▲▲▲▲▲

wanted but nevertheless within the realm of possibility. Much like the Iteso ritual, the Athenian nonritual exhibits the acceptance (indeed the tolerance) of a subversion to the order of things, the resistance to that which is official, namely, the prescription and expectation of specified feelings.

## Untouchables

The dead body creates feelings of terror both through the actuality of its existence and through the abstraction of its presence. Hence others commented about my presence while Yerássimos was washing the body (the actuality of the dead object) and my sleeping on YiôrgoPanourgiás' bed (the abstraction of its presence).

I had seen this terror before, particularly at Marika's funeral, when Elenitsa would rise from her chair from time to time and kiss dead Marika on the lips. After several unsuccessful attempts by all the relatives to dissuade her from doing this, they came to me and asked me to intercede, "because of the ptomaine. It's poison. Besides, who would ever kiss Elenitsa after she has kissed her mother like this?"

But when the dead body has been classified as untouchable and soon disappears into the grave, the desire, all too human, for it does not disappear. Hence, the mother in Papadiamantis' story felt twice robbed, first

122

tire from head to toe, which mandates black stockings. I recognized the feet immediately. I looked up, and there was YiórgoPanourgiás' granddaughter Vangeliô, who had arrived with her husband, Yiôrgos, having left her children in the care of her mother. Dressed in black, she could hardly restrain her tears; her eyes red and puffed from crying, she wandered around, her eyes unfocused, as if she were absent, not present at the scene. She sat on the bench with us, and all three of us started speculating on who would be present at the funeral. I looked around. Kyria Chrysánthē had disappeared. Her cousin Iákōvos was there, and off in a corner her husband was talking with his older brother. One of her other brothers-in-law, Frangiskos, was recounting his father's last moments to a group of distant relatives who had just arrived.

I could not see YiórgoPanourgiás' siblings anywhere, so I moved inside, into the cool shade of the krýptē. The coffin was placed parallel to the walls on a high table, which brought it to chest height. It was made of walnut with a cut crystal cover, lined with white taffeta. YiôrgoPanourgiás was laid there, in his light gray suit, his head resting on a white pillow, his

▲▲▲▲▲▲▲▲▲▲▲▲▲▲▲▲▲▲▲▲▲▲▲▲▲▲▲▲▲▲

of her daughter's body in its actuality, and then of the embodiment of her soul in the little swirling moth. In ancient Greek the word *psychê* is used to indicate both soul and moth, and the use has been carried over in the purist version of Greek, the katharévousa. The play on the meaning of the word by Papadiamantis, the famous Greek proto-ethnographer and novelist, is most effective. His story "A Soul" ("Mia Psychê"), first published in 1881, is one of the finest pieces of the period.

Vernant (1986) has placed the desire for communication with the soul of the dead within the analytical framework of *pothos*. The bereaved, Vernant argues, make the dead one present, but in the moment they see the dead's double, the *eidōlon*, the reflection (in this case the moth), and try to speak to it, the dead one disappears. The presence of the dead is always their irrefutable absence.

## Carrion

Magpies (*káryies*) and crows are both birds of prey, and the connection between the anticipation of an inheritance and the proclivity of *synyphádhes* for gossip, on the one hand, and the professional attributes of an undertaker (the crow, *koráki,* par excellence), on the other, is apparent. Rushton (1983:57–68) has observed that in the Macedonian town of Velvendos women associate themselves with magpies—a divergence from the ideal,

hands crossed on his thorax, in a profusion of flowers that Kassimēs had arranged around him. He looked pale but serene. People kept coming into the krýptē, bringing bunches of flowers, which they deposited on the dead body. They kissed his hand or his forehead and exchanged a few words with his sister and brother. His sister Militsa was sitting on a chair at the head of the table, resting the palm of her hand on the coffin. Next to her, at the opposite corner, was her brother, Yiánnēs, who was standing, looking at his dead brother.

Along the sides of the table were other relatives, and standing opposite to Yiánnēs, I found Kyria Chrysánthē, drenched in tears, talking to her father-in-law, caressing his face, reproaching him for having left us, wondering what would happen to the family now that the head of it was gone. I thought it strange that she exhibited all this grief and pain. I knew that their relationship had been a strained and difficult one. I assumed that this was the performance of a good nýphē, the public exhibition of feelings that did not exist, simply for the perpetuation of an acceptable social persona. Or then again, I thought she might not really be crying for him: she might

▲▲▲▲▲▲▲▲▲▲▲▲▲▲▲▲▲▲▲▲▲▲▲▲▲▲▲▲▲▲

which is the dove—as they, introspectively and self-critically, mark characteristics of the bird (ceaseless noisemaking and mischievousness) in themselves. This is done in a very serious manner in the case of the Athenian women and the undertaker, where traits of the magpie, such as preying on the unsuspecting and stealing eggs from other birds' nests, are accepted as metaphorical markings of the characters of the synyphádhes and the undertaker, in a construction where social identity is conceived within a framework of inherent characteristics. In Velvendos, Rushton reports, the connection is made laughingly and jokingly, as if women were telling inside jokes about themselves. I would argue that, in opposition to the Athenian critical and caustic hue of the metaphor, in Velvendos this might constitute a self-empowering praxis of the women through the appropriation of traits and attributes which they are not expected to exhibit or possess, but which they savor nonetheless, and through the rejection of the official ideal tying them to the unattainable (and sometimes undesirable) perfection of the dove (peristerá).

## To Fear the Exotic

Seremetakis (1991:165–66) notes that a funeral she attended in Athens, without laments, without loud cries, with the dead covered with flowers, made her fear death, whereas funerals in Mani, with their laments and

be crying for her own parents, her dead brother, and her own inevitable death. Many other people, besides the one being buried, are cried for at funerals. Kassimēs came about ten minutes before the service was to start and coaxed everybody out of the krýptē so that the coffin could be moved upstairs into the church.

We walked outside into the bright, hot sunshine. I looked around at all the relatives, YiôrgoPanourgiás' daughters-in-law and his granddaughters. I had the distinct impression, which I had first felt at his apartment, that his granddaughters felt some resentment and suspicion directed toward their own mothers and aunts regarding genuine feelings of loss at this death. I was not wrong. Vangeliô turned to Myrtô, who was sitting next to me, and said, "Is your mother crying in there?" Myrtô answered yes, with an uneasiness in her voice. Léngō came up to us. "Did you see all four magpies [*káryies*] in there crying for Grandpa? Now they are sorry for him? When they were calling him names, before he died, did they love him back then, too? Has your mother forgotten that she was wishing a few days ago that he would die a thousand times?" She was addressing Myrtô. Vangeliô

▲▲▲▲▲▲▲▲▲▲▲▲▲▲▲▲▲▲▲▲▲▲▲▲▲▲▲▲▲▲▲

noise, gave her peace. Conversely, I have never been as terrified by death as when I chanced upon a funeral in Mani several years ago. The voices of the women, the deep wailing and crying, still ring in my ears. I have never made my peace with death, and I never find it peaceful (except when pain and suffering preceded it). I have never made my peace with the fact that we are brought into this life so that we can die later, as if we are unwillingly part of a joke or an experiment. Thus my opposition to death is almost political and ideological. I always cry at funerals, not so much for my own (I hope distant but nevertheless imminent and certain) death, but for the deaths of all who have preceded me, for the unfairness in the deprivation of their lives. No funeral has ever made me feel at ease. The funeral in Mani, however, with the wailing, the lamenting, and the loud voices, upset me and terrified me in ways that no other ceremony had before.

The easy explanation for these two very different approaches to similar events would be to classify Seremetakis' position as "folklorization" (in the case of the Maniat funeral) and mine as "modernization" (in the case of the Athenian funeral). That, however, would be too easy and would not explain much. What is at play here is the element of familiarity. What is familiar, no matter how frightening, is manageable and containable, as it rests within a known and accessible frame of reference. Nevertheless, we should bear in mind Vovelle's position that ultimately there has never been

sighed. She turned to me. "If the person [*ho anthropos*] is not of your own blood, you should not expect them to cry for him," she said. She thought for a while and qualified what she had just said. "A friend perhaps. But the in-laws never. Unless they are friends first, and then in-laws."

More people had arrived, mainly relatives, waiting for the signal for everyone to move inside the church. We moved inside en masse, friends supporting relatives and distant relatives talking with acquaintances. The church is relatively new, built in the 1960s, much larger than the old fifteenth-century chapel of Saint Nikólaos (also on the premises of the cemetery), where Vangeliô's funeral had taken place eleven years earlier. This church, dedicated to the patron saints Kōnstantinos and Eléni, is a large-domed basilica, a rectangular structure with a central dome, facing east, as all Greek churches and ancient temples do. There is no colonnade inside, just a large open space, lighted by the sunlight that floods in through large stained-glass windows. Above the entrance is the loft that in parish churches is reserved for women who do not want to mix with the rest of the congregation (the *gynaikōnitēs*) but which in cemetery churches like

▲▲▲▲▲▲▲▲▲▲▲▲▲▲▲▲▲▲▲▲▲▲▲▲▲▲▲▲▲▲

a time when human death was taken as "natural" and accepted serenely, without fear or apprehension (1990:67).

## Descent into the Grave

A Greek grave (*táphos*, also *mnêma*) is a hole dug three meters into the ground, where the coffin is placed. Unlike some graves in America, Greek graves do not contain vaults made of concrete or metal. The body and the coffin disintegrate directly into the ground (affecting, perhaps, the ground-water), an issue which at the turn of the century gave rise to a theory concerning the usage of the dead as fertilizers, which has been, rightly, questioned by Humphreys (1983:164n9). As the undertakers dig the grave, they place the removed soil around it, and they will use this soil in order to cover the grave again, after the coffin has been lowered into it. Hence Kassimēs advised us to leave, for "it will be very dusty here in a moment." After the coffin is placed into position and the soil has been restored over it, the grave is allowed to stay as it is for up to a month, "so that the soil will sit." After that, and before the fortieth-day memorial, the top of the grave is covered with concrete, which is in turn covered with marble, usually white. The styles vary, so that some graves are covered with a continuous marble slab with a bronze cross on it and the names of the dead engraved

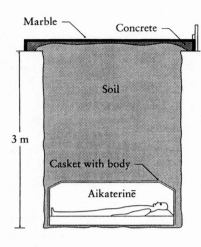

*First Burial (Aikaterinē)*
1. 3 meters of soil removed
2. Perishable casket (wood) placed
3. Hole filled with soil and mounded
4. 20-35 days later concrete placed
5. Concrete claded in marble
6. Mnēmósyno performed
7. Wooden casket decomposes

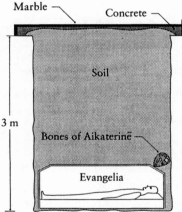

*Second Burial (Evangelia)*
1. Marble slab / concrete removed
2. Dirt removed
3. Bones of Aikaterinē gathered and placed in bag
4. New casket with body of Evangelia placed in hole
5. Bag with bones of Aikaterinē placed on end of casket
6. Repeat items 3-7 of first burial

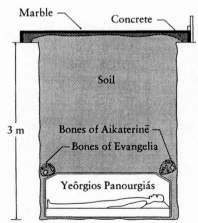

*Third Burial (Yeôrgios Panourgiás)*
1. Marble slab / concrete removed
2. Dirt removed
3. Bones of Aikaterinē placed in new bag and bones of Evangelia placed in 2nd bag
4. New casket with Yeôrgios Panourgiás placed in hole
5. Two bags containing bones of Evangelia and Aikaterinē placed at head and toe of casket
6. Repeat items 3-7 of first burial

The stratigraphy of mnemonic usage. Based on an idea of Eugene Humbles.

this one houses the choir. In funeral and memorial liturgies, as in weddings and baptisms, the separation in church of men and women to two flanks is not kept. Thus men and women stand next to each other in a semicircle. In an imaginary rectangle in front of the templum the coffin is placed. The rectangle is separated from the congregation by flower stands draped in white taffeta.

The coffin, without being taken outside, was transported as if miraculously through an inner staircase and placed in front of the templum, feet facing east, among a cluster of flower stands, with three series of chairs placed along its southern flank. Militsa, Yiánnēs, Violétta, Kyria Chrysánthē, and Vétta were seated in the first row of chairs. YiôrgoPanourgiás' sons, their daughters and sons, and their sons-in-law were seated in the second row. The third row was provided for the rest of the close relatives. I stood next to Myrtô, with her friend, Nikē, standing next to me. I heard Nikē's voice whispering, "He looks so serene! Are you sure he is dead?" No one answered. The choir chanted the first hymn, and the priests materialized from behind the templum. The service had begun. Suddenly

▲▲▲▲▲▲▲▲▲▲▲▲▲▲▲▲▲▲▲▲▲▲▲▲▲▲▲▲▲▲▲▲

around the cross; some have another marble slab at the head, bearing the names of the deceased sharing the grave; other graves have marble ledges around them, with a depression in the middle of approximately thirty to fifty centimeters, where colored marble gravel is placed. All invariably have at least one lantern, either at the head or at the foot of the grave, where the photographs of those buried in the grave are kept, along with oil and wicks for the lamp, candles, and incense. Privately owned graves are used for multiple, consecutive dying members of the family, thus creating a stratigraphy of death which records the temporal spacing of deaths through the years, possible family disputes (by the absence of some family members), and the accordance of family status to various others.

One such example is the family grave (indeed, an *oikos*) that Héllē had built for her parents. Now in her nineties, Héllē is the only surviving member of her immediate family of origin. Her sisters and their husbands have been dead for many years. The grave originally contained her parents, her grandfather, and her elder sister, Iólē, who died fairly young. Some years later, Timos, the son of her younger sister, was killed in a motorcycle accident and was buried there. His parents lived only a few years after his death. His mother, Anna, and his father, Dēmákos, died within a few years of each other and were both buried in the family grave. Shortly afterward, Iólē's husband, Lalákos, died, but Héllē, judging that he had not been adequately

Kyria Chrysánthē stood up, approached the coffin, and started crying and wailing. There was a general feeling of discomfort. It seemed that everyone in the church knew, somehow, that she had not been very fond of her father-in-law. The wailing continued until her husband summoned her. "Chrysánthē," he said, "that's enough. Come sit down." She protested, but he, rather forcefully, convinced her to sit down. Vangeliô, all this time, was sitting quietly between her husband, Yiôrgos, and her cousin Léngō. Myrtô, behind her dark glasses, looked as expressionless as a statue. The priest prayed: "Give rest to your servant, O God, and place him in Paradise, where the companies of saints, O Lord, and the righteous will shine like stars. . . . Give rest with the saints, O Christ, to the soul of your servant, where there is no pain, no sorrow, no suffering, but life everlasting. . . . Give rest to the departed soul of your servant Yeôrgios in a place of light, in a place of pasture, in a place of peace, where there is no pain, sorrow, or suffering."[9] The priest continued with a prayer for forgiveness. What should *he* be forgiven for? Aléxēs thought, he confided to me later. We should be the ones asking for forgiveness, for all the *kônio* (hemlock) we

▲▲▲▲▲▲▲▲▲▲▲▲▲▲▲▲▲▲▲▲▲▲▲▲▲▲▲▲▲▲▲▲▲▲▲▲

overwhelmed by Iólē's death some twenty years before, did not allow him to be buried in the grave. When Anna's daughter-in-law, Paulina, died recently, she was buried alongside her young brother-in-law. Now Paulina's mother has expressed the desire to be buried beside her daughter, so that the family will be complete. Although all interested parties consider this a family grave, it actually is more of a *soï* grave.

I do have the suspicion that the reluctance to leave anything of value on the buried person might be a lingering practice from the times of grave robbers. Grave robbing, although never widespread in Greece, primarily because of the aversion toward the grave as a physical object, did exist until around the Second World War. Then by a strange twist of circumstances that pitted together the worst economic crisis in the country (thus far) with the highest number of students admitted to the university system, a sharp demand was created for human skeletal bones to be used by students in the schools of medicine, education, and physical science. Since there was no organized entity that would collect and make the bones legally available to the students, the students themselves had to rummage either in the ossuaries or in old, unattended, and obviously forgotten graves, in order to procure the bones needed for their education. My mother, Dêmētra, was very proud that she was able to find a *complete* (the word was stressed to me) skeleton in a grave, which she kept throughout her studies at the uni-

gave him through his life. The service approached its end. "May your memory be eternal, our blessed and ever memorable brother," recited the priest three times, and then he invited us to the last kiss: "Let us give the last kiss, brothers, to the one departed."

Militsa, Yiánnēs and his wife, Tsikō, Katina (another sister), and YiôrgoPanourgiás' sons proceeded in a line, kissed the icon of Saint George that had been placed on his crossed hands, kissed his forehead, kissed the icon of the Ascension to Heaven that was on the stand to the left of the coffin, and headed toward the exit. Léngō, Vangeliô, and Myrtô's turns came. Kassimēs was there and directed them toward the coffin, Nikē following closely. I stood right next to Nikē, hearing every word, every whisper, that she uttered: "I am here for you," she whispered in Myrtô's ear. "Don't get lost, my sweet little bird. Don't let go, don't let go."

Standing next to her, I could hear her voice, trying to coach Myrtô, ready to support her in case she collapsed. They got to the coffin. Léngō paid her respects first, her shoulders shivering from crying as she bent into the coffin to kiss her grandfather, almost carried by her husband. Vangeliô

▲▲▲▲▲▲▲▲▲▲▲▲▲▲▲▲▲▲▲▲▲▲▲▲▲▲▲▲▲▲

versity and which she used to frighten her older sister (I have been assured by both parties) by displaying it erect in the space between their beds.

### Seeds and Coins

"The *Kóllyva* or *Stári* (literally 'wheat') is the custom of boiled wheat. According to the canon, adorned with dried fruits and sugar, these are offered at churches and cemeteries to commemorate the dead" (Souliotis 1986:11). Usually kóllyva contain the following ingredients, always in an odd number: wheat, sesame seeds, raisins, sugar, ground coriander, walnuts, almonds, Jordan almonds, parsley, pomegranate seeds (in season), and bread crumbs. If all ingredients are not available, schemings begin in order to produce an odd number of ingredients. Thus, salt might be added, two different kinds of raisins, a pinch of flour, or any of the ingredients might not be included (or counted) in order to produce the desired numerical outcome.

Grains have been associated with the dead since ancient times, along with eggs, pomegranates, and celery (Garland 1985:70). The symbolism of grains and eggs is easily discernible, since both regenerate life on their own. Pomegranates have been associated with the dead since the mythical time of Persephone, who, after eating only one pomegranate seed, com-

came next. Crying and shaking, she caressed his arms, his cheeks, his forehead, kissed him on the crown of the head, and headed toward the exit. Myrtô approached the coffin calmly, lowered herself to it, worshiped the icon, kissed her grandfather's fingertips, and moved toward the icon of the Ascension, where, after having kissed it, she rested her forehead and broke down weeping. A long, wailing sound came from her, which drew both Nikē and Vangeliô, who returned, close to her. Léngō left the arm of her husband and rushed to her. Thus the three cousins together, all three sobbing, followed by Nikē, walked through the church, past the friends and relatives who, stunned at this outburst, watched them as they came out to the front patio.

On the stairs their parents waited for Kassimēs' men to bring out the coffin for the procession to begin. Myrtô's mother turned around, looked at her daughter, and tried to pull her toward her. Without turning to see who it was, Myrtô murmured, "Leave me." Her mother insisted, trying to take her away from Léngō and Vangeliô by pulling her arm. "Leave me," Myrtô screamed, pulling her arm back, then turned and saw her mother.

▲▲▲▲▲▲▲▲▲▲▲▲▲▲▲▲▲▲▲▲▲▲▲▲▲▲▲▲

mitted one-third of her life to Hades. Clay replicas of pomegranates have been found in the Eleusinian cemetery dating from the Geometric period (Farnell 1907:226). Seed remnants were also found in an ancient cemetery in Larissa, in one of five excavated tombs. A small basket contained "a large array of fruits, very well preserved: almonds, filberts, one small pomegranate in the middle, next to it other smaller fruits, and remnants of one or two figs" (Souliotis 1986:25). The pomegranate is used to "cool the souls, and to symbolize the return of the body to earth" (22). The almonds, according to Souliotis, symbolize the bones freed of their flesh; the parsley (in lieu of the ancient celery?) symbolizes the grass, the coolness of the point of arrival of the dead; the raisins testify to the fact that after the death and Resurrection of Christ death is bitter no longer.

The kóllyva of the third day (*trimera*), composed of wheat boiled with salt, is called *pikrokóllyva*. It is unadorned and unsweetened. The kóllyva on any other occasion is sweetened and adorned, usually (in the case of a memorial) prepared by professionals. The practice—which is found only among the Orthodox, and primarily among the Greeks—is believed to stem from the ancient practice of offering *panspermies* or *pankarpies* (boiled grains) at the Anthesteria, the festival of the commemoration of the dead, in ancient Athens. According to Nilsson (1969), the first three days of the festival were dedicated to the dead. On the third day seeds

She broke away from her cousins and walked through the patio, where Violétta intercepted her. "Let's go home, Myrtoula. I want you to help me with the tables," she said.

Myrtô looked at her, rather disturbed. Her father, Kýrios Nákos, came to her rescue. He hugged her, stroked her face, looked at her. "Can you think about me, how *I* feel, just for a moment?" he said. Myrtô looked at him, leaned on his chest, and wept. Vangeliô motioned to them that the coffin was being brought out. Nikē approached and held Myrtô's arm. The coffin appeared at the doorway, we crossed ourselves, and the procession started. The closest relatives were at the head of it, husbands supporting their wives, Kyria Chrysánthē supported by her son-in-law, Léngō walking with Vangeliô. Myrtô, Nákos, Nikē, and I fell behind. Kos Nákos started telling a story to Myrtô: "Do you know that Maria Nikoláou's sister died in her twenties from cancer? Her father a medical doctor, eh? When she was this close to death, she said to her father, 'You cure the children of strangers. Can't you cure me?' Ask Nikoláou sometime to tell you the story. It's terrifying." Myrtô was almost completely calm by now.

▲▲▲▲▲▲▲▲▲▲▲▲▲▲▲▲▲▲▲▲▲▲▲▲▲▲▲▲▲▲▲▲

were cooked and set out for Hermes, the guide of the dead souls to the Otherworld (*psychopompós*).

The term *kóllyva* resembles (and might be related to) the ancient term *kóllyvos*, which originally meant the grain of wheat used as a measurement for gold. Later it came to mean the nugget of gold itself, and even later it identified a very small coin (Souliotis 1986:11–12). In early Christianity *kóllyvo* came to indicate the *tragêmata:* dried fruits (walnuts, almonds, raisins) and cooked wheat (Souidas quoted in Souliotis 1986:24n5). The practice of kóllyva was sanctioned and adopted by the official Church after the "miracle of the kóllyva" in A.D. 362, during the reign of Julian the Apostate. It is based on Saint Paul's example of the grain of wheat that falls on the ground and through its burial is reborn (1 Corinthians 15.35–44), an illustration that comes from Christ's teaching that unless a grain of wheat falls on the ground and dies, it remains alone, by itself; if it falls and dies, it gives life to many more. The seed, as symbol, contains the idea of regeneration, "a sense that out of the mystery of death there will unfold the mystery of transformation. The grain must die that it may be transformed into new life" (Herzog 1983:90).

The Canon of the Apostles (canon 14, bk. 8, chap. 52) prescribes the days that kóllyva should be offered, and Metrophanes, the patriarch of

They arrived at the grave. Militsa wailed, "*Ah, Yiôrgē mou,* look at this grave now. Where are the flowers you had here for your Vangeliô? Where is the sparkling marble? Who will take care of your grave now, *Yiôrgo mou?* Who will care for your Vangeliô now that you are gone?" She turned to Myrtô. "*Móy Myrtoula mou,* why haven't you put Grandpa's picture here yet? You have Grandma's here alone, my little girl." Myrtô started explaining that she had commissioned the duplication of a picture from one of the custom photographers but it wasn't ready yet.

The priest summoned us to order. He began the Thrice Holy Prayer (Trisáyio). It sounded quick and impersonal. The undertakers started lowering the coffin into the grave with thick, sturdy ropes. I remembered that it was exactly at this point at Vangeliô's funeral, eleven years before, that Frangiskos broke down, crying, sobbing, and wailing, and tried to fall into the grave along with his mother. It took his three brothers and his father to restrain him. I looked at him now. He was crying uncontrollably, with tears drenching his face, his handkerchief soaking wet, but there was no indication that he would lose control again.

▲▲▲▲▲▲▲▲▲▲▲▲▲▲▲▲▲▲▲▲▲▲▲▲▲▲▲▲▲▲

Alexandria (1589–1639) canonized the practice, which should take place on the first, third, ninth, twentieth, and fortieth days after the death, and in the third, sixth, ninth, and twelfth months. After that time has lapsed, kóllyva should be offered once a year, on the anniversary of the death, on All Souls Saturdays, and whenever the relatives wish to offer them (Danforth 1982; Souliotis 1986:25; Dubisch 1989). Claims of Greek cultural continuity aside, this is a remarkable example of the geocultural texture of ritual, of the power of survival and perseverance that ritual (and kóllyva should also be counted here) has over time, despite cultural change and persecution by state and religious authorities. As in Vovelle's formulation, we see here the astonishing obstinacy of ritual, of the whole system of deeply rooted gestures, reproduced even when they are no longer understood (1990:69).

The prescriptions governing memorials in general, are not always kept. Often, instead of kóllyva, a family might choose to provide a dinner for the elderly at a local senior citizens' center, or at a nursing home, in memory of the deceased. This option became available in the 1970s, with the creation of special centers in Athens where elderly people who could not be cared for by their families (or who had no family) were put up at municipal nursing homes or were cared for during the day at the senior centers. Funds are limited for these centers and must be generously supplemented by the

The wailing this time came from YiôrgoPanourgiás' sisters and his sister-in-law. The moment the coffin started being lowered into the grave, these four women, in their seventies and eighties, dressed in black from head to toe, with long black head scarves wrapped around their faces in the manner of the Arvanitisses, formed a circle around the grave and started wringing their hands, lightly slapping their faces, and crying out their brother's name, sobbing and wailing. Their husbands moved toward them, embraced them, and tried to pull them away. The priest sprinkled some ayiasmó and a handful of earth on the coffin, instructed us to do the same, and then left. Each one of us in turn performed the rite. Léngō turned to me. "You see this grave right here, at the foot of ours? It's that friend of mine who died at thirteen, in high school, from an aneurysm. Do you remember her? Her mother comes every day and cleans the grave. I think she is a little touched in the head." [10] We were told by Kassimēs to leave the grave. Myrtô, Vangeliô, and their fathers lingered behind. "Go now, go," Kassimēs said. "It will be very dusty here in a moment."

We took the short winding concrete path that connects the graves to

▲▲▲▲▲▲▲▲▲▲▲▲▲▲▲▲▲▲▲▲▲▲▲▲▲▲▲▲

public. One of the most appreciated forms of help is the provision of a day's meal for the group at a center. A priest is always on hand at the center (which is usually run through one of the parishes of the municipality) who reads the benediction and a quick Trisáyio (the Thrice Holy Prayer) for the soul of the dead. Dinners are also offered as supplications for the health and well-being of the family or the quick recovery of an ailing member. As Behar notes about the "ordered" masses in rural Spain, these affairs become "the private property of their purchasers" (1991b:362). Thus, the person who pays for the dinner has the exclusive rights to decide the names of the persons (dead or alive) who will be mentioned in conjunction with the dinner.

If the dinner is offered on the anniversary of someone's death, then the dinner is provided only for the memory of the particular person. If the dinner is offered on All Souls Saturday, or during the lenten periods (before Christmas, Easter, and the Dormition of Mary in August), then it is considered as a collective memorial for the family. Kyria Chrysánthē often opted for a dinner instead of a memorial at church as soon as the option became available. For the collective memorials she would make a note not to include people in the family that she did not get along with (namely Violétta, Pétros' wife, and her brother's wife, Tassia, who lives in the United States). As she put it, "Let them have their own prayer." Explaining her preference for the dinner, she said that the elderly really appreciate it, they enjoy

the coffeehouse of the church. The coffeehouse (owned by the municipality but leased to individual concerns after a high-bidding auction) is a wide oblong structure between the old and the new churches, adjacent to the flower shop (leased to a different proprietor). Its long tables and wooden chairs are placed perpendicular to the walls, along both sides, with a large area in the middle of the room furnished only with low comfortable arm-chairs for the immediate family. Bitter coffee, stale *paximádhia* (a sort of sweet melba toast), and a brandy of dubious origin and very objectionable quality were served. Within a few minutes Kassimēs came back with a tray of *kóllyva*. Militsa came up to me and asked me to inform everyone that she would hold the ninth-day memorial at her Old Calendrist church in Markópoulo. I promised I would relay the message and told her that Myrtô, Léngō, and I would make the kóllyva for the fortieth-day memorial at the same church as the funeral.

I then sat down next to Léngō and Vangeliô, since they had decided not to sit with the rest of the family. "See what they serve us?" Léngō commented. "All the money Kassimēs charged us, and this is the quality he has

▲▲▲▲▲▲▲▲▲▲▲▲▲▲▲▲▲▲▲▲▲▲▲▲▲▲▲▲▲▲▲▲

their dinner and give "genuine thanks and blessings," the soul of the deceased rests more easily, as it is blessed by people with "clear hearts," and giving a dinner is a much more humane gesture than giving the money for the memorial to the "goats" (staff at memorial parlors and priests), who simply perform a professional duty.

What happened in YiôrgoPanourgiás' memorial in regard to the preparation of the kóllyva was very unusual. Almost invariably in Athens kóllyva are prepared by professionals through the funeral parlor. This gives the family greater flexibility in order to be prepared for the liturgy—funeral or memorial, whichever it might be—and to concentrate on the mourning itself. (One could argue that the preparation of the kóllyva could, and until some decades ago did, constitute part of the mourning process in Athens. Since it no longer does, there is no point in making an argument for its validity as part of mourning.) Myrtô, Léngō, and I , however, wanted to make the kóllyva ourselves, for a number of reasons. First, we enjoyed making kóllyva. Second, we had always enjoyed the conviviality of making things together. Third, it was a way to occupy ourselves until the time of the memorial without having to mingle too much with the rest of the family. Violétta offered to provide the wheat: "It is good, white, thick, from the fields at Thebes," she said. It turned out to be old, hard, and wormy. We cleaned the wheat and gathered the rest of the ingredients, but since it was

to offer. But how can you trust a gravedigger? If he had any sense of self-worth [*filótimo*] he wouldn't be doing what he is doing. Making money off people's pain!" Violétta, uninvited, had sat across the table from us. She was smoking and looking around, noticing everyone who was there, smiling at everyone. She turned to Vangeliô, obviously angry. "Asses of a lineage [*kolóssogo*]," she said bitterly. Vangeliô looked at me, embarrassed and amazed. "I wanted to ask her," she told me later at the table, " 'You stupid whore, what do you have against this *soï*? It's no one else's fault but ours that we got you from the gutter and made a lady of you.' "

For the moment, though, she remained silent. We finished our coffee. The guests started approaching the family, especially Kyria Chrysánthē, who was sitting in an armchair, offering their condolences and then leaving. Myrtô saw her cousin Achilléas, whom she had not seen for more than a decade. "It's a good thing we have some funerals in the family so we can meet from time to time," he said. It was true. The last time they had met was at Myrtô's grandmother's death. It was also prophetic. They would meet again almost two years later, when Myrtô's uncle, cousin, and cousin's

▲▲▲▲▲▲▲▲▲▲▲▲▲▲▲▲▲▲▲▲▲▲▲▲▲▲▲▲▲▲▲

late September, it was still too early for the pomegranates to be ripe. Persephone always died in the winter. Léngō remembered that a neighbor had a pomegranate tree that produced fruit early. She went over to ask for a pomegranate. The neighbor asked what she would make with it, and when told that it was intended for a memorial, the woman gave the fruit along with a profusion of blessings and good wishes. Léngō thanked her and turned to leave. As she stepped on the first step, she slipped and tumbled down the thirty-six steps of the marble staircase. The neighbor rushed to her, apologizing—although she had nothing to apologize for—crying, and saying that she had given the pomegranate with all her heart, not begrudgingly. There was no reason at all for this fall to have happened. Léngō came back home horribly bruised, shaken, and sobbing, all her grief for her grandfather's death having been released through this very physical, very painful, very suggestive channel.

Until recently in Athens, women of the mourning family would stand at the crossroads in the neighborhood of the deceased on the day of the memorial and distribute kóllyva to the passers-by, something that is still occasionally practiced in smaller cities and villages, such as Aigeion and Akráta. Each person would be given a spoonful of kóllyva on a napkin and would say, "May God forgive him," and eat it. My last recollection of the practice is from the ninth day after the fall of the Polytechnic School in

mother died within forty days of one other. The coffeehouse started empty-ing. Militsa informed Kyria Chrysánthē that she would hold the ninth-day memorial at her church. We were among the last to leave.

At the apartment, tables had been set in both Kyria Chrysánthē's and YiôrgoPanourgiás' households. White linen tablecloths, Sunday-best crys-tal and porcelain—this funeral meal lacked no extravagance. The tables looked as beautiful as wedding tables. Iōánna had left nothing to chance; everything was in perfect order. Negotiations about the seating arrange-ments were begun. Finally Pétros, Violétta, Violétta's mother, Vangeliô and Yiôrgos, Léngō and Kyrilos, Myrtô, and I were assigned to YiôrgoPanour-giás' apartment. The rest of the brothers and their wives and children stayed at Kyria Chrysánthē's. Loukianós cornered me again. "Is Grandpa ever coming back?" he asked. I answered that no, he would not. By now he was three meters into the earth. "And Tzoutzoulomýtēs? What about him?" Loukianós asked, referring to the little bird with the bright red beak that YiôrgoPanourgiás had sheltered for a few years after it flew into his bal-cony and perched on his head. Who would care for it? Loukianós wanted to

▲▲▲▲▲▲▲▲▲▲▲▲▲▲▲▲▲▲▲▲▲▲▲▲▲▲▲▲▲▲▲▲

Athens, 26 November 1973. It was the day of the coup d'état of Ioannidis. The woman at the crossroads was a neighbor, the mother of a young stu-dent who had been killed at the Polytechnic by an army officer. She stood at the corner, the same one that my father identifies as the one that German and government soldiers used during World War II to hunt down members of the Resistance. She stood there passing out spoonfuls of kóllyva to any-one who would accept them. No one dared ask who the kóllyva were for, and she wouldn't volunteer such information. This is the terror of silence that Taussig (1987) mentions. Martial law was in effect, the country was in a state of emergency, and it was dangerous enough for Kyria Komnēnou to be so forthcoming about a death that had occurred in her family during that time. There was deathly and deadly terror everywhere. Our prayer of "May God forgive him" was a whisper. We were afraid of who would be listening.

### Esoterics

The term *soï* was used by Violétta to denote the patriline, that is, the line of YiôrgoPanourgiás which includes his siblings and their families. Con-trary to Campbell (1964), Herzfeld has noted that soï should be viewed as a "patrigroup" whose members share a common surname and are said to "have the same blood" (1985:52). This reading of the notion of soï, how-

137

know. I offered the care of Tzoutzoulomýtēs to him, which is what he had been implicitly negotiating for the entire time. That matter settled, with Loukianós pleased with the outcome of his bravery, Iōánna summoned all the children below the age of fourteen and took them to her house. They had been around death for too long.

Food was served, and everyone agreed that wine should be drawn from YiôrgoPanourgiás' personal supply, which he kept in a small oak barrel in his kitchen. At his farewell supper, it was only proper to drink his wine. It was the last time he would be, in some form, incorporated in a family meal. After this his place would be strictly in the grave. The conversation mainly centered on reminiscences of YiôrgoPanourgiás' life—the time he had spent at Eskişehir during the war with the Turks, his capture by the Germans, his escape, the Polish Resistance leader who had sought refuge at the family house. Pétros remembered, "He was very tall, very blond, didn't speak a word of Greek. He spoke with everyone in French. Grandma—she must have been in her seventies then—tried to teach him Arvanitika. They had a jolly time together. One night, late—Father was still a POW—we

▲▲▲▲▲▲▲▲▲▲▲▲▲▲▲▲▲▲▲▲▲▲▲▲▲▲▲▲▲▲▲▲▲

ever, excludes the female members from belonging to it once they marry and change their surnames, while, we assume, other women are admitted into this same patrigroup once they marry into the family and acquire the surname. Under this logic the Panourgiá granddaughters sitting at the coffeehouse after the funeral, all of them married, could not belong to the same soï any longer; but this comes into direct opposition with the statements of these same women, who decisively consider themselves (as does everyone else around) as still belonging to this soï. We know here that Violétta referred to her husband's patriline because this is the only soï (in its near entirety) collectively present at this funeral.

The term is also used in the vernacular when quality is being explored, criticized, or disputed, as in the expression "Ti soï prágma einai autó?" "What sort of thing is this?"), already implying a suspicion about its dubious quality. It is also used about people, when asking about their qualities, as in "Ti soï anthropos einai?" "What sort of a person is he or she?" It is used to express dismay: "Ma, ti soï anthropos eisai esý, vre paidhi mou?" ("But, what sort of a person are you?") Finally, it is used to indicate total lack of quality, as in "Then einai soï to psōmi" ("The bread is not good"), or "Then einai soï ánthrōpos" ("He is not a good person"), which should not be confused with "Then einai apo soï" ("He is not from a good lineage").

heard the signal about a German raid. The Pole didn't know what to do. We tried to hide him in the pantry, but he was too tall, too big. Then Grandma came out from her room and dragged him inside, with her. She made him lie in her bed, and she lay next to him. The Germans came, searched the whole house—you see, somebody, a relative, had told on us—looked in Grandma's room, saw her 'asleep,' and left. After that he decided it was too dangerous for us to keep him, so he left through the river. They caught him and hanged him at the bridge. A week later they arrested me too."

I drifted into Kyria Chrysánthē's apartment, where equal amounts of food and wine were being consumed and where a heated discussion had developed. They were talking about the property. Léngō had walked up behind me without my hearing her. She heard her mother's raised voice talking about the future ownership of the fig groves. "Let his body cool off first in his grave, and then you can disagree about the farms and the houses," she said. The discussion stopped. I followed Léngō into the kitchen to help her with the dishes. Shortly afterward our relations started leaving.

▲▲▲▲▲▲▲▲▲▲▲▲▲▲▲▲▲▲▲▲▲▲▲▲▲▲▲▲▲▲

## Glimpses

Weddings, funerals, and (to a lesser extent) baptisms, are usually the occasions when family connections are reaffirmed and the solidarity of family and friends is demonstrated to the outside, indifferent world, much the way military marches exhibiting the military might of the country, are opportunities to demostrate to any real, present, potential, or imaginary enemies the military advances and advantages of the exhibitor. In the case of Achilléas, however, a deeper plot was at play. Achilléas is the first cousin of Nákos, their fathers being brothers. Achilléas has lived all his life in Markópoulo except for three years (1968–71), which he spent attending the technical university in Athens, while living as a houseguest of Nákos' family. Subsequently Nákos intervened for him, and Achilléas landed a job at the company that Nákos had helped to spawn, where Achilléas is still employed. After 1971, however, the relationship between the two cousins and their families became progressively cooler, and finally was reduced to casual meetings at weddings and funerals, which resulted in Achilléas' statement to Myrtô. The reasons that created and precipitated this cooling of feelings and relations require a psychoanalytical rather than a sociocultural explanation. I am not willing to undertake such an approach here, first, because it would be rather painful to do so, and second, because it would not add anything to the overall argument. You have to take my word for it.

1. A *nýphē* is a bride; the term also refers to the inmarrying woman, who is called, collectively, "our bride" (*he nýphē mas*).

2. See de Certeau 1984:190–98.

3. *Pappou* means Grandpa (vocative of the noun *o pappous*); *Pappoulē* is "little Grandpa," a term of endearment.

4. They use a mixture of Greek and Arvanitika expressions: *móy diáliyth,* "my good child"; *theia mou,* "my aunt"; and *móy koitçi mou,* "my good girl."

5. See de Certeau 1984:191.

6. An *ekforá* is a carrying out (of a corpse for burial) or the burial or funeral. The term derives from *ekférō,* "to carry out," "to carry away," "to carry off as a prize" (Liddell and Scott 1871; Kyriakidis 1908).

7. *Brikia* are small contraptions used for making Turkish coffee.

8. Papadiamantis 1988:82.

9. Zanetos 1975:19–21. All translations of the liturgies are Zanetos'. The incantation inevitably suggests a similar passage from Homer about the Otherworld: "And where life is most free from care for men; / There is neither snow, nor much cold, nor rain, / But always Okeanos rouses blasts / Of the whistling-breathed Zephyr to cool men" (*Odyssey* 4.565–68).

10. For an opposite view on the matter of daily attendance at the grave, see Danforth 1982.

The small side of the *prósforo* seal

# Part III

# FRAGMENTS
# OF MEMORY

*I am politically minded. I mean, I think about death daily and compare it with a vastly better system: life.*

—Katerina Anghelaki-Rooke, "Twilight"

# 6

# La Longue Durée

## PALIMPSESTS OF MEMORY

Only the conscious horror of destruction creates the correct relationship with the dead:
unity with them because we, like them, are the victims of the same condition and the same
disappointed hope.
— Max Horkheimer and Theodor W. Adorno, *Dialectic of Enlightenment*

Anyone else's funeral could be your funeral. In any one of the caskets you
see being lowered into the ground could be your body. And it will be.
Whether you speak of it or not, whether you name it or not, the devastation
of death is counterbalanced only by the totality of its existence. Naming
it, speaking it, is simply the act of memory and the means by which you
measure your relationship with your past. It was not self-absorption that
led "Pétros" back, in narrative time, to the times that he himself had been
arrested and almost executed (although it was a tragic irony that in two
years' time he also died of cancer). But the knowledge of the imminence of
death is never too far away. Pétros had been arrested at the age of sixteen
by the Gestapo and, along with a few hundred other teenagers, had been
held for four and a half months in one of the prisons of Athens. He would
not speak of the tortures. "I will not put them on paper and thus perpetuate
them," said Judith Elkin (in Behar 1991a), writing about a similar situation. Pétros only spoke of the terror of the repeated torture, the fear of the
*eikonikê ektélesē* (mock execution), and the fear of real death, which also,
ironically, would mean the cessation of torture and pain.

This is what mock execution is: They place you in front of the firing
squad. They have blanks, and they know it. You don't know it. They fire at

you. You think you are going to die, but you don't. You just get terrified. They do that over and over again, every so often. They take you to solitary confinement, leave you there for a few days, torture you, then take you out and again pretend to execute you. Sometimes after that they bury you, only it is still not real. They make you lie down in a small trench, like a hurried grave, and they put a piece of corrugated metal over it. Then they take you out, and the cycle starts all over again.

Only the conscious horror of death can inform the horrific feelings present in our contact with its simulations. As Pétros was held by the Gestapo in Athens, his father was being held as a prisoner of war in Crete, after that fateful battle with the Germans. At home in Athens Pétros' two brothers, Kōnstantinos, and Nikólaos (thirteen and eleven years old, respectively), were teasing death as *saltadhóroi*. In small gangs of children aged six to thirteen, they accosted German trucks full of provisions, and while a few of them diverted the guards' attention with various tricks, the rest emptied the truck clean. Sometimes the German soldiers did not realize what had happened until much later. Other times they realized it almost immediately, and then "we had to run as fast as possible, then diving onto the pavement, then meandering on the road, so that they couldn't take good aim at us," Kōnstantinos said. "Some of us got hit, died on the spot, on the same spot that the little boy was killed in '73."

I remember the case of 1973 very well. It happened in front of our house the day after the fall of the Polytechnic, Saturday, 17 November. The students (primarily university students but also a good number of high school students from around Athens) had barricaded themselves in the campus of the Polytechnic School, starting on Tuesday evening, 13 November. The colonels drove their tanks into the Polytechnic grounds on Friday night, 16 November. The following weekend, on Friday, after a whole week of curfews, another generals' coup d'état took place. Saturday, 17 November, was the first day that we were able to go outside and do some shopping, after a week of curfews. Yiôrgos Panourgias and Lea, my sister, were standing in front of our house. I was a little way behind them. A young woman was just returning from the fish market holding her five-year-old son by the hand. We heard two shots: one went right in between Lea and Yiôrgos Panourgiás, between their heads, and got stuck on the wooden light pole. The other, also between their heads, struck the boy on the head, killing him instantly. The woman must have felt his hand go limp in hers. She jerked him up a few times, and then Yiôrgos Panourgiás rushed to her, held the boy, and told her he was dead. I remember her looking at my grandfather as if what he was saying did not make any sense. She then looked all around

144

her and started giving away her fish to all of us who had gathered there. The soldier who had fired the shots was still sitting on the steps of the church up on the hill, looking down onto our street.

Altogether three people from Zográphou died during the Polytechnic uprising. In addition to little Dēmêtrēs, Diomêdēs Komnēnós, a seventeen-year-old high school student, died when a bullet pierced his heart on the grounds of the Polytechnic on the night of 16–17 November. Michálēs Mavroyiánnēs, a university student, died on 18 November. The students' graves, by coincidence, are merely a stone's throw away from each other at the Zográphou cemetery, thus fixing their ideological and symbolic proximity and affinity in space and time.

Yiôrgos Panourgiás was not new to danger. He knew all too well (as the rest of us either already knew, or soon learned) that you are never really out of harm's way, that life is only a series of overlappings and parallelisms, ever so fluid in their positions. Let us take the case of Yiôrgos Panourgiás' life, as presented to us in a photograph, with its layered messages, a palimpsest of memory that shows us, in three small and seemingly insignificant instances, the span of twenty years (his most productive). The photograph itself is image 1.

In this photograph we see Yiôrgos Panourgiás (on the left) with Dēmêtrios Tsalapátēs, the brother of Evangelia Panourgiá (then still named Drakou, as she was not yet married, but only betrothed) in front of the White Tower in Thessaloniki. In a strange twist of history, Yiôrgos and Dēmêtrios served in the same regiment in the army during the expedition to Asia Minor. After the defeat of the Greek army, Yiôrgos was arrested by the Turks and taken prisoner in the hinterland of Anatolia, whence he escaped in the spring of 1923. He made his way to Thessaloniki, where he managed to rejoin Dēmêtrios, who had evaded imprisonment. They had their photograph taken then, and Yiôrgos sent the picture to Evangelia, dated 2 September 1923 and signed "Yeôrgios," in the purist katharevousa that he always used and in his elegant calligraphic writing. This is image 2.

The photograph, with its inscription, was kept by Evangelia in her jewelry box. What caused the photograph to surface twenty years later nobody knows. Somehow, however, the photograph was taken out of the box while Yiôrgos was away during the Second World War, when he was sent to fight in Crete against the Germans. After the battle of Crete and the eventual capture of the island by the Germans, Yiôrgos was once again taken prisoner. Somehow he was able to send word to Athens that he was being kept at the Fourth Center for Prisoners of War in Fourné, Crete. No one can remember any longer who brought the message. It must have been

Image 1: Yiôrgos Panourgiás, *left*, with Dēmêtrios Tsalapátēs in front of the White Tower in Thessaloniki in September 1923.

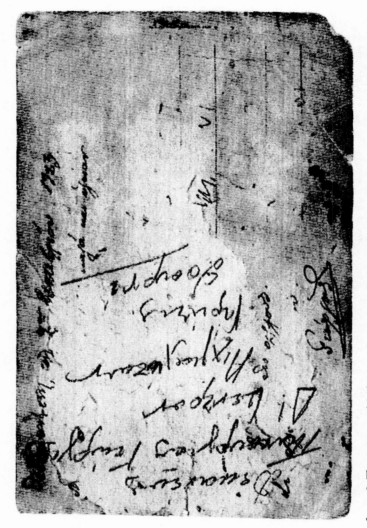

Image 2: The remnants of the horizontal message read: "Thessaloniki, on 2d September 1923 . . . well and health . . . to all. Yeórgios."

147

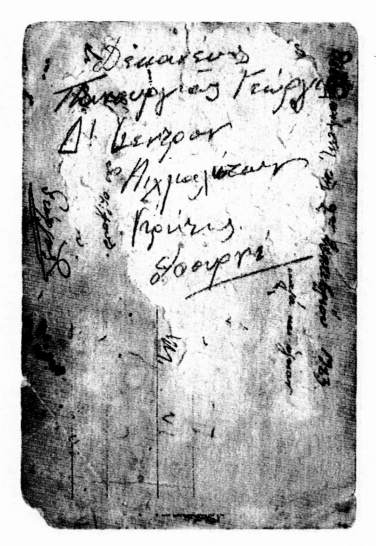

Image 3: The vertical message reads: "Sergeant Panourgiás Yeôrgios D',
Center for Prisoners of War, Crete, Fourné."

given in a hurry, because Yiôrgos' mother-in-law, Katina, was the one who received it. She wrote the address vertically on the back of the photograph that Yiôrgos had sent from Thessaloniki. Apparently Katina tore off part of the top layer of paper, vertically, to create a blank space on which she could write the second message. This is image 3.

Could she not find a piece of paper anywhere in the house? Is there any intended significance in this multiple layering of messages, this reconstruction of history, this peeling of *mneme?* We will never know. Katina died in 1963, long before anyone knew that these questions might eventually interest a great-granddaughter anthropologist. Before his prisoner unit was sent to Germany, Yiôrgos managed to escape and, along with another seventeen Resistance fighters, to get safe passage to Egypt in a small fishing boat. From there he made his way, on foot, to the "Middle East" (*stēn Mésē Anatolê,* he said, probably referring to Palestine). Hidden again in the belly of a small fishing boat, he safely landed in Piraeus, whence he walked home to Athens. It is this absence, then, this almost perpetual presence of his through his photographic image, that is recorded in the preceding sequences of mnemonic gestures.[1]

Telling the story of the Polish Resistance fighter at the funerary meal for YiôrgoPanourgiás, then, was not out of place. He whose name has not survived in the family memory is always considered a hero and, to recall Vernant's words, "thanks to his exploits, and through his heroic death, the warrior fallen on the front line of battle remains forever present in men's lives and memories" (1986:54). The connecting thread among these men—and the women whose lives are also strung on this same thread—is their concurrent brushing with death. What sets them apart is the different times during which their deaths occurred.

The Panourgiádhes were the last ones to see the Polish soldier alive. He left the house, entered, through a manhole, the covered banks of the tributary of the Ilissos that runs along the main road of Zográphou, and came up at the bridge, almost a kilometer down the road, where the Germans (notified by the traitors) were expecting him. He was killed on the spot. Through the realization that no one saw him between our house and the bridge, he was admitted as a member of the family. He became part of the family memory, of its symbolic property. He is *our* Polish Resistance fighter (*Ho Polōnós mas*). Now, in the small society of our family, he is one of our dead, for a society comprises its dead as well as its living.[2]

## RAPTURE

Ἄφκιαστο κι ἀστόλιστο
τοῦ Χάρου δέ σέ δίνω.
στάσου μέ τἀνθόνερο
τήν ὄψη σου νά πλύνω,

Μήπως καί τοῦ Χάροντα
καθώς θά σέ κοιτάξῃ,
τοῦ φανῆς ἀχάιδευτο
καί σέ παραπετάξῃ.

To Charon, unadorned, undecked
I shall not hand thee o'er.
O wait that I might lave thy face
With sweet perfume once more.

Ill would it be if thou shouldst seem
Uncared for to his eye,
And Charon, deeming thee unloved,
Should scorn and pass thee by.
—Kostis Palamas, "The Grave"

In what follows we—that is, you as readers and I as author—will experience a discursive rapture, one that stems from an epistemological ambiguity that existed in this phase of my authorship. Let me take things from the beginning.

The writing of the next section started in the spring of 1984, not as part of an anthropological-ethnographic analysis, but as a diary. At that time I had no intention of creating a work on death in Greece. As you might recall from Part I, I planned to study the rembétika, and I was hoping that my visit in 1984 would produce valuable material on that subject. Moreover, and more important, I had not yet fully resolved the epistemological and political implications of being simultaneously an anthropologist and an informant. Therefore, I had not yet developed a strategy through which I could manipulate my inclusion to things and situations or my simultaneous academic distance from them, so as to create the analytical advantage that I managed to achieve years later with the death of my grandfather.

In 1984 my childhood friend (and a possible prospective life companion) Panayês died in an automobile accident. My pain was immense, and I was immersed in it. When I visited Greece that spring I was not yet the anthropologist; I was simply a pained "native," trying to cope with my pain. It was only approximately four years later that I was able to see Panayês' death from an analytical and theoretical perspective. It is from this angle, the angle that bears the fissure between the gaze of the anthropologist and the voice of the native that the following text has been written.

150

## Springtime

*Death is a whore*
*who takes everyone*
—Yiorgos Chouliaras, *Fast Food Classics*

*Ti terástia anōnymia ho Thánatos.*
*(Kai ti mnêmē,*
*Theé mou!*
*K a n é n a n*
*Dhen xehná!)*

*How vast an anonymity is Death.*
*(and what Memory,*
*my God!*
*It forgets*
*n o   o n e!)*
                              —Yiannis Patilis, *Warm Midday*

It is springtime again, Good Friday, as I am writing this in Princeton, where the bell of the Russian Orthodox church tolls the Apokathêlōsis, the liturgy of the unnailing of Christ from the Cross. The sound and its effect are only too familiar and too painful. It is the same sound, the same timing, the same feeling, as that created by the Holy Week church bells in Greece.[3] The droning sound, mixed in with the voices and the loud cries of the undergraduates, replicates the children's voices in Akráta.[4] There they play with their friends, begging their mothers not to drag them to church, oblivious to the memory of pain that will be replicated in the evening liturgy, the tears that some women will shed on Maundy Thursday, thinking of the pain of Christ's mother watching her son being crucified.

During this evening twelve Gospels are sung, each recounting a part of Christ's Passion, followed by chants and responses between the priests and the cantors. The liturgy is in two parts, each containing six Gospels, with a dramatic break in the middle, during which the representation of Christ's Crucifixion takes place. The central object of the representation of the Crucifixion is, of course, the body on the Cross. A wooden replica of the original Cross, almost to size, is kept throughout the year behind the altar (the Hagia Trápeza). This cross is movable and has a detachable figure of Christ on it. After the fifth Gospel the priest takes the cross, brings it out of the sanctuary, and presents it to the congregation, who are singing the Crucifixion hymn. Then he places it on a block of marble and secures it there, erect. While the cantors continue to sing the Crucifixion hymn, the priest stands on a small stool and, with a hammer, taps on the nails that keep the effigy in place: they pass through the two palms and the feet. Thus symbolically recrucified in public, Christ regains once more his corporeality (in the full essence of the term: the reality of his corpus, his body) as the son (of the woman) and the Son (of the Christian god).

Much more than during the ensuing funeral, people grieve for this public execution. At this point it matters little whether the act is symbolic or not, annual or singular. Thus, in the middle of this dramatic performance, at the peak of it, the congregation venerates the site (and the sight). They leave flowers to be used in tomorrow's funeral, cross themselves underneath the cross, and kiss the feet of the executed. And they sigh. And some tears trickle down their cheeks, because here there is no divine abstraction, only the reality of the crucified body. It is this same body that will be brought down from the cross by the priest in the Friday morning liturgy, the Apokathêlōsis, when he will reverse the previous night's gestures and will climb back on the step stool, only this time behind the cross, not in front of it. He will tap with his hammer on the nails again, only this time to loosen them, not to tighten them; and he will bring the wooden body down from the cross and give it to the sexton, who will take it into the altar, place it on the Hagia Trápeza, and wait for the priest to come and wrap it in the shroud. Then the priest will take it out into the nave of the church, where the bier has been placed on the pall, and he will place the shroud-wrapped body onto the gold-embroidered icon of it. Almost all day the body will remain there, until the evening, when the procession starts, when the priest will take the body back to the altar.

What all this leads to is the Epitáphios, the procession that takes place on Good Friday night throughout Greece and is the reenactment of Christ's funeral, with the official participation of the authorities. The Epitáphios is the preclimactic moment in the performative drama of Holy Week. As G. A. Megas notes, "Flags are flown at half-mast. Sentries carry their arms reversed, and church-bells ring a funeral knell" (1963:99). Schools (throughout the week), public services, theaters, movies, and clubs are closed, and most of the restaurants serve only lenten dishes. (It has become almost a ritual of adulthood, however, for teenagers and older children still living at home to sneak out of the house and procure some of the forbidden foods for themselves, to be consumed outside the house. They take great pains to obliterate all possible traces of the transgression: they immediately brush their teeth, wash their hands, and assume famished looks to ward off the watchful parental eyes.) *Epitáphios* is also the term used for the gold-embroidered icon carried on the pall (*kouvouklion*), the piece of cloth bearing a representation of Christ's crucified body.

The procession starts inside the church on Friday evening. Placed on the bier, which is an effigy of a church, adorned with flowers, and flanked by soldiers or boy scouts, the pall is taken on procession around the *enoria* (parish). The structure of the procession is very precise. First go the altar boys carrying the six-winged-angel portraits and the banners of the church, followed by the choir and the cantors. Then follows the Epitáphios, then the priests, then little girls carrying white calla lilies, and finally the enoria and church notables and the congregation.

Epitáphios, more than anything else, is the affirmation of the death of Christ. As the pall is carried around, in plain view for all to see, it underlines the desire of the church to convey "the reality of death, as it would never wish to neutralize it by coverings" (Harakas 1990:152). On the same level operates the open casket at the funerals of mortals. This conceptualization of the reality of death is the main operative point in the celebration of Christ's death on Good Friday; his death is not only acknowledged but also celebrated. As a friend commented as we were coming out of the church one Good Friday, only through the celebrations of the Holy Week can one realize exactly how corporeal a dogma Greek Orthodoxy is. And it is precisely this corporeality that refers back to its own symbolism, the sublimation that governs religion, that crystallizes in ritual. The procession starts at the church and makes the rounds of the main streets of the enoria and then returns to the church. It stops three times during its rounds, each time for the choir to sing laments to Christ.

Nothing is associated in my conscience with Panayês' death as the Epitáphios. Here's why. In 1984 I arrived in Akráta on Good Friday, shortly before the Epitáphios procession began, a few weeks after Panayês was killed. Exhausted from the transatlantic flight, devastated by his death, anxious to go to his grave and to see his mother, I bathed and left for the procession along with my parents, my sister and her family, and two American friends who were visiting us.

We caught up with the beginning of the procession around the central square, a couple of blocks from the church. Everything looked the same: balconies and patios were once again decorated with luminarias made with hollowed-out oranges in which candles had been stuck; yellow candles had been affixed to the balcony rails; boy scouts were there, keeping order; young girls from the schools were preceding the Epitáphios, dressed in blue and white and holding white calla lilies in their hands.[5] Then followed the band, the church banners, and the icons draped in mauve and black ribbons. Then came the people carrying their yellow tapers, shielding them from the spring breeze. The band started playing the first stasis of the laments for the death of Christ. Everybody stopped and listened to the lament sung by the choir:

| | |
|---|---|
| He zoë en táfō | O Christ, Life, You were |
| katetétheis Christé | placed in the Tomb |
| kai aggélōn stratiai | and the armies of |
| exeplêtonto | angels were dazzled |
| syngatávasēn doxázousai | glorifying Your |
| tēn sēn | condescension |
| | |
| He zoë, pôs thnēskeis? | O Life, how do You die? |
| Pôs en táfō oikeis? | How do You Live in the Tomb? |
| tou thanátou to basileion | You unbind the kingdom |
| lyeis the kai tou Adhou | of death and You raise |
| tous nekrous exanistás | the dead from Hades |
| | |
| Póte idō, Sôter | When do I see You, Savior |
| se to áhronon fôs, | You the timeless light, |
| tēn harán kai hēdonên | the joy and pleasure |
| tês kardias mou? | of my heart? |
| he parthénos anevóa goerôs | the virgin cried loudly |

The lament, in the A plagal sound of the Byzantine chant, with its arrangement in the minor scale that is so reminiscent of later Western classical music, immediately sets the tone for mourning. I looked around once more, and I saw Panayês' mother, dressed in black from head to toe, holding on to the arm of Kōstês, her older son. I broke away from the rest and walked over to greet them. Yiôta was in a daze; she hardly recognized me. "Kyria Yiôta," I said, "it's me. It's Neni." It was obvious that she could not quite fix her memory on me; she wasn't really sure. I repeated what I had just said. She kept looking at me, without crying, without tears, but as if she could see through me. "He's gone," she said. "What am I doing following the funeral of someone else's child?" I bent over and kissed her cheeks. Then I kissed Kōstês and joined the procession with them. We walked for a while silently, listening to the chanting by the priests. Then the second stasis was sung, in the same plagal again. We all stood motionless, listening to the choir:

| | |
|---|---|
| Axion esti megalýnein | It is meet to magnify You |
| se ton zōodhótēn, ton | life-giver whom Your hands |

en tô stavrô tas heiras
ekteinanta kai syntripsanta
to krátos tou ehthrou

stretched onto the Cross
and crushed the might
of the enemy

Mónē gynaikôn hōris pónon
étekón se, téknon,
pónous the nyn férō
páthei to oh aforêtous,
élegen he semnê

Alone among women
I bore You with no pain,
child, now I bear the pain
unbearably painful, said
the modest one

Efrixen hē gê,
kai ho hêlios Sôter ekryvē,
sou tou anespérou féggous,
Christé,
dýnantos en táfō sōmatikôs

The earth shuddered
and the sun, Savior, hid
from you unsetting light,
Christ, at Your
bodily grave

We started walking again as the priests resumed their chanting. I felt
Yiôta's hand holding on to my arm and squeezing it. I looked at her. "Welcome back," she said. It was time for the third stasis, the most beautiful of
all in lyrics and in music, the one that gets most of its stanzas sung, this
time in the third sound:

Ai geneai pásai
hýmnon tê tafê sou,
prosférousi, Christé mou

All the generations
offer a hymn at Your funeral
my Christ

Myrofóroi êlthon
mýra soi, Christé mou,
komizousai profrónōs

Myrrh-bearing women
came anxiously to anoint You,
my Christ

Oh, glyký mou éar,
glykýtatón mou téknon
pou édy sou to kálos?

Oh, my sweet springtime
my sweetest child
where has Your beauty set?

Hē dámalis ton móschon
en xýlō kremasthénta
alálazen ōrôsa

The heifer wailed
seeing the calf hanging
from the wood

Oh fôs tôn ofthalmôn mou,
glykýtatón mou téknon,
pôs táfō nýn kalýptei?

Oh, light of my eyes,
my sweetest child, now
how can a grave cover You?

Anékrazen hē kórē
thermôs dakryroousa,
ta spláchna kentouménē

The girl cried out
shedding warm tears, feeling
pierced in her vitals[6]

155

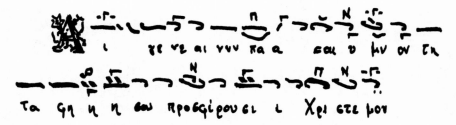

The Byzantine notation for the third stasis

"I want to go home now," Yiôta said to Kôstês and me. I kissed them both, promising that I would come and visit the next morning, and Kôstês led his mother away. I went back to my family and friends and followed the rest of the procession with them. The mood for me, however, was decisively different than at any other Good Friday. I realized that I had not joined my father in whistling the music of the laments as we did every year (thus always provoking my mother's reprimand that "this is not a club, and this is not a popular song that we can whistle"), and I actually caught myself *listening* to the lyrics of the hymns. I was not even participating in the gossip that was going on around me, between my sister and my mother and friends and relatives that we chanced upon at the procession. The aesthetic of the Epitáphios was the same—the light breeze, the candle and flower smells, the colors—but my mood, the way I sensed things around me, had changed. For the first time I felt the Epitáphios as it actually is: a funeral (of a god, the son of the god of the Orthodox Christians). We returned to the church, waited for the bier to be brought back, revered the pall, and left. We went home to our lentil soup and steamed shrimp. "Let's put some oil in the soup. The stars are out now. God can't see us," my father said jokingly. My mother also sautéed some shrimp and kalamari.

We mourn for the particular dead at a particular funeral or memorial (*mnēmósyno*) along with our own dead (see Alexiou 1974; and Danforth 1982), and there is also a clearly articulated connection between the laments for Christ and the recognition of his human (thus mortal) essence, but we are implicitly discouraged (culturally and theologically) from connecting the Epitáphios with mourning for our own dead.[7] First of all, the mood at the Epitáphios is almost gay; people chat with each other, gossip, exchange news, and make plans for the rest of the celebration, much the way they act during any other church liturgy. Second, when Epitáphios is experienced as mourning (as it is by practicing Orthodox Christians), it is experienced as the moment of mourning for the one, collectively owned,

156

dead; in that instance Christ is instituted and reaffirmed as the singular object of collective mourning (Papayiorgis 1991:69).

That is why in the Orthodox tradition Good Friday is the strictest lent. No consumption of oils, fats, meats, anything that contains blood, anything that would indicate excess is allowed. (Some people go so far as to actually drink a whole wineglass of vinegar, in commemoration of the vinegar that Christ was given on the Cross when he asked for water to quench his thirst [John 19.28–30].) And that is why a practicing Orthodox Christian should never mourn his or her own dead during the Epitáphios; it is the ritual mourning for the one whose death promises eternal life for the many. Only through the death of Christ can Christians hope for the eventual resurrection of their dead and for unending spiritual life in Paradise. And that is why Yiôta's mourning that Good Friday was so much, and so strangely, out of place. To her the death of Christ and the death of her son had the same sense of finitude. For her neither of them would be resurrected. Hence, her objection to following the procession was not an objection to the Christian understanding of Christ's nondeath (as it should have been, perhaps) opposed to her son's definitive death, but rather to her inability and unwillingness to participate in someone else's sorrow (that of Panayia, the mother of Christ) because she was too deeply involved in her own. The dividing line between her two worlds, the spiritual and the secular, had been erased.

This eradication of the difference between two cosmologies produced in turn a homology where these two worlds, our same and the Other of the dead, collapsed, and reality, Yiôta's reality, became simply a metaphor for her existence. The cruelty of the usually accepted division between the dead and the living became the focal point of rejection of death within the context of life, because, as Horkheimer and Adorno note, "it is not possible for the consciousness to perceive of death as absolute nothingness, since absolute nothingness is inconceivable" (1972:215). Hence various strategies are developed and employed in the analysis of this inconceivability (on the local level) and its inevitably exigent resynthesis into a possibility of things that may become conceivable and accepted.

The next evening was the celebration of the Resurrection. A little before midnight we put on our finery and went to church, my parents, my sister, her husband and son, my two American friends, and I. As urban custom has it, although the liturgy of the Resurrection starts at half past ten in the evening, most people do not appear until shortly before the reading of the Gospel, approximately twenty minutes before midnight, when the hymn of Resurrection is sung.[8] Thus we also arrived at the church, the same church that had now given up the aesthetic of mourning of Friday's tomb to the whiteness of the tapers and bright clothing of the congregation, ready to celebrate the Resurrection. The church was packed primarily with the older people who wanted to secure a seat, as they would stay until the end of the liturgy, approximately one and a half hours later. The younger ones (that means anyone below the age of sixty) and the visiting Akratinoi were outside, on the large patio in front of the church, spilling over into people's front yards and into the streets, so that they could make a quick exit after the Resurrection hymn was sung. Out on the patio a large platform had been placed on which the priest and his deacons would stand to carry on the celebration. It was shortly before To Fōs (the Celebration of the Lights), when the lights inside and outside the church are put out except for the Asvestos Lycnia (the Ever-Burning Candle) on the altar. From this flame the priest lit a candle and passed the light around, and from that flame the congregation lit their candles. A favorite (or simply a speedy) child from each of the families pushed ahead, toward the entrance of the church, trying to catch the light first, to bring it to family and friends and receive the blessings for the year.

For twenty years that was precisely what Panayês would do: he would bring the light to us, receive my parents' blessings, and teasingly demand a prostration from Lea and me (as the custom is) so that we could light our candles from his. Not this year, nor any year hereafter, would this happen. I felt the swelling of tears in my eyes. I took Oréstēs' hand—he was not two years old yet—and headed toward the church, in search of Kōstês, Panayês' brother. I found him with his wife. We kissed, and I showed Oréstēs how to light his candle from Kōstês'. Yiôta was nowhere to be seen, of course. As Megas says, "Nobody fails to attend the Resurrection, except widows and those in mourning" (1963:105), and Yiôta was in the deepest mourning. "How's your mother tonight?" I asked Kōstês. I had not been able to bear to visit her that morning. He shook his head and hand at the same time, as if to say, "How could she be?" He started crying. I kissed him again and took Oréstēs back to the place where our family was standing, where all the rest of us prostrated to this half-meter-tall person who had brought us the Paschal light. The priests came out, the Gospel was read, the Resurrection hymn was sung, deafening fireworks went off, we all kissed the Kiss of Love, we said "Christ has risen" to each other, and then we went home to eat our *mayēritsa* (goat-innards soup).

The morning of Sunday, Easter Day, the sky was overcast and a light drizzle was falling. My father roasted a goat kid and a *kokorétsi* (the goat's

Kōnstantinos and Dêmētra Panourgiá preparing the Paschal kid and Kokorétsi

entrails wrapped in its intestines) on two spits, my mother stuffed eggs and made salads, and we brought out fresh feta cheese and yogurt, the first from the year's milking. We set the table outside under the African vine and brought out ouzo and my father's wine; the radio was playing popular and demotic music, and Oréstēs was whirling around in a dance of his own. In Akráta, in the Peloponnese, the custom of roasting a kid on a spit does not exist, nor is kokorétsi known; both are foods of the Attika and Roumeli regions. Because my father is an Athenian, our house is the only one in Akráta where these two foods are found. This is one of the reasons that friends come to have a taste and a glass of wine and to visit with us. Old friends of my grandparents', people who have known the family long before any of those now living were born, stop by and exchange news and toast with us. It was so this morning. Everyone started nibbling and joking. Only my father noticed that I was doing neither. He sat next to me. "What's up?" he asked, rather provocatively. I turned to answer him, and my mother came to my rescue: "Leave her alone, don't you understand? It's the first time she's here since Panayês' death." My father turned to me solemnly and austerly: "The dead with the dead, and the living with the living," he said. I asked my mother to prepare a couple of plates with some

159

roasted meat and kokorétsi for me to take to our neighbors who are too shy to come around on their own. I took Oréstēs by the hand, and we started our rounds of the neighborhood.

## PARERGA

1. The Greek term for the logic that drives the act of photography is *apathanatizō,* "to immortalize," or, literally, "to un-die" someone. Cadava, drawing on Benjamin, goes even further, to note not only that photography is the immortalization of the photographic object, but also that photography itself is a "mode of bereavement" (1991:90). Benjamin (1968) not only establishes the connections between death and photography but further draws out the importance of the photographic image in the mnemonic process. See Cadava 1991 for commentary on Benjamin's position.

2. See also Ariès 1974, on the incorporation of the dead into the collective identification of society as a result of the rise of nationalism in the late eighteenth century, and Kearl and Rinaldi 1983, on the political uses of the dead. See also the exhaustive treatise by Prior (1989), especially on how the dead have been treated as political and cultural commodities in the British-Irish war, much the way they have been treated in Greece by opposing political factions, and much the way their use is evidenced in the political capital invested in the Tombs of the Unknown Soldiers throughout the world.

3. The drama of Holy Week starts with the commemoration of Christ's entrance into Jerusalem, on Palm Sunday, and ends with the celebration of his Resurrection at midnight the following Saturday. Easter in Greece is a movable feast, as is the case with the rest of the Christian dogmas, but its determination depends upon the lunar, not the solar, calendar. Thus it is always celebrated on the first Sunday after the first full moon that follows the Jewish Passover. Holy Week itself is the culmination of Lent, of the forty-day period of abstinence from meat and dairy products (even oil on Wednesdays and Fridays), sexual abstinence, and the absence of the celebration of all joyous sacraments, such as marriages, baptisms, and ordinations of new priests. It is catachrestically called Forty-Day Lent (Tessarakostê, or Sarakostê in the vernacular: the act of abstinence, *nēsteia,* from the verb *estheiō,* "to eat," and the module *nē,* "not"), as it usually lasts closer to fifty days than forty. It is computed from the beginning of Lent on Clean Monday (Katharê Deutéra, or Koúlouma in Athenian), which is the first Monday after the last Sunday of Carnival (Apókries, literally "distance from meat"), roughly corresponding to Ash Wednesday (which

comes on the first Wednesday after the last Sunday of Carnival). Although few people observe the forty-day prohibition as strictly as the Church mandates, most bow to the dictate (*nēsteúoun*) during Holy Week. During that week the clergy dresses in black and mauve vestments (*ámphia*), instead of their usual colorful ones, and in the church mauve and black ribbons are wrapped around the chandeliers, the icons, and the entrance to the altar, the Ōraia Pýlē.

On Palm Sunday evening a reversal of liturgical time takes place in the church. Matins are celebrated in the evening, and vespers in the morning. Thus, matins of Holy Monday are sung on Palm Sunday evening, Tuesday matins on Monday evening, Tuesday vespers on Tuesday morning, and so forth. On Holy Wednesday, however, the only service that takes place is that of the Holy Unction for the faithful, not in anticipation of Thursday but as a commemoration of Christ's anointment by Mary Magdalene on Tuesday. That is why there always seems to be a lag between the Catholic Church's celebration of the events and the Orthodox celebration of them. With this in mind, it becomes obvious why crucifixion in the Orthodox Church takes place on Thursday evening instead of Friday morning and resurrection on Saturday evening instead of Sunday morning.

4. Akráta is a small community (a *kōmôpolis*) where the Panourgiás family has property, through Dêmētra's family of origin. The term *kōmô-polis* indicates an administrative district that is larger than a village (*hōrió*) and smaller than a city (*pólis*). The permanent population of Akráta is four thousand, not counting the vacationers of the summer months and major holidays. It has an elevation of 130 meters and is located on the northeastern shore of the Peloponnese, between Korinth and Patras (the first being the capital of Korinthia, the latter the capital of Achaia, to which Akráta belongs administratively). Akráta played a major role in the War of Independence, first by being among the first places where revolt occurred (on 16 March 1821, before the official date of the beginning of the war) and later by participating in the demise of the Turkish army that was headed by Drámalēs in 1823.

Akráta has experienced a revitalization, along with other semiurban or rural places throughout southern Europe (cf. Behar 1991b:380n). Emigrants return to spend weekends and vacation time after they refurbish their paternal or maternal homes with cash earned through labor in the urban centers, through the liquidation of their spouses' property, and through revenues from close relatives long migrated to Australia or the United States. Behar also notes correctly that the children of these emigrants are not expected to participate intimately in the agricultural life of the village or town, beyond the level of casual (however deeply felt and appreciated) contact with the permanent residents. The only difference with places in the rest of southern Europe that Behar discusses is that revitalization occurred in Akráta before the Second World War, sometime in the mid-1930s.

The financial situation of the returned emigrants freed them from anxieties and enabled them to provide their children with good educations, both in Greece and abroad. In the last twenty years these children have studied medicine, dentistry, architecture, engineering, art, and forestry and have returned to Akráta, where they have taken up permanent residence. Hence in Akráta, unlike other places in Greece, the pattern of migration is inward rather than outward. Today Akráta counts among its permanent residents three civil engineers, two architects, three dentists, two pharmacists, an ethnologist, two lawyers, one Supreme Court judge, one retired university professor, four retired high school principals, one electrical engineer, two agricultural engineers, three physicians, and twelve nurses. Among those who consider themselves Akratinous but only visit seasonally are three parliamentary deputies (two with PASOK and one with Nea Demokratia), one retired general, a large number of educators, a few lawyers, and one retired undersecretary of the interior. Both the permanent and the nonpermanent residents of Akráta own plots of land, which they cultivate (some on their own, others with contracted help), primarily tending citrus and olive groves. Those who produce more than they consume sell the surplus to the local (very profitable) co-operative in exchange for cash and/or fertilizers and chemicals or manure. The co-operative also owns three (of four) commercially owned oil presses. Undoubtedly much of the prosperity and financial security of the community must be attributed to the influx of monies from the migrants during the financially and politically crucial and turbulent years 1930–60. My connections with Akráta have always been those of a visitor.

5. Thus these girls close the symbolic circle that started with the Annunciation of Mary with a white calla lily, carrying it all the way to the fulfillment of the prophecy regarding the Crucifixion, burial, and Resurrection of Christ.

6. I am indebted to Photios Ketsetzis, professor of Byzantine music at Hellenic College/Holy Cross School of Theology, for providing me with the Byzantine notation of the staseis, and to Dean Lymberakis, professor of music at the same institution, for providing the Western notation.

There are many more stanzas in each one of the staseis, but each enoria is very selective about which ones will be sung at the Epitáphios, because of time restrictions. Should all the stanzas be sung (as I am told they are in

Mount Athōs), the whole liturgy could take up to five hours instead of the usual three. Each choir, then, in collaboration with the priest of the enoria, decides which ones will be performed, depending largely on the priest's and the choir's preference for particular lyrics. In Akráta the stanzas that are chosen are admittedly among the most beautiful ones, and also the ones that give the most important role to the Panayia and her position in the understanding of the drama of Christ's death.

7. See Baud-Bovy 1936, on the island of Nisyros; and Panourgiá 1983, on the island of Kalymnos. In Kalymnos men and women gather in church on Maundy Thursday evening for the wake of Christ. They sit mingled, on the marble steps in front of the templum, on the chairs, on the floor. They form small groups, and each group holds the lament for a few stanzas, until another group takes over and continues it, until morning. Structurally this event closely resembles the way laments are performed for mortals. There is enough time in the night for the lament to go around approximately ten times. The lament is very long, and some of its stanzas have been lost, so the opening and closing of the plot are almost never sung. This is almost appropriate, since in death there is no entrée or closure, but only ever-moving process.

The text of the lament, as complete as I was able to record it in the church of Aghios Mammas in the capital town of Pothia, on Maundy Thursday night, 15 April 1982, is as follows:

| | |
|---|---|
| Sêmeron hóloi krývontai | Today everybody is hiding |
| kai ta vouná lyghoúntai | and even the mountains are bending |
| | |
| Sêmera évgalan voulê | Today they decided |
| hoi ánomoi Hevraioi | the lawless Hebrews |
| | |
| hoi ânomoi kai ta skyliá | the lawless and the dogs |
| ki hoi treis katēraménoi | the three cursed ones |
| | |
| gia na stavrósoun to Christó | to crucify Christ |
| ton pánton vassiléa | the king of all |
| | |
| . . . . . . . . . | . . . . . . . |
| | |
| tas prosefhás tēs ékane | She was saying her prayers |
| gia ton monogenê tēs | for her only son |
| | |
| fōnê exêlthe ex ouranoú | a voice came from the heavens |
| ki ap' archaggélou stóma | and from the mouth of the archangel |
| | |
| sônoun kyrá m' oi prosefhés | Enough praying, mistress, |
| sônoun kai oi metánoies | enough prostrating |

| | |
|---|---|
| kai to yión sou piásane | because they caught your son |
| oi ánomoi Hevraioi | the lawless Hebrews |
| | |
| oi ánomoi kai ta skyliá | the lawless and the dogs |
| ki oi treis katēraménoi | the three cursed ones |
| | |
| san kléftē ton epiásane | they caught him like a thief |
| kai sa phoniá ton páne | and they are taking him as a murderer |
| | |
| kai stou Pilátou ta skaliá | and at Pilate's steps |
| ekei ton tyrannáne | that's where they are torturing him |
| | |
| ki hē Panayiá san tó'kouse | And Panayia when she heard it |
| épese kai lighôthei | she fainted |
| | |
| stamni neró tes rixane | They threw an urnful of water |
| tria kanátia móscho | three pitchers of musk |
| | |
| kai tria me rodhóstamo | and another three of rose water |
| gia nárthei ho logismós tēs | to bring her back |
| | |
| kai san tês êlthe ho logismós | and when she gained her thoughts |
| kai san tês êlthe ho nous tēs | and when she gained her mind |
| | |
| tên pêran paramáschala | they took her from the arms |
| phōtiá mên páei na pései | so that she wouldn't throw herself into the fire |
| | |
| eite gremó na gremistei | neither would she fall from a cliff |
| gia ton monogenê tēs | on account of her only son |
| | |
| láve kyrá mou ypomonê | Get patience, my mistress |
| láve kyrá mou aréstē | get a repose, my mistress |
| | |
| kai pôs na lávō ypomonê | And how can I get patience |
| kai pôs na lávō aréstē | and how can I get a repose |
| | |
| pou échō yió monogenê | now that I have only one son |
| kai keino stavrōméno | and he is crucified? |
| | |
| páne he Mágdha he Mariá | Magdha and Maria go there |
| kai tou Lazárou he mána | and Lazarus' mother |
| | |
| kai tou Iakôvou he aderphê | and the sister of Jacob |
| ki oi téssereis antáma | all four together |
| | |
| kai piásan to strati strati | and they took the street |
| strati to monopáti | they took the path |
| | |
| ki ho monopátēs évgale | and the path took them |
| mbrostá s'éna 'klēssáki | in front of a chapel |

164

| | |
|---|---|
| ki he Panayiá edhipsase | and Panayia became thirsty |
| 'skypse na piei neráki | and bent over to drink water |

.  .  .  .  .  .  .  .  .  .        .  .  .  .  .  .  .  .  .  .

| | |
|---|---|
| pou 'he karphiá kai éftiachne | who had nails he was making |
| karphiá me ta paidhiá tou | with his children |
| | |
| karphiá me tê gynaika tou | nails he was making with his wife |
| kai me tê fameliá tou | and with his family |
| | |
| hôra kalê sou Atsiggane | Greetings to you, Gypsy, |
| ti na 'nai autá pou ftiáchneis | what is it that you are making? |
| | |
| kai ho tsiggános apêntēse | And the Gypsy answered, |
| karphiá 'pan na tous ftiáxō | They told me to make them some nails |
| | |
| ki ekei' moú 'páne téssera | and while they asked for four |
| ki egô tous ftiáchnō pénte | I am making them five |
| | |
| válte ta dhyó sta héria tou | Drive two into his hands |
| kai t'álla dhyó sta pódhia | and two into his feet |
| | |
| to pémpto to pharmakeró | The fifth one, the poisonous, |
| válte to stên kardhiá tou | drive into his heart |
| | |
| na tréxei aima kai neró | so that blood and water run from it |
| na ligōthei he kardhiá tou | and his heart gives out |
| | |
| ti les mōré Atsiggane | What are you saying, Gypsy? |
| psōmi na mê hortáseis | May you never have your fill of bread |
| | |
| eite tê trahêlitsa sou | and may you never change |
| poté na mên alláxeis | your shirt |
| | |
| kai piásan to strati strati | And they went on to the street |
| strati to monopáti | the street and the path |
| | |
| ki ho monopátēs évgale | and the path brought them |
| mbrós stou lēstoú ten pórta | in front of the thief's door |
| | |
| ánoixe pórta tou lēstou | open door of the thief |
| kai pórta tou Pilátou | door of Pilate |
| | |
| ki he pórta apó tón phóvo tēs | and the door was so frightened |
| ánoixe monahê tēs | that it opened on its own |
| | |
| tērá dhexiá tērá zervá | She looks to the right, she looks to the left |
| kanéna dhen gnōrizei | She does not know anyone |
| | |
| kyttáei kai dhexiôtera | She looks further to the right |
| vlépei ton Háyio Yiánnē | She sees Saint John |

165

Háyie mou Yiánnē Pródhrome
kai vaptistá tou yiou mou

Saint John Prodhrome
and baptist of my son,

dhen eidhes ton yióka mou
kai se didáskalo sou

you haven't seen my little son
and your teacher?

dhen éhō stôma na sou pô
heilē na sou milêsō

I have no mouth to tell you
no lips to say it to you

dhen éhō héri eúchero
dhiá na sou to deixō

I don't have available hand
to show him to you

vlépeis ekeino ton ghymnó
ton paraponeméno

Do you see that naked one
the sad one?

hópou phorei poukámiso
sto aima boutēgméno

the one who wears
a blood-soaked shirt?

ópou phorei sten kephalê
agáthino stepháni

the one who wears
a thorn crown on his head?

ekeinos ein' ho yioúkas sou
ki emé dhidháskalos mou

That one is your son
and my teacher

ki he Panayiá plēsiase
glyká ton erōtoúse

And Panayia approached
sweetly she was asking him

dhen mou milás paidháki mou
dhen mou milás paidhi mou

Do you not speak to me, my little child?
Do you not speak to me, my child?

ti na sou pô manoúla mou
pou dhiáforo dhen échei

What can I tell you, my little mother?
It does not make a difference

páne mána sto spiti mas
kai sto noikokyrió mas

Go, mother, to our house
Go to our household

vále krasi sto mastrapá
ki aphráto paximádhi

Put wine in the pitcher
and nice springy rusk

móno to Méga Sávvato
kontá to mesēméri

Only on Holy Saturday
close to midday

pou tha lalêsei ho peteinós
tha paixoun oi kambánes

when the rooster crows
and the bells toll

(pou tha lalêsei ho peteinós
sēmainoun ta ouránia

(when the rooster crows
and the heavens toll

semainei ki he Hagiá Sophiá
me tis chrysés kampánes)

Hagia Sophia also tolls
with the gold bells)

tóte ki esy manoula mou
tha 'cheis harés megáles

then, my little mother, you also
will have great joy

| ki hópoios to léei sônetai | and whoever says it is saved |
| ki ópoios t' akoúei hagiázei | and whoever hears it becomes a saint |
| | |
| ki hopoios to kaloaphougrastei | and whoever listens closely |
| parádeiso tha lávei | will receive Paradise |
| | |
| parádeiso kai livano | Paradise and incense |
| apo ton Hágio Tápho | from the Holy Tomb |

. . . . . . . . . . . . . . . . . . . .

This is not the place to embark on a close reading of the lament, but I should point out the similarities between this (lay) lament for Christ and the official (ecclesiastical) laments of Good Friday, in the construction of the narrative and in the emphasis given to the corporeal dimensions of Christ and his relationship with his mother, all of which give precedence (this one time) to his human, rather than his divine, nature. Also, the narrative addresses the *chronos,* the moment and the manner in which Panayia finds out about the death of her son, something which acquires an importance of its own in the whole sequence of events, gestures, and rationalizations that surround the death of a loved one.

8. Akráta is not an urban center, but returning Akratinoi and their friends consider themselves fundamentally urbanite, as we saw in parergon 4.

167

# 7

# Space

## SÊMATA

The interpretation of the moment of death is informed by an acknowledged interconnectedness of all spheres of life: space and time, animate and inanimate objects, the souls of the loved ones, and supernatural structures. Much the way that tradition holds that all these forces and energies came together at the time of Christ's death—the roof of the Temple collapsed, clouds covered the skies, heavy rain overtook the city, the animals started howling, and Mary felt her womb move—people identify similar signs at the time of the death of mortals, not because of their occurrence at the moment of Christ's death but because *even* Christ's death was subjected to them.

Owls (*Athene noctua*) are the birds connected with the warning of death. The owl is a bird of specific significance for Athens. In ancient Athens it was the symbol of the goddess Athena, the protectress of the city. In modern times it has retained its significance as the most abundant night bird (*nychtopouli*), which could be heard throughout the city until recently, before the dramatic explosion of population of the 1980s. Nowadays it is almost impossible to hear an owl in Athens, a fact that makes the occasional hearings of it even more poignant.

Other *sêmata* (signs) include the howling of dogs, the stopping of watches and clocks, and the physical discomfort of individuals who are close to the one who is dying. Anything out of the ordinary is interpreted as connected to the death, such as an unusually cool or hot day in the summer, or the opposite in the winter. "It was a really lovely day, warm and sunny," Dêmētra always says of the day that her mother died, noting thus that her mother was indeed a person worthy of a lovely dying day.

168

Some time after YiôrgoPanourgiás' death I was talking with Iōánna about the particular details of his last few hours. I told her that I had been monitoring his breath very closely, ever since his lungs collapsed, so that we would all be somewhat prepared at the time of the actual death. "Oh, I knew about it from the previous night. Irma [the family dog] started howling. She wouldn't stop. And you know what else? I swear I heard an owl," she said. Other people in the polykatoikia attested to the fact that Irma was, indeed, howling the night before the death. None seemed to have heard an owl, and I did not hear one either, but Iōánna is convinced about it. My friend Nikē told me that when her grandfather died the big pendulum clock they had in their living room broke, and they had to have it fixed. Vivê said that the night before her daughter died, she had a dream in which her daughter was telling her not to worry since she was well. "That's the way she told me that she was going to die, my sweet little daughter," Vivê said, tears streaming from her eyes, eight years after her daughter's death.

Occasionally a dream is interpreted as an attempt by the dead person to take the dreamer away to the world of the dead. Katerina, a medical doctor and an old friend of the family, now in her early forties, has told me a story, the like of which I have not encountered anywhere else, except in Seremetakis' dream analysis in Mani (1991:50–56). Shortly after her father died from a household accident, Katerina said that she had seen in a dream a youth whom she had known when she was a teenager on the island of Skopelos. This young man, slightly older than she, died when he was very young and very much in love with her. In her dream he came up to her, and after they greeted each other and exchanged news, he asked her to give him something of hers to take along with him to keep. She asked what he would like, and he pointed at her ring—a beautiful silver ring with a large amethyst on it. Katerina said she would not give him the ring because Sotērēs, her fiancé, had given it to her. " 'Give me something else, then,' he told me. And I took off this necklace, that my father gave me years ago, and gave it to him. A few days after that my father fell from the ladder, and you remember, he died very soon afterward," she said.

Seremetakis (1991) has also mentioned the significance that birds (the *nekropouli,* "the bird of the dead," in particular) and dreams have in Inner Mani, as signs that frame the understanding of death. It must be understood, however, that as frightening as these signs are, they are perceived as just that, as signs, with no causal relationship to the particular death (see also Badone 1989:302).

## THE TERROR OF THE *TOPOS* (THE CEMETERY)

The next morning, the day after Easter, which was also Saint George's Day, Lea and I went to the cemetery, to Panayês.[1] We went on foot. We took the long winding path that goes through the citrus groves, past the newly built houses, until we got to the cemetery.[2] It is a small one. There is a low white iron fence around it and a white iron gate. We went past the gate, ignoring the grave of our mother's stepmother, and went straight to Panayês'. His is halfway between the gate and the cemetery church. The cemetery, fairly new, has good coordinates; you can find your way around it easily. We came upon the grave, sparkling with its white marble, full of flowers and lighted candles.

This grave is a rectangle framed by a fifteen-centimeter band of white marble, with a ten-centimeter depression in the middle, covered by colored gravel. Next to the plaque bearing the names is a silver picture frame containing a picture of Panayês' father. There are two *kandêlia* (candle cases) on either side at the foot of the grave, where Yiôta keeps incense, a small bottle of olive oil, matches, wick (*louminia*), and *karvounákia* (small pieces of coal, especially manufactured and sold for incense burning). She also keeps there a few paper napkins, three small candles, and the *livanistêri* (censer), the small contraption made out of copper and used by lay people to suffuse their houses, icons, and graves with incense. On the foot of the grave is a built-in jardinière where flowers are always planted, and on either side of the jardinière are marble vases to hold fresh-cut flowers. Panayês was much loved in his community, so fresh-cut flowers are never missing from his grave and his *kandêli* is always lit, even on the days that his mother does not visit the cemetery.

Yiôta wanted to be able to see her son, to see his face, even after his death; she wanted to remember him the way he was, a young, attractive, healthy man. She requested the negatives of some pictures I had taken of Panayês a few years before his death. She had them enlarged, along with as many other pictures as she could find, and she hung them in every room of her house. For the same reason she had a marble bas-relief bust of Panayês commissioned by a famous Athenian sculptor, and she had this fitted to the grave, to replace the black iron cross that had previously adorned it. She had the relief placed next to the plaque bearing the names of Panayês, his father, and his father's parents.

Yiôta also wanted to have a marker at the spot of Panayês' death. She agonized greatly about it. "I thought of having something very simple, but I really have no idea what it would be. Panayês didn't believe in all this,

The Petrópoulos family grave. On the right, is Panayês' relief, on the left, his father's plaque. Lea is sitting on a grave looking at a woman in the distance who is tending her mother's grave. Next to Lea, in the stroller, is her son Iásōn, two years old.

anyway," she told me. Some time later she acquired a wrought-iron cross, very simple and truly understated. She kept it around the house for some time. When I saw her in the summer, she asked me to take her in my car and go with her to the 105-kilometer post on the Patras-Korinth highway to install the cross. When I showed up she had changed her mind. "He really didn't believe in these things. Why should I do something that he didn't believe? Although this is really simple, isn't it?" she said to me. I agreed. The cross was indeed unobtrusive. "Let me think about it some more. We've got time," she said again. She finally went with her brother. From time to time she and I go to the 105-kilometer post together to cut down the wild oleanders that grow around the cross.[3]

The construction of a *proskynētári* (usually translated as "shrine") is a usual practice for a family when one of its members is killed on the road or as a marker of good fortune in the event that the person involved in an accident escaped death (in the latter case the person who survived takes the responsibility for the construction of the proskynētári). In essence this practice is the abstract reconstruction of the *space* of the dead (which is the grave) into a space where death should not exist; indeed, it is intended to help avert it. It is not an attempt to negate the occurrence of death, but

171

The photograph I took of Panayês Petrópoulos in 1978

172

Two proskynētária, side by side, on a particularly treacherous stretch of the road in the mountains of Euboea

rather an attempt by the space of death to invade the space of life, so as to underline the finitude of death in an effort to prevent it from occurring at the specific place. It serves as a memory marker for the accident; in the case of death not only does it mark the death, but it is also a reminder of the fluidity of life and the fact that no one has any real power over one's own life. In the case of survival, it serves as a public declaration of thanks to Christ, Panayia, or a saint for having intervened and saved the lives of those involved, and to God for not having allowed a death to take place. Motorists generally do not know which of the two is the case at any particular proskynētári, unless they knew the particular person and knew about the specific accident. The proskynētári, however, always evokes a prayer from the passers-by. These edifices are meant (and sometimes successfully so) to suggest to motorists to slow down, to be careful, and to drive defensively. The vast number of proskynētária throughout the Greek countryside, of course, suggests that the reality of driving practices in Greece is rather the opposite.[4]

These proskynētária are built to resemble churches, while simultaneously giving a partial impression of the grave. They are not large—
usually measuring fifty by fifty centimeters—they are set up on pedes-
tals, and instead of walls, they have pieces of glass, like windows. Inside
are placed an icon of the particular saint, Christ, or Panayia (according
to whomever is thought to have intervened), sometimes a photograph of
the deceased, a kandêli, and a bottle of oil, some charcoal, incense, and
matches.[5] I remember, as a young child, that when we happened to stop
along the road to stretch out and a proskynētári was around, my mother
always lit its kandêli and burned some incense, even though we knew nothing about the accident and we never had been in an accident ourselves, nor
had anyone else in the family. We would not make a point of stopping at
a proskynētári just to tend it, in the same way that we would not, on purpose, visit and tend a stranger's grave. Since we were there, however, we lit
its lamp, just as we might light the lamp at the grave next to our family's
when we visit the cemetery. On a grand abstract level, all dead belong to
our collective universe (whichever way we decide to construct this universe,) and we recognize a certain affinity with them. After all, that's what
we all are: prospective dead.

The practice of visiting graves of loved ones other than the one specifically visited is a very old one. Sally Humphreys comments on the pre-
Solonic practice of making the rounds of other graves—she presumes members of the same family—making offerings and lamenting, which Solon
forbade (1983:153). This offers an explanation of why Panayês' grave is
always clean, his kandêli is always lit, and his flowers are always fresh. I am
not arguing that this is a point of survival of classical Greece into modern,
but rather that our relationship with our dead changes little over time.

Orthodox death is a public death. The notices in the newspapers are
also invitations to everyone who knew and loved the deceased to come
and attend the funeral. The more people that come, the more loved and
important the deceased is understood to have been. Chrysánthē thus commented about the multitude of people who attended Evangelia's funeral
and reminded her family that even the mayor of Athens was present. When
my mother phoned me to tell me about Panayês' death, four days after it
had happened, she also told me that close to four thousand people had attended the funeral. She did not say this in order to impress me—obviously
I did not need to be impressed—but in order to calm me down, to assure
me once more, once again, that this person whom I loved so deeply and
dearly was also loved by a vast number of people. This love of the people
was what accompanied him to the grave. "He didn't go alone," she said.

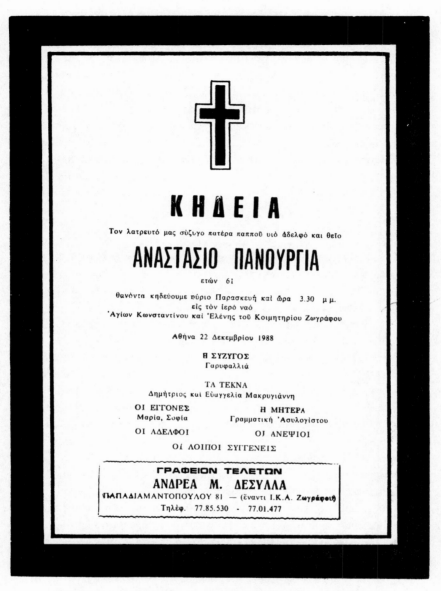

The *nekrósēmo* (death announcement) for Anastásios Panourgiás' funeral

Panayês was a classificatory member of everyone's family; he was a nonkin family member, much the way Iōánna is nonkin family to Myrtô. This means that while the institutional circumscription of the familial boundaries is well defined along kinship lines, the symbolic understanding of family is much more loosely structured, allowing for Bakhtin's "permeable boundaries" (1981), where boundaries of a unit can be, and are, negotiated by those who are bound by them in order to accommodate the institutionally unincluded. As a family member, even a classificatory one, Panayês was included in the rounds that other mourners made at the cemetery. The pain of his death was felt throughout the community.

## PÓNOS (THE PAIN OF THE LOSS)

Despite what the "objective truth" might be, many people are unwilling to concede that a sibling will feel greater *pónos* (pain) on the loss of a sibling than a mother would for her child. "The pain of the mother is unmeasurable" ("O pónos tes mánas dhen metriétai") is offered and usually accepted as the axiomatic truth of a mother's love for her children. This gives mothers the right to rule over matters that concern their dead children and to have the final word over everyone else's, because, as Anna Caraveli-Chaves notes, "As a mother, a woman has taken the first step in the hierarchy of 'understanding of pain,' an understanding which is the privileged territory of women and which increases with age and experience" (1980:146). People also often indicate that the mother is the only one who will keep her child's memory alive. As Kyria Yiôta said, "So many times I sit here alone and think about Panayês and say, 'Ah, *Panayê mou,* only your mother remembers you.'"

Perhaps it is the "preemptive expansionism" of motherhood, the "privileged territory" of female understanding that in Greece associates women with mourning and tending of the dead, although women are not the only ones who tend the graves, nor are they the only ones who feel the pain of the loss. A look at the obituaries and the memorial announcements that appear in the daily news and are posted throughout the neighborhood of the deceased can be very illuminating on the issue at hand. If we take a look at the order in which the bereaved are mentioned, we will see a clear distinction in that order according to the family status of the deceased. If the deceased was unmarried, the order starts with the family of origin (parents, siblings, grandparents, aunts and uncles, cousins, and finally friends). If the deceased was betrothed, then the fiancé or fiancée is mentioned after the siblings. If the deceased was married, then the spouse and the children head the list, followed by the parents (if still alive), and then the rest of the relatives, friends, colleagues, and occasionally a beloved godparent.[6]

In Potamia, Loring Danforth has reported that the pónos of death "prevents the full acceptance of death and leads those in mourning to believe that a return from the dead is possible" (1982:142). The situation we have encountered here, however, is the reverse. The pónos is experienced because of the faith in the impossibility of a return from the dead. As Yiôta said, "It does really not matter how long you stay abroad, Neni, because your mother knows that she will see you again. What can I say? I know that I will not see Panayês ever again."

This ordering of things and lived experiences (death set against *depaysement*, against physical separation) reevaluates the reality of death and displaces it into a game of illusions where the deceased can be thought of as still being alive and the grave is believed to be a real, not a symbolic, home. This illusionary game permits the appropriation of the discourse on death to be used as a neutralizing agent that empowers the interlocutors to look at their own deaths through the prism of (neutralizing) humor. While still living, people often make pointed jokes about their deaths and their graves. Galáteia told me the story of a conversation that took place among her grandmother, her sister Naná, and herself quite a few years ago. It was the time when they were constructing the *oikos* (literally "house") on their family grave. An oikos is a cross between a proskynētári and a church, in size and in appearance. It is never larger than one meter in width, two meters in length, and two meters in height. Most of the time it resembles a basilica, which in its turn resembles an ancient temple, although I have occasionally seen oikous that resemble domed churches. Other times they are built to resemble classical Greek or Roman structures, and there is at least one oikos at the Third Cemetery of Piraeus which resembles the Minoan palace of Knossos.[7] Oikoi are always lined with marble inside and outside, and inside, along their flanks, they have drawers the length of an average person, which are hermetically sealed with cement. That is where the coffin is kept.

Galáteia's family's oikos would have four drawers, two on each side. Her grandmother was worried that she would be buried in one of the bottom drawers and it would be too "heavy" for her. "I am claustrophobic," she said. Naná interrupted her, saying (according to Galáteia's recollection of the conversation), "Don't you worry, Grandma. You die and I will put you in the penthouse [*sto retiré*]". Naná was killed shortly afterward, in an automobile accident during her honeymoon, approximately a month before her grandmother died.

Nineteenth-century neoclassical graves at the Syros cemetery

Akráta has two cemeteries. One, the oldest, is known by the name of the church to which it is attached: Ai-Yiôryēs (Saint George). Ai-Yiôryēs is built on a bench of the hills overlooking most of Akráta, the river, the Korinthian Gulf, and the Roumeli coast. On a clear day, I was told many times, not only can you see Itea (the main port on the Roumeli coast), but if you look very closely you can see Delphi. The view of Parnassus is magnificent, and the blending of the colors—the green of the citrus and the pine trees, the silver of the olive groves, and the deep blue of the gulf—composes a picture that one cannot forget. Ever. As hard and as genuinely as one might try.

That is the cemetery where Dêmētra's parents were buried, but it was relocated in the 1970s to the hanging valley, in the middle of a citrus grove. Her mother died during the German occupation, in 1942, at a young age. Her father remarried several years later, but none of his children ever accepted Regina as a substitute for their mother. She was not meant as one, in any case, as they were all grown by then. She outlived him by twelve years. When she died Dêmētra had her buried, after a private funeral, in the new cemetery in the hanging valley. She said that this woman was never to meet her mother, and that her bones would not be mixed (*na mberdheftoun*) with those of her parents, which, Dêmētra's sister contends, were lost dur-

178

ing the relocation of the cemetery. As it is apparent how important the grave is in the conceptualization of the family history, it is (almost) understandable why Dêmētra did not want to introduce a body that was foreign (to her) into the neat package that she wanted to consider her parents and her line of descent.

On a larger scale, Maurice Bloch has reported a similar practice and belief in Madagascar, where the common grave of the state is the marker of the state itself, and only through the blending of the bones of all the deceased of the state can harmony be achieved (Bloch and Parry 1982). Conversely, Michael Kearl and Anoel Rinaldi mention that in another case of common burial strong opposition was mounted against it, as it was perceived that the common burial erased the individuality of the dead. It was the case of a proposed mass reburial of some of those who were killed in the American Civil War, under a memorial with the inscription "Now We Are One." It was vehemently opposed by veterans because it altered the symbolic value of the dead in their relation to the temporal and spatial connections with the living, while it negated the idea of individuality after death (Kearl and Rinaldi 1983:701).[8] Dêmētra's objection to the blending of the bones of her stepmother with those of her parents, and of Garyfaliá with the rest of the Panourgiá's family, should be viewed also within this perspective.

Similarly, some families in Greece can be assured eternal companionship, unity, and everlasting remembrance through a common grave for all their members. It is the last home of the family, and by virtue of its finality and definitiveness, it positions the specific family against other families, much the same way the physical, actual home does for the living family unit.[9] Therefore, excellent care is taken to provide each grave with unique and original markings which will distinguish it, physically and symbolically, from the rest of the graves of the cemetery.

Actually, the individuality of the grave parallels the individuality of the Greek city, in its architectural and structural anarchy. The city (Athens in this case) is a conglomeration of styles, rhythms, and structures, giving the (correct) impression that every effort has been made to evade characterization, to resist classification, to present a nonunit, to underline the fact that each house has been designed for the specific customer, in the same way that each grave has been designed and built for the specific dead, the specific family.[10]

The grave itself, however, is perceived as a dark, musty, cold place, not only in folklore (where it is believed to be much deeper than the actual three meters), but also in the writings of the Church and in literature (see Alexiou

1974:42–44; Ariès 1981:157; Danforth 1982; Hirschon 1989:206–18). In this scheme of things, there is no place for tender feelings toward the grave such as Gilbert Durand reported, describing the euphemism of the grave as a cradle. Depending on the feelings toward the deceased, the grave is viewed either indifferently, as simply a burial place, or negatively, as the physical preventer of communion between the living and the dead. This aversion was very clearly explained to me by Yiôrgos Panourgiás when Evangelia died.

In the beginning he refused entirely to go to her grave, much to the dismay of his children, who, incidentally, did not go either. I asked him why he did not want to go. He replied that he had difficulty believing that my grandmother, the woman to whom he had been married for fifty years, was dead and placed in a grave. His distaste for that was such that he channeled his anger toward the grave. He could do something about that anger—he did not go to the grave—but he felt totally helpless against the reality of death. After that initial rejection, however, he would walk to the cemetery once a week, on Sunday, after the morning liturgy. He washed the marble, cleaned the glass, changed the water in the flower pot, lighted the kandêli, and burned some incense in the livanistêri. He would also take a piece of *antidōro* (bread offered to those who did not take Communion) and scatter it on the grave. "The birds come and eat it," he would say. Now my grandfather is also dead, buried in the same grave, which no one ever visits. This, though, is not totally out of cultural order. I was told by parents (some mothers, also some fathers) whose children had died that they never visited the graves, although they loved their children very dearly. A friend of mine told me that her father had never visited the grave of her sister, who had died very young, nor did he ever visit the grave of his three sisters. And I know people who refuse to go to funerals altogether.

Nadia Seremetakis, then, is correct, to an extent, when she says that the grave "talks" about the moral condition of the living kin and/or the dead (1991:175). An unkempt grave can be viewed as almost analogous to an unkempt house. YiôrgoPanourgiás' grave is just as unkempt. The lack of visitations to his grave, however, does not indicate a moral degradation of the family, nor does it imply that he has been forgotten or is not missed by his family. But since he did live a full life, and died a "good" and almost enviable death, the cycle of his life, and the grip of his presence on the living, have all been completed. No one visits his grave because mourning for him has come full circle. Now he is part of the collective order of the family dead. Now he has become part of history, not of everyday lived experience. Still, from time to time, one of us goes to the grave, cleans it up, lights the kandêli and the livanstêri, and pays one of the cemetery priests to say a Trisáyio on the grave.

Alongside the aversion toward the cemetery and the grave as topos, however, exists a completely opposite disposition toward the specific grave of the specific dead, which is largely determined by the relationship between the dead and the mourner during their life together. Thus, although the grave might be detested and resented, it is also treated as the home of the dead, where the bereaved go to pay a visit (*episkepsē*), bringing presents—flowers, *kóllyva*, a new photograph to replace the old one—or bringing a new addition to the family, such as a child, a new in-law, or someone visiting from abroad. Then the bereaved do not refer to the grave by its name but by the name of the dead, just as when they go to visit someone still alive. "Let's go to Panayês" ("Páme ston Panayákē"), Yiôta tells me every time I visit her. And YiôrgoPanourgiás seldom would mention the grave as *táphos,* but he preferred to say that he visited Kyrá Vangeliô (Mrs. Evangelia, as he affectionately called her).

Even more indicative is Vivê's story about the grave of her first husband. Vivê, now in her eighties, was married when she was eighteen to a man who had returned to Greece after a twenty-year sojourn in the United States. He had been married in Pennsylvania, where he lived and worked, and had had two children. By a strange twist of fate, a few years before his return to Greece he was involved in a car accident in which his wife and children were killed. After his return to Greece he saw Vivê, whom he had known when she was a child, and they fell in love and married. They lived a blissful eight months together, until he died suddenly of a heart attack.

Vivê was a few months pregnant when her husband died, and she was quite desperate with his loss. She used to visit the grave daily, as it was on her way to and from work. One evening she went to the grave again, on her way home, and as she was sitting there, she hurt so much for this untimely death that she started crying uncontrollably. She cried so much that she finally fell asleep on the grave. "The guard did not notice me when he locked the gates at night, and I spent the night there. Then it started raining, one of those heavy summer rains that we get in Athens," she said. "Were you afraid?" I asked. "No. Not at all. I was happy there. It was the first night that I spent close to him after he died. I fell asleep leaning on the cross. When I looked up in the sky, after the rain stopped, I felt as if the rain had been sent for me. I slept well that night. No, I was not afraid for a second."

In at least another two cases, however, the aversion toward the grave was questioned, but both were considered extremely perverse and hilari-

Vivē's daughter, Petroula, sipping ouzo after a swim at the family's shore house several summers before her death.

ous. The first involved Kōnstantinos Panourgiás and his friends during the early years of the German occupation. Kōnstantinos has repeated the story many times, first to my sister and me, his daughters, then to his grand-children: "It was one night in the summer, around Saint John's, and we thought we would play a prank on the Vlachs, the shepherds around the cemetery. So we got some old sheets from home, and eight of us [he gave all the names] went up to the cemetery. There was no moon that night. So we went to the cemetery, we found a few graves that were old and had caved in, and we got the skulls from there. We had brought some candles from home, and Skiountzēs [one of his friends] somehow had found some fire-crackers. So we put the candles inside the skulls, we covered ourselves with the white sheets, and holding the skulls and burning the firecrackers, we made for the huts of the shepherds. You can't imagine what happened. They woke up from the noise, ran outside to see what had happened, and there we were, holding the skulls with the lighted candles, screaming and yell-ing, and running after them. After them came their dogs barking, and they awoke the pigs, which started squealing. And that was nothing, because with all the commotion the Germans woke up, and we heard the trucks coming up from the hill. You should see how we all ran, the shepherds to their huts and us to the graves. We hid in the graves until the morning. And I shouldn't tell you the beating we got from our mothers."

For some people the cemetery and the graves offer a good hiding place. In 1993 the following incident acquired notoriety not so much because of its content but because of its space. The priest of a village (married with children) and the sexton of the church (who was also the wife of the grave-digger, also with children) fell in love and started an affair. Their affair became known because some of the villagers were hearing strange noises at night, coming from the freshly dug and unused graves. In the beginning they were afraid, one of the villagers said, but upon closer inspection, and after a few months had gone by, they realized that there was nothing to be afraid of, since the noises they heard coming from the graves were part of the sexual encounters between the priest and his lover, who used the graves as their meeting place. Just for the record I mention that the priest was deposed, and they both left their respective families and came to live in Athens.

The reaction of the public, however, was not centered so much around the affair of a married priest with a married member of his congrega-tion and an employee (something which is thought of as almost a given in Greece, as is evident from folk songs and anecdotes; see Michael-Dede 1991; and Orso 1981). It was centered, rather, around the issue of a sexual encounter inside a grave. Of course, here we see the juxtaposition of feelings toward the grave (as an abstract concept) between the general public (who only come into contact with the grave when someone they know dies, thus setting the relationship to the grave on a personal level) and the professionals surrounding death (the priest who officiates over it and the gravedigger who profits from it, without having a ritualistic relationship with it). The other point mentioned regarding this incident was that the graves did not belong to either of them anyhow; they were owned by the families of the deceased who were soon to be interred there. These remarks imply that beyond the conceptual boundaries the priest and his lover had violated (in changing the use of the grave from a space of death to a space of an act of life), they had also trespassed on someone else's property. They had violated the integrity of the space of a strange family.

The intimate connections of the family with its property cannot be overemphasized. Thus, as a point of delineation for each family, a marked priority is given to the ownership of the grave over its renting, the same way that a priority is given to owning a house over renting it. A general feeling of discomfort is expressed on the part of those who cannot afford to purchase their own lots, and conversely, a sense of pity is felt toward them by those who have managed to acquire one. In the cemetery of Zográphou, only in the last ten years has it become difficult to purchase a grave lot because of the recent popularity of the cemetery, owing primarily to its location and the quality of its soil.

But the pity one feels at the thought of one's burial in a leased grave cannot compare with one's horror at the thought of having one's remains stored in a common ossuary (*osteophylákeion*), as it is often considered to be the fate of paupers and is a matter of indignity to be avoided at all costs.[11] Therefore, many families join forces to buy "family graves" (*oikoyeneiakous táphous*) in the hope and the certainty that the family will stay together in eternity.

Lately, however, due to the lack of space and to the fact that a lot of families live far away from the cemetery, and also to the fact that efforts for a clean and well-tended grave can be financially taxing as well as time-consuming, the phenomenon of osteophylákeia has acquired different use and signification.[12] Instead of being simply the final burial place for the indigent, they have become an accepted alternative to a large permanent grave. The osteophylákeia have become personalized, and they figure as private niches placed on low-level walls, built along the paths of the cemetery. Each can contain only one skeleton and the skull, in a box, and each also has space for a photograph. These are much more economical than regular graves (which can reach the prices of small downtown apartments); they are accessible and easy to maintain. The remains are placed there after an initial three-year period in a typical grave is completed, provided that the bones come clean, with all flesh dissolved. With the three-year interment there is no conflict between the use of osteophylákeia and the need for the fulfillment of the Orthodox dogma regarding the regeneration of life through the dissolution of the dead body into the soil (on the recent rise of the use of niches among Catholics in Spain, see Behar 1991b).

Thus, since so much importance is given to the dissolution of the body and its blending with the earth, it is apparent why the grave is considered as a marker of the family unit. A family grave ensures the spiritual perpetuation of a family's distinct identity, asserts beyond death their established individuality, and alters the axiom that death levels everything by affirming that individual choices made in life can outlast the nonidentity of death. That is a reason why no two graves are alike. Financial concerns aside, one family's grave cannot resemble any other family's grave. Even when grave lots are leased, if a structure is already on the grave, it is removed, and a new one is constructed, even if the new construction consists only of a differently shaped cross or an altered kandêli. Graves are appreciated as aesthetic objects for their beauty, for the color of the marble, the shape of the cross or of the plaque, the fresh and planted flowers (see Petropoulos 1988). Well-tended graves give a sense of tranquility and serenity. They are shady in the summer and sunny in the winter and have good combinations of marble and flower colors; they are clean, and their kandêlia are always lighted and scented. Kyria Yiôta has planted red and white geraniums in Panayês' jardinière, while the mother of a friend of my sister's has planted mauve bougainvilleas. The floral trademark of a cemetery, however, is the cypress tree (*kyparissi*). The association is so close that the two have become synecdochical, and the mere utterance of the word *cypress* can be taken as a reference to the cemetery.[13]

Not only does the grave delineate a family's identity, but the cemetery as a whole is a marker of the community of the dead as decisively separate from the community of the living. As is common throughout Europe, cemeteries in Greece are municipal, hence public. The cemetery, although it administratively belongs to the municipality (the *dêmos,* which draws on its generous revenues), conceptually it belongs to the fringes of the dêmos, to its liminal point along with that which does not belong anywhere, that which is public and impersonal.[14] This is precisely why cemeteries in Greece, where death is accepted as the total Other—that which cannot be avoided yet perpetually resists appropriation and life—are placed away from the domain of life, have perimeter walls that clearly delineate the topos of the dead from the topos of the living, and are built away from the city. (Now, however, with the expansion of the city, development has encroached on the topos of the dead, with apartment buildings facing the cemetery. Those apartments, however, have a much lower price attached to them than they otherwise would, precisely because of their proximity to the space of the dead. Cemeteries have not yet become aesthetic objects in Greece, except in the case of the First Cemetery in Athens.)

## THE TERROR OF THE *ÁTOPOS* (PARADISE)

"How did you find out about Paradise and hell?" I asked Lea once, in the course of a conversation. She said she asked her grandmothers. "That was a memorable exchange," Lea said. "Do you have your tape recorder on?" Yes, my tape recorder was on. This is what it recorded:

"I went first to Evangelia. 'Where is hell?' I asked her. 'Oh, hell is in the core of the earth,' she said. I knew I detected mirth. 'And what happens to people who go to hell?' I continued. 'Ah, there they take you away, and they use big cauldrons with boiling water, and they plunge you in there, and then the little devils come and stir you, just like with soup.' I decided to play along for a while. 'And where is Paradise?' I asked then. 'Ah, Paradise is high up on the clouds, and you go there and it's really nice, you don't have a worry in the world, you don't get hungry, you don't get thirsty, you don't get tired, there are some *uris* there [the reference is to the Islamic version of angels], and they come around and dance for you, and you just sit and do nothing.' But I wanted answers. 'Come on, tell me, where is Paradise?' I pressed. 'Paradise is here,' Grandmother answered. 'And where is hell?' I pressed again. 'Hell is here too,' she answered, dead serious.

"Totally unsatisfied with her answers and determined to find out where exactly it was that we were all about to go after death, I went to Regina, not with a question but with a firm request: 'When you die I want you to write me a letter telling me what it is like wherever it is that you are going.' I do not remember whether I asked her if she was going to Paradise or hell. She laughed and promised she would. I was about eight years old at the time, and these were among the first entries in my first diary, which I started keeping during that Holy Week."

Unlike the grave (the *topos*), then, Paradise (*Parádeisos*, the *átopos*), the nonspace, the imaginary other world, is considered as that which can only exist in dreams, the perfect, the pleasant, the desired. Otherwise, why would anyone want to go there? It is the space at the end of the end of the world, the wonders of which are exalted: eternal sunshine without the scorching of the desert, lack of precipitation without undue heat, as Bruce Lincoln has put it, "the dreamland of any tourist" (1991:39).[15] And that is also the impression we get from the ecclesiastical references to Paradise (such as the passage from the funerary liturgy), as the place "where there is no pain, no sorrow, no suffering, but life everlasting. . . . a place of light, a place of pasture, a place of peace." This strangely suggests the Homeric references to Paradise, which is found

> with golden Rhadamanthos at the world's end,
> where all existence is a dream of ease.
> Snowfall is never known there, neither long
> frost of winter, nor torrential rain,
> but only mild and lulling airs from Ocean
> bearing refreshments for the souls of men
> the West Wind always blowing
> (*Odyssey,* 4. 600–607)

In both cases, existence in Paradise is circumscribed by absence, by that which it is not: it is not cold, it is not worrisome, it is not scorchingly hot, it is not desolate, it is not lonely (see Lincoln 1991). Nothing exists there but perpetual existence. It is a place marked not so much by the presence of desirable objects but by the absence of desire.[16]

Paradise, however, which is so much marked by absence, is thought of as a very specific place, the place where the pious souls rest. Therefore, although neither Christian nor pagan poets venture to make a statement that would fix the nature of Paradise, both traditions give the specifics regarding the space of Paradise (at the ends of the world) and its inhabitants (the rewarded pious). The opposites of that are reserved for the truly Other world, Ho Allos Kósmos, that conceptually murky space that is dark, cold, musty, and uninviting, just like the grave. Persephone worries whether Odysseus has "gone in death to the sunless underworld" (4.889). This sentiment is also expressed in complaints by some Athenians when they are made to sit in dark, or dimly lit, rooms. They say that they want light, more light, as they will be perpetually in the dark in the Otherworld (*ston Allo Kósmo*).

Although there are clear references in both religious traditions regarding the existence, the space, and the nature of Paradise and the Otherworld, there are nowhere in the funerary literature references to the space of hell (Kólasē). Perhaps that *is* the logic of religion, since the funerary liturgy is but one long invocation to God to place the deceased among the pious ones in Paradise. Images of Kólasē, however, abound in the Apocalypse of Saint John, where it is circumscribed as the place where all known torture is present. And maybe this is the fundamental difference in the conceptualizations of Paradise and hell: human experience has not yet found the serenity, happiness, and fulfillment that it seeks in the constructions of Paradise, whereas, conversely and unfortunately, it has too concrete a knowledge of the projected tortures and abandonments that it seeks to displace into the distance, into yet another level of understanding.[17]

## THE TERROR OF THE FLESH

*. . . because our limbs are tied together with impudent hope*
—Pindar, *Nemean Ode* 11.45–46

In the gestures of death, then, what is the position of the grave, beyond its tripartite significance as a physical, spiritual, and social marker? Within the context of the Greek Orthodox Church and its construction of ideal Christian behavior, the grave should be the burial place of every Greek, and thus the only sanctioned depository for dead and decomposing human flesh. Since death is not considered the end of life, but rather the beginning of another dimension of life which will be judged in the Second Coming, the dead person is automatically transformed into a possession of the religion and the Church, which acquires sovereignty not only over the soul but over the body of the dead as well. Hence cremation is prohibited in Greece by decree of the Church, and so is embalming, so that the biblical pronouncement of "dust thou art, and unto dust shalt thou return" (Genesis 3.19) should be fulfilled.[18] Therefore, the utmost care is taken to facilitate and expedite the dissolution of the body and its eventual blending with the earth. The coffin is of perishable material (wood), and only its decorations are allowed to be of nonperishable materials, so that if an *ektaphê* (exhumation) takes place later, those nonperishable decorations can be distinguished and removed from the remaining bones. It is essential that the body dissolves and that at the exhumation the bones appear white and without any remnants of flesh adhering to them. These concerns have acquired spiritual and religious dimensions. /

Ektaphê, as a ritual, is particularly interesting and significant in the context of funerary rites among the Greek Orthodox. The rules that govern it, although set not by the Church but by custom, are canonized by the construction of an eschatological discourse that involves the appropriation of the otherness of death in both organizing the cosmos of the living and in offering post hoc explications and rationalizations of the past. Of course, it also serves as the final test of the separation of the dead from the living and their incorporation into the world of the ultimate Other. Although it is widely practiced throughout Greece, its prescriptive canons are neither uniform nor universal. The general rule is that ektaphê is to be performed no earlier than two years after death and no later than five, if it is to be performed at all. Strictly speaking, it is not an ecclesiastically prescribed rite, but rather one which, Danforth suspects, must have arisen because of necessity (Danforth attributes it to lack of space in Potamia) instead of spiritual need (as Bloch maintains) and was adopted as one of the distinguishing markers of a community.[19] Bloch notes the spiritual need in Madagascar for exhumation and secondary burial, where the blending of the bones in communal ossuaries ensures the metaphysical blending of the community in a domain of eternity (Bloch and Parry 1982). Danforth (1982) has reported that in Potamia, where land is scarce and all graves are rented, an exhumation always takes place five years after death. Elsewhere, however, exhumations take place in the third year, even in the case of privately owned graves, except when extenuating circumstances are present, as in the case of fear over partial dissolution, as we will see. There are exceptions, however.

I always believed that exhumation was a prescribed rite, until Dêmētra, my mother, contested my position when I challenged her about Tássos. Tássos died almost three years after his father and was buried not in the family grave (along with his parents and grandmother) purchased by Dêmētra and Kōnstantinos, but in a leased grave in a different zone of the cemetery. My mother's answer to my question was that my grandfather's body had not completed three years in burial, and consequently an exhumation could not be performed. Another answer to the same question (my sister's this time) was that if Tássos was buried in the same grave, then his wife, Litsa—and by now we know the disposition of the family toward her—would have burial claims for herself on the grave. Needless to say, such an arrangement was inconceivable to Dêmētra, who shivered at the thought of an afterlife cohabitation with her synypháda.

In a sense the cemetery is thought of as a homeland (*patridha*, as Papayiorgis has acutely noted [1991:46]), where all those buried together are compatriots of sorts. The grave is considered as a home within that patridha, as I have already pointed out. Therefore, Dêmētra, by not allowing Litsa the prerogative of being buried in the family grave, was replicating the actions of the family during Tássos' lifetime, when Litsa (although tolerated, and usually included in family gatherings because of the love that the family had for Tássos) was never accepted as belonging to the same "house." Dêmētra was trying to perpetuate the integrity of the household even in the grave. The moment Tássos died, Litsa stopped being considered as having any ties with the family (especially since no children were produced from this marriage, and there was, already, a child from Tássos' first marriage to fill that gap). In the family structure, Litsa became expendable.[20] "You want me to allow Litsa to be buried in the same grave with us, along with your grandparents? Your grandmother's bones will rattle and creak [*tha trixoun ta kókkala tês yiayiás sou*]," she told me angrily, when I pressured her over Tássos' burial site.

In order to make her point more plausible, Dêmētra reminded me that her mother-in-law had not been exhumed either—until the grave was dug for her father-in-law—but I had attributed that to the fact that when the three years after her death had been completed the family had opted against an ektaphê because she had undergone heavy dosages of chemotherapy and they feared only a partial dissolution of the body. I thought that once the three years were over without an exhumation, then the deceased had, in a way, lost his or her rights to one. I was admonished for my ignorance by the parish priest when I went to him, perplexed and confused. "You should be ashamed of yourself," he said, half mockingly. "Your grandparents were such good Christians, you should know these things. Have you ever heard me say anything about an exhumation at a funeral or a mnēmósyno? The Church does not have a position on this."

Later Father Iōakim expanded on that. He said that very often people call for advice and confide to him that they want him to think of ways whereby he can claim that certain things and practices are prescribed or prohibited by the Church, depending on the occasion, so that they will be in a position to substantiate their claims. He said that Dêmētra's claim that her father-in-law had not been dead for three years and therefore could not be exhumed for Tássos to be buried with him was the commonest claim of all and the most incorrect, since the Church does not allow an ektaphê to take place in less than two years, not three.

It is intriguing, however, that the appropriateness of an ektaphê can create the emotional arguments it usually does. Galáteia, an archaeologist studying prehistory, said that she felt violated on behalf of her sister when her mother insisted on an exhumation of Naná's remains three years after her accident. She referred to all those "strange hands" (*xéna héria*) handling Naná's bones. She thought that there was no point in it, since, above all, the family owns their own grave.[21] "I knew anyhow," she said, "at any given moment what was the status of Naná's body. I knew how dissolution was progressing—now the eyes, now the nails, now the hair. I knew when her limbs would fall apart. I didn't need anyone to dig up her bones to show us that they were really clean." Her mother, naturally, won. Naná was exhumed, but Galáteia was not present. But as she had said, she didn't need to be present. She knew the periodization of decomposition, the dismantling of the connecting tissues, the outcome of the boning process.

Even in cases where the dissolution—or lack thereof—of the body of the deceased is easily explainable for physical or natural reasons (e.g., large doses of chemo- and radiotherapy, or exceedingly alkaline soil), an exhumation will be postponed or, in the case of privately owned graves, not be performed at all, so that the relatives will not have to face the potential hardship of a partly dissolved body. (Slightly alkaline soil is preferred for the facilitation of decomposition of organic matter, with a range between ph 6.6 and 7.6, with an optimal ph of 7.1 [Fry 1974:45].)

The implications of an undissolved or partly decomposed body are multidimensional. Admittedly, a partly decomposed body is indeed a disturbing sight, with its flesh darkened by exposure to the moisture of the soil, partly clinging to the bones, hairs dangling here and there, eyes partly gone and partly remaining. The sight conjures up the image of mummies, something outworldly, something that belongs somewhere else that is unknown, something unlike anything we know. It goes beyond the point of aesthetics. It offers itself to a number of alternative explanations and explications, which are locally accepted with a greatly varied degree of "belief." It can be explained primarily as a sign of the possibility that the deceased is not at rest; this, in its turn, may be perceived as the result of a sin committed by the deceased person or a relative, or even an old score with the living which prevents the deceased from separation from the earth (see Danforth 1982:22, on Potamia). Or it might indicate a vampire (du Boulay 1982).

On the opposite end of the spectrum, lack of dissolution of the body in the case of reverent Christians might constitute adequate grounds for their elevation to holiness, as in the cases of Saint Spyridhon in Corfu, Saint Dionysios in Cefallonia, Saint Nektarios in Aegina, Saint John the Russian in Euboea, and Saint Rēginos in Skopelos (a similarity can be found in Portugal, where an undissolved body may also denote holiness; see Piña-Cabral 1986).

Thus an ektaphê is usually done as a means to offer some sort of assurance to the bereaved that the deceased, *ho nekrós,* has indeed been admitted to Paradise. Although it has been suggested that the exhumation and the secondary burial indicate the final acceptance, on the part of the bereaved, of the departure of the dead, this seems inadequate as an analysis (see Danforth 1982; Huntington and Metcalf 1985). If that were correct, then mourning, pain, and grieving should stop by default after the performance of the secondary burial. Some wounds, however, never heal, and some deaths are never accepted, despite ektaphés, secondary burials, and frequent visits to the grave. The dead return again and again, invading the lives of the living either through the trigger of other deaths (as Seremetakis correctly notes [1991:178]), or through the perpetual harsh confrontation with their profound absence.

## PARERGA

1. Saint George's Day is an almost movable feast, as it is determined by the date of Easter. The canonized date for the celebration is 23 April if Easter Sunday falls before that date. If Easter falls after 23 April, then Saint George's Day is celebrated the second day of Easter, on Monday.

2. By governmental decree (1128/80), cemeteries should be at least 250 meters away from the city limits and 100 meters from isolated houses. See Schizas 1991.

3. One might be tempted to see this change within the framework of commodification and to explain it as a wish of Panayês' mother to display the magnitude of her pain at his loss through a monetary equation. Such an explanation, however, would be very limited theoretically and equally limiting analytically.

Following Taylor's arguments about the commodification of death, Dubisch presents death in Greece as a stratagem exploited by actors for the furthering of their social and material ends. She argues that death "becomes a secular opportunity to display wealth and social accomplishments (and in this sense, at least, a reaffirmation of the material), rather than being an occasion to express the equality of all members of the community in the face of a shared physical and spiritual destiny" (1989:195).

Throughout her article Dubisch takes this position, informed by an ontological and teleological discourse on the reification of death, which inevitably attributes to death (a biological happening) a power possible only through its social constructs. In other words, death is used here metonymically for its rituals and its material consequences (e.g., memorial services, clothing, cemeteries, graves), which are interpreted as the props of a the-

192

atrical scene in which people are (theatrical) actors acting out parts and roles prescribed and predetermined by a Grand Playwright.

Things are not always so predictable, however, and people are not always as obedient to what Dubisch sees as cultural prescriptions; some individual choices are always made in defiance of possible expectations. One example (among the many that we see in this text) that can illustrate this point is Yiôta's decision to erect the proskynētári for Panayês. If she were interested in an ostentatious display—either of her wealth or of her pain—she would have chosen a much more expensive marker than the simple wrought-iron cross.

I do not mean here to minimize the importance that rituals and practices that surround death have in the reaffirmation of the social position that the specific family has, and also the importance of public display and performance of feelings and goods. I am, however, suggesting that things are much more complicated than an analysis based on commodification allows.

4. Greece has a horrifying record pertaining to highway automobile accidents. During the Serbo-Croatian war of 1991, there were more casualties on Greek highways at one weekend, due to excessive speed and illegal passing, than during the bombing of the highways in Serbo-Croatia. See Mintsis and Patsiava-Latinopoulou 1990 for a good study of traffic accidents in Greece and the correlations between accidents, driving behavior, and structural conditions of the Greek road network.

5. In older times, when people were more diligent about keeping the proskynētária clean and functioning, many summer fires were thought to have started from sparks from the kandêlia.

6. The order in which the bereaved are mentioned in the *nekrósēmo* coincides with the order in which the bereaved should be informed about the death. See Sudnow 1967, on the same issue in the North American context.

In the announcement for Tássos (Anastásios) Panourgiás' funeral, I should point out an anomaly. Tássos' parents died before him: his mother, Evangelia, died in 1975, and his father, Yiôrgos, in 1986. Somehow Garyfaliá, his wife, managed to put the name of her mother, Grammatikê, under the heading for mother. This caused great distress in the family, since a mother-in-law, although addressed as "Mother," is never actually considered as such; the term is used as a social convention, not as a marker of a biological or emotional relationship. Moreover, there is a separate category in these announcements for in-laws, which Garyfaliá ignored. The incident would not have had the same weight had Grammatikê been Tássos' only mother-in-law. But Tássos had been married before, and the whole incident was thought of as "corny" (sahló), in Chrysô Pintzou's words, and audacious (thrasý), in Dêmētra's words. Vangeliô, Tássos' daughter from his first marriage, was enraged because, as she said, "My father had only one mother, and she in fact hated both Garyfaliá and Grammatikê."

7. The "Minoan" grave was built in the 1980s for a young Cretan man who died in a car accident. It is the only contemporary private funerary structure with references to antiquity that I have noted. The rest of them, primarily in the First Cemetery of Athens but scattered around the rest of Greece also, are the products of the age of neoclassicism and nineteenth-century modernity. As I have argued elsewhere (1994), this turn to antiquity in architecture and sculpture should be viewed within the perspective of the dominant architectural and artistic language of nineteenth-century Europe, not just as an atavistic quirk of nineteenth-century Greek nationalists. One of the prime examples of this funerary architectural and sculpting style is the cemetery on the island of Syros.

8. While the analysis by Kearl and Rinaldi is absolutely correct, I would like to note two additional factors which further compound and confound the issue. The first is that Americans are largely unfamiliar with collective graves, even for families, where each member usually has his or her own grave. The second one is that Americans are even more unfamiliar with the notion of a secondary burial. Overarching all this is the issue of mixing together the bones of people who fought in different camps, a post hoc homily of the hegemonic culture that seeks to make its peace with its own past, through the political use (and manipulation) of its collective dead.

9. For a discussion of family identitary delineation through the home, see Herzfeld 1982a. Badone (1989) has also developed the idea of the connection between a more individualistic, less anonymous approach to death and burial through the introduction (since the Second World War) of family tomb monuments, the abandonment of ossuaries, and the use of skull boxes in Brittany.

10. It is worth noting that Mrs. Bonsanquet, in 1914, also referred to this distinctiveness of the grave in regard to the ancient cemetery of Kerameikos in Athens. She wrote: "Each tomb had its own slightly different angle, and in the monuments themselves there was infinite variety" (1914:310). Greeks talk with great amazement about the Cemetery of the Allies, in Phâlēron, which is a perfect rectangle, with rows of perfectly symmetrical and identical gravestones, and identical flowers on each one of them. Many people wonder how can anyone find a particular grave in

there. Although the whole cemetery is admired as a prototype of order and method, there is always implicit the thought that such order and method, albeit effective and attractive, must simultaneously be stifling and suffocating.

11. In Potamia, however, Danforth (1982) has reported that the general practice is that of leased graves and common ossuaries.

12. The cemetery of Zográphou draws people from the municipalities of Zográphou and the separate municipality of Athens, for lack of adequate space anywhere else in the area.

13. Panayiôtēs was well into his forties, an Air Force commander and a lawyer, married with two daughters, when his mother, Kōnstantina, died at the age of ninety-eight. Panayiôtēs was distraught, although his relationship with his mother had been a difficult and strained one. A few weeks after the funeral he chanced upon a friend of his who had not heard about Kōnstantina's death.

The friend commented to Panayiôtēs that he looked drawn and pale, in bad spirits. Panayiôtēs replied that his mother's death had shaken him deeply and he was trying to cope with it. At that his friend answered, jokingly and cheerfully, "Ah, Panayiôtēs, may *I* live to be ninety-eight, and I won't give a damn if they plant not one, but even two cypress trees over my head."

Beyond offering an illustrative point on the symbolism of the cypress tree, the incident provides us with further commentary on the expected and prescribed place of mourning within the conceptual and cultural framing of composure and excess.

Old Athenians also use the term *Thymarákia* (literally "little thyme shrubs") to denote the cemetery, because for a long time the only cemetery serving the greater Athens area was the one in the district of Thymarákia, southwest of the center of Athens. The First Cemetery of Athens existed then, but it was primarily used by people in the heart of the city. On the importance of the First Cemetery in Athens as an exhibitory topos of the aesthetics of Hellenicity, see Dubisch 1989; for a more historically situated analysis, see Mikoniatis 1990.

Dubisch, drawing primarily on Herzfeld (1982a), concludes that the neoclassical statues that adorn the First Cemetery should be viewed within the framework of the desire of modern Greeks to be considered the biological, cultural, and political heirs of ancient Greeks, appropriating simulations of ancient Greek art and architecture in the construction of their modern identity. What eludes Dubisch in this instance, however, is the fact that the aesthetic of the First Cemetery conforms to the aesthetic of neoclassicism, a much broader construct that in the early and mid–nineteenth century encompassed the idea of modernity, much more than an explanation basing it on archaeolatry and cultural survivalism suggests. In other words, if Athens wanted to be a modern city, Athens had to turn back to antiquity and reinterpret its aesthetic and its ideology, much the way the rest of the European cities had done earlier in the century. See also Tsiomis 1983 and 1985a, for detailed analyses of Athens as a modern city, situated within the project of nineteenth-century neoclassicism.

14. According to Vovelle, Ariès, and McManners, the modern European relationship to death was set by the victory of Enlightenment thought over the hegemony of the Church. For an excellent analysis of the connections between the Enlightenment, the uses of the public space, and European conceptualizations about death, see both Vovelle (1990) and Ariès (1974). Also see McManners (1981), for an epistemological approach to the same issue.

15. What seems to slip by Lincoln here, of course, is that tourism always entails return to the point of departure, whereas as inviting a place as Paradise might be, no one has ever returned from there.

16. This might appear to be a very boring existence. The Greek punk band Trýpes (Holes), however, in its latest album has a song entitled "It Is Very Nice in Paradise" ("Einai Hōraia ston Parádeiso") exulting over precisely this idyllic absence.

17. What lurks as an idea here is the following inconsequence: in Orthodox dogma there are two afterlife images, Parádeisos and Kólasē, and as we saw, both places are conceptually set and defined, even through their indeterminacies. There is no Purgatory, no place where souls can be cleansed through punishment while waiting for the Second Coming. This, however, comes into direct opposition with the gestures that surround the point for three years after a person's death, whereas there is the expressed hope that through these supplicatory gestures the living can actually change the outcome of the final judgment for their beloved dead. That is, they hope they can actually impress Christ in favor of the specific dead—hence the kóllyva, the mnēmósyna, the Trisáyio, and the other prayers.

The question (which I am not prepared to answer yet) is the following: Are these religious gestures incorporated into Orthodoxy from the preexisting ancient Greek religion, a syncretism whose nature has eluded us completely? Or is this something that was adopted from Catholicism, through the repeated contacts of Orthodox Christians with the Catholics, both before the Schism and afterward through the succession of occupations of Orthodox lands by the various Catholic nations of the Middle

Ages and the Renaissance (Venetians, Catalans, Francs)? Or is it, perhaps, the result of a sinister religious realpolitik of the thirteenth century, which implicated, once again, a matter of dogma in real politics? Le Goff presents the idea that the formulation of the theory of Purgatory grew out of the papal fight against the heretics. The first dogmatic formulations on Purgatory came in the thirteenth century. The Eastern Church had not developed those dogmatic positions, as Le Goff notes (1981:376). The Church was perfectly satisfied with the vague faith in the possibility of redemption after death and in a practice of prayers and commendations for the dead that was very different from the Latins'.

The Latin belief rests on the idea of ποιναὶ πουργατορίου ἤτοι καθαρ-τηρίου (retributions of Purgatory or *catharteriis*, the term καθαρτήριον being the Greek translation of the Latin term, as in *poenis purgatoriis seu catharteriis*), but the Greek clergy and congregation never accepted the idea of *kathartêrion* as inclusive of the idea of retribution or punishment, as the term ποινή (*poinê*) implies. The first proposition on the doctrine of Purgatory came in 1204, the year that a Latin empire was established in Constantinople, after the city fell into the hands of the Crusaders of the Fourth Crusade. In 1231 the Greek metropolitan of Corfu, Georges Bardanes, held another round of discussions with the papal envoys, in which the metropolitan denounced the idea of Purgatory as absurd. In 1254 came the first papal definition of Purgatory by Innocent IV. In 1274, as political conditions in Constantinople worsened, the Greeks sought to reestablish relations with the Latins at the Council of Lyon. Gregory V led the Latin side, and Michael Palaeologos the Greek delegation. In 1274 Michael Palaeologos, assessing the political situation in Constantinople and recognizing that help from the West was direly needed, tried to force the union of the two churches (which rested on the Byzantines' acceptance of the doctrine of Purgatory and of *filioque*) on the Greek Church. Mount Athōs revolted, and the revolt was crushed by the imperial police in 1276. The idea of Purgatory, however, never took hold in Greece.

18. I have not encountered even one case of embalmment of a Greek Orthodox person. When I suggested the possibility to friends, I was confronted with expressions of disgust and terror—disgust at the idea that a body might be preserved almost indefinitely without any life in it, and that it would have been emptied of its blood and had chemicals added instead; terror because such a body (physically) reminds people of a cadaver, and cadavers are associated not with the medical profession as much as with horror films.

Although there is a minor movement—led and followed primarily by leftist intellectuals—toward the institution of cremation as an alternative burial practice, the proposition has not found many followers among the general public. According to Kassimēs, there are no provisions made by the funeral parlors in Greece to accommodate cremations. When cremations happen, the desire that leads to their occurrence has less to do with a break with Christianity (as is attested by the fact that even in the case of a cremation an ecclesiastical funeral takes place) and more with an affirmation of modernity or, as Ariès has also noted, "a manifestation of Enlightenment" (1974:91). Very convincing also is the proposition put forth by Badone that the bereaved also desire to relate to the deceased loved one as *homo totus* after death (1989:156).

Although cremation is not allowed for the average Greek citizen, it seems that it can be accommodated for Greeks who die abroad, especially famous ones. This does not occur without some considerable stir, however. Maria Kallas, Dimitri Mitropoulos, and Konstantinos Dimaras were cremated abroad, and their ashes were subsequently brought to Greece. Maria Kallas wanted her ashes to be scattered over the Aegean, which was done without any problems. Dimitri Mitropoulos had wanted his ashes to be buried in the First Cemetery in Athens, but they were not interred until eight months after the urn had arrived in Athens because of the major objections of the Church of Greece.

The only two instances of cremation that were recounted to me belonged to the same family and had taken place in the United States some twenty-five years apart. They involved the mother of a friend and his father's brother. The latter was the first to die, in a motorcycle accident, and was cremated in California; his ashes were later transported by his parents to Greece, where the funeral took place. After the funeral, the box containing his ashes was placed in a drawer in the family *oikos*. Twenty-five years later, when the mother of my friend died, she was also cremated in California. Her ashes were carried to Greece a few months later, in a box in her son's suitcase, to be eventually placed in the same drawer in the family grave. The official Church in Greece declares ignorance of the practice of cremation for Orthodox Christians abroad. Although the burial is a matter of tradition and not of dogma for the Church, the Greek Church insists on its objections to cremation. When pressured on the issue, the spokesman for the Church said, indicatively, that he could not understand all this desire for cremation. Is it not enough, he joked, that we will burn in the afterlife? Do we really need to be burned when we die? Should we add one more burning?

There is a rapture, however, experienced in the process surrounding death when the dead body is not present. The ashes—the product of cremation—suggest, as much as they forge, an abstract relationship with the dead that disorients the bereaved, as it further distances (conceptually and physically) the deceased from the bereaved—hence the agony of recovering the bodies of those killed in acts of war and accidents.

19. Bloch attributes it to the conviction that eternal unity comes through the constant blending of the materials that constitute a society materially, spiritually, and politically. The bones of the dead become one with the physical soil that constitutes the political and social space (Bloch and Parry 1982).

20. We should resist the temptation to explain this expendability of Litsa to the lack of children by her marriage to Tássos. It really has to do with the way she has treated the family as a whole, and to the way (very objectionable to most of us in the family) that she treated Tássos during his illness. An opposite example further supports this point: Evangelia had an elder sister, Militsa, who died within a year of her marriage, without leaving children behind. Her husband, Moysês, remarried after a while and begot two sons with his new wife, Déspoina. Although there are no kinship ties between our family and theirs, we always called them Uncle and Aunt and counted their sons among our cousins. If Litsa were expendable simply because her link with the family had been severed (through the death of Tássos), then the same should have happened in the case of Moysês after Militsa died.

21. Galáteia and I have had discussions lasting well into the night regarding this particular issue in connection with her own professional relationship to death and to her own "strange hands" handling all those ancient, long dead, and utterly forgotten bones. My debt to her for this portion of the analysis is immeasurable.

# 8

# Positions and Signs

## EMOTIONAL CAPITAL

The mortal has no sight of his own death. Each one of us, that's what we are . . .
prospective dead.

—Kostis Papayiorgis, *The Living and the Dead*

This human praxis upon death (the Foucauldian void) is manifest in things
that surround, circumscribe, and mark death, such as mourning attire,
grieving, and the grave.[1] It is a void accurately positioned in the expression "Oi nekroi me tous nekrous kai oi zōntanoi me tous zōntanous" ("Let
the dead be with the dead and the living with the living"), with which
my father had admonished me, years ago, when I was grieving (exces-
sively, he thought), at the table again, for the death of his mother. To him,
my "excessive" grief constituted an act of digression from the social code
which posits the two worlds (the living and the dead) into an antithetical
and mutually exclusive relationship with each other. Through my grieving in the presence of others—who were not grieving, but eating—I was
abolishing this cosmological division.

It is easy to justify grieving for an untimely death, especially the death
of a young person who has not yet been given the chance to live a life. My
grandfather, who knew Panayês but was not related to him, was told about
the accident by my mother. He called me to offer his condolences. "Why
should he die, *paidi mou* [my child]?" he said to me. "Why he and not I?
Why should I, eighty-four years old, go on living when a twenty-six-year-
old man gets killed? And that poor mother of his! She hardly got out of
her black a few months ago for her husband.[2] Now she will get drenched
in black again. And still a young woman. May God forgive him."[3]

This conversation brought to mind a similar passage in Papadiamantis' "A Soul." After the death of Anghelikoúla, her grandfather laments his old age: " 'Why didn't he take me and leave you!' cried the old man, who only the other day had come home from the Eye Hospital. He had undergone surgery on his eye to regain his sight so he could see well and find his way to the other world" (1988:81).

It is much more difficult to justify grieving for a person who died full of years. People talked scornfully when Frangiskos wanted to jump into Evangelia's grave at the age of forty-two. "He lost his little mother and is an orphan now," someone said laughingly. Markos Dragoumis, the noted musicologist, insisted that I include his experience with grief at his mother's funeral when I related this incident to him. He told me, "Did you remember to include my mother's funeral? Do you remember, I was very shaken by her death, and at the funeral I was crying and wailing and pulling my hair out, and all my relatives came up to me and told me to compose myself and act with some dignity. Only Loukatos [the folklorist, an old friend of the family] came to me and said, 'Don't you listen to them. This is the proper way to mourn for your mother, since you loved her as much as you did.' And that calmed me down more than anything anyone else had so far told me."

The acts of mourning have an indeterminate length and force that is proportional not only to the relationship of the deceased to the bereaved but also to the relationship that the bereaved has with death and mourning. Thus, lack of adherence to the proscriptions is not taken as lack of care of the particular dead. Although kóllyva should be made until the third-year memorial and occasionally thereafter and the grave should be visited at least on the occasion of the memorial, people make their own decisions which do not necessarily coincide with those of the others. Dêmētra has never visited Regina's grave. Kōnstantinos never visited his parents' grave, except when someone else died and was buried in the same grave (after Evangelia's death, he visited the grave next at his father's funeral). I have never visited my cousin Thēklē's grave. Yiôta visits Panayês' four times a week. Léngō, Tassoulês' mother, visited his daily in the forty days that lapsed between their deaths.

Although there is no set number of visitations to the grave that the bereaved should make, an implied sense of balance organizes the expression of grief and bereavement. No one can give an answer to the question How often should one visit the grave? It is only contextual. In the beginning of the mourning period no one comments on the fact that some people visit the grave of their loved ones daily. After some time, however, which is never fixed and always changing, it becomes more and more difficult to justify daily visits. Recall Lea's remark about her schoolmate's mother: "I think she is a little touched in the head."

Two points are implicit here. First, there is a lack of trust regarding "genuine" (*gnêsia*) feelings of grief and loss, and the daily visits to the grave are generally regarded as affectations, simply to draw the attention of the public. When I visited Panayês' grave with Yiôta in the summer of 1993, we saw two women, mother-in-law and daughter-in-law, visiting the grave of the mother-in-law's mother, who had died almost seven months earlier. Yiôta said, "Look at them. They come here every evening and go to the grave. What do they want, coming here daily?" "Did she love her mother so much?" I asked. "Oh, come on now! They just come so that we see them here and we say how devoted she was to her mother! *And* they come to gossip. They go around, see who's visiting, if the graves are clean and neat . . . They haven't got anything else to do," Yiôta answered.

And this might be the most important point in the relationship of the living to their dead: the point of the sincerity of their emotions. Why is it so important that the emotions be "authentic"? This has been the recurrent question, a question that I have posited to myself, to my friends, and to my family, and one that friends and colleagues have in turn posited to me. Why is it so important that people do not fabricate their emotional expressions, that they do not show an emotion that does not exist, or does not exist on the same level as it is exhibited? Why does the affectation of emotions draw such reactions of indignation from those who observe it? What is at stake?

On a certain level it touches (unknowingly, no doubt) upon the Heideggerian formulation of death and the authentic, where death is understood as the lever that forges the authenticity of the self. Through this authenticity we are "most ourselves, most at home," Eduardo Cadava notes (1991:90), because we are forced to think of the possibility of our own death, which, Adorno has told us, "sets our correct relationship with our dead." Hence, the emotions that surround death should be "authentic" because this is the only way for the living to oppose themselves to death, and thus to respect death as that which one can neither mock nor resist. On a more pragmatic level, however, it seems that much of the opposition to "inauthentic" emotions has to do with a perceived challenge to the exhibition of "authentic" emotions, and the possibility of reproduction that is inherent in everything that is not "authentic." If the reproduction has occurred once, then it can occur again ad infinitum, extinguishing the space that is created from one reproduction to the next. This removes the necessity for the original stimulus of production (the dead body, the grief of loss, the pain of the moment of death) and relegates the process of reproduction to the realm of mechanicity. In this way tears, sighs, cries, and wailing can be reproduced at will, without the subject ever achieving the state of excess (grief, pain, mourning, loss) that is the necessary stimulus for the production of the original emotion, the "authentic" tear, the "true" lament.[4]

Now the parameters that help us gauge which emotions are authentic and which are not are a matter of the interpersonal history of the community, whichever way community is being construed. Relationships among people and the emotional ties that govern them are usually known around the community. If a daughter used to argue and quarrel with her mother frequently and violently and then appears at the cemetery exhibiting all the outward signs of grief (tears, wailing, a drawn face) in addition to the signs of mourning (black clothing, kóllyva), then the assumption is that the grieving emotions are not real, not "authentic," as Yiôta's comment indicated. This, again, is altogether different from the cases where it is conceded that "although they fought a lot, they loved each other"; in such circumstances people would accept these same outward signs of grief as "authentic."

The second point implicit here is that in cases where the loss was really tragic, the assumption is that daily visitations are a symptom of a disturbed psyche due to excessive grief. Lea's comment was accompanied by a sense of pity at the fact that the mother had been "a little touched" by the loss of her daughter. Nor do we need to evaluate a death as a "tragic" one. It is always tragic if it comes in a particularly violent or painful manner, or to an individual who has not met the statistically determined mark of life expectancy. In those cases all grief is understandable. In the opposite case, however, grief not only is not understandable, but often it is ridiculed.

I gave my friend Galáteia a much earlier draft of this section, and she returned it with this comment:

After the funeral of my grandfather (on my mother's side) some relatives of ours came to our house and were sitting on the veranda (we were vacationing at Kastri). I stayed inside the house, crying and writing a poem. I still remember a verse: ". . . and who will come up the steps / leaning on his cane . . ." At some point I heard this soprano laughter coming from my grandmother. I still remember it.

My mother mourned her father for a long time, and one day my grandmother told her: "Now, tell me, why are *you* crying? I should be the one to cry, because he left me an old widow, and I can't remarry now."

And the following: My father died on 16 July. On 22 July is the celebration of Sainte Marcella's day, my mother's name day, and three of her cousins came to visit her at Loutraki, along with their husbands. All of us, my son William included, were eating at Margarita and were wishing many happy years (*Chrónia Pollá*) to my mother. Then William says to my mother: "*Chrónia Pollá*, Grandma, and may you remarry soon." You can imagine how we all laughed, except for William, of course, who meant his wish very seriously.

What was not written in the note but had already been communicated to me by Galáteia was the fact that at lunch on the day his grandfather died, William (who was born and brought up in the United States by a Greek mother and an American father, in what we would call an untraditional home) put down his fork and announced, with all the seriousness of his fifteen years, that from now on his name would be Adam, his grandfather's name.

Some grief is mitigated, though. When Tássos died Lea phoned me to tell me the news, although I had already been told of the death by other relatives. Lea phoned crying, obviously shaken. She asked me if I knew and how I was holding out. I said that I was hurting emotionally. Lea cried a little more, and then she said, "You know, I just found out that I am pregnant." I stopped crying immediately. I knew how much she had wanted a second child, and how much Oréstes had wanted a sibling. I asked her if Tássos knew before he died. No, he did not. She had just found out. "But you see, Nenaki," she said so sweetly, "one person leaves, another one comes. That's how life goes on."

Allowances in the interpretation of grief are thus made according to the importance that is placed on the relationship with the dead. The grief for a child is always immeasurable (as "the pain of the mother is immeasurable"). Then follows the grief for a spouse, then for siblings and parents (as it is difficult to distinguish between the two in emotional attachment on part of the bereaved). Then follow the rest.[5]

When a new death occurs, however, it overshadows the previous one, provided that the second death is of equal or greater importance to the first one. Panayês' death overshadowed the death of his father, which had occurred four years earlier. Panayês' death, however, could only be overshadowed by the death of his brother or of his brother's children, God forbid. The death of Tassoulēs, on the other hand, who was forty-eight years old, was not overshadowed by his mother's, since she was in her nineties and it was thought that she had lived a full and good life.

Which are the gestures of mourning, then? Here I will identify two: the narrative about the death and the verbalizations about its quality. In other

Lea with her younger son, Iásōn

words, acts of mourning are not only the rituals but also the attempts for the construction of a framework of cultural logic which could contain the existence of death.

## *Voices of the Speechless*[6]

3 January 1984, Tuesday, at 12:50 A.M.

A ring on Panayês' telephone breaks the silence of the night. A cold voice—fierce, if you wish—says from the other end: "Madam, are you the wife of Panayês Petrópoulos, the dentist?"

I feel a numbness, I get upset and start shaking, but I must compose myself and hear what is happening. . . . "No, I am his mother. What do you want?"

"Listen, madam, your son has had an accident on the road, and he is seriously hurt at the Korinth Hospital. We are calling you from the Aigeion Highway Patrol." . . .

We went to the hospital. The news is unpleasant. They say: "He is in the operating room. He has had head injuries. He is undergoing a serious operation." Everything tells me that these are excuses, lies—because the truth is that Panayês is dead. They took him there dead. I understand that it is all over. I say it out loud, I shout it, and no one has the courage to deny it. No one says the opposite. Besides, what can they say? The news is shocking for everyone. Panayês . . . dead.[7]

Summer 1985, Athens
We had lost Arē for three days, Neni. His father and I almost went crazy. Sometimes, I knew, he was late coming home, but when he didn't show up in the morning, no phone call, nothing, I went crazy. I combed Athens. I went to all his friends, all the bars he used to go to. . . . To think that he had been dead for three days, with all that heroin in his blood. . . . I tried to think of all the things I had done during those three days, I tried to see if any particular hour could have been the hour of his death. . . . But then the coroner said he died in the middle of the night, when I was asleep.

These narratives, and the others that we have already seen, seek to determine and mark the precise moment, the exact *chronos*, the context, and the texture of the content with which each of the narrators came in contact with a specific experience of death. There are two forces at work in these narratives: one is the need for knowledge, for gnosis, about the death of a loved one. The other is the simultaneous need for the placement of that knowledge within a framework of logic, something that will bring a historical and social perspective to an occurrence that is profoundly individual. Hence in these narratives we see the secant of Victor Turner's knowledge of the narrative and Cornelius Castoriadis' formulation on sublimatory objects. Turner (1986) positions the role of the narrative within the framework of "experiential knowledge," where gnosis and action find each other in the attempt for interpretation of antecedent events. Castoriadis talks about the processes by which the psyche opens itself up to a sociohistorical temporality, through its encounter with "objects" that initially had other meanings and another existence from the present one, in its search for a logic that will place its experience beyond the realm of the unconscious magma (1984:95).

These two formulations offer a possible explanation for the (native) conceptual and analytical constructs about death. Seen only as "objects" of sublimation aiming at the conversion of the drive for self-preservation— since the logic of death is directly opposite to the logic of self-preservation —can narratives concerning the *quality* of death, the narration of its happening or the time of it, be positioned within a framework of "logic" (even a native, or a Geertzian "local" one)? A logic that has as its expressed "object/nonobject" a negotiation over the acceptance not only of death but also of the absurdity of life, which comes into direct opposition with the very existence of this "logic"? This negation/acceptance of "logic," however, legitimates also the possibility of a negation/acceptance of death, which is sublimated because the drive for self-preservation is blinded, and terror

206

is part of the sublimation (Adorno 1973:155). Furthermore, these "objects," as Castoriadis argues, not only are imaginary (e.g., the "goodness" of death, or the "mode" of its narration), but they can only exist as "socially instituted" objects (1984:36). In this sense, they cannot but be socially acceptable and readily recognizable (hence the kóllyva, the ornamentations of the graves, the significance given to the informing narrative).

The ultimate objective, then, is to put death in its place, to challenge its hegemony without denying its existence. The tameness of death here is not understood in the sense of Philippe Ariès' formulation of it, which implies a nostalgia for the ancient blissful and consented death, but rather in Michel Vovelle's formulation of a "tame" death, where death's hegemony is challenged while its existence is still understood and experienced as a rapture in the social life of the survivors. Thus the domestication of death shifts in significance from addressing the dying to addressing the living. As Greeks say often, "All the gestures of mourning are for the living, not for the dead, who are three meters under the earth." All of us who are concerned with the understanding of the logic of death, if there is such a thing, want then to resist even this final, totalitarian, absurd condition of alienation, of otherness. We want to keep our dead among us, not as living but as dead whose material existence has ceased. Jean-Pierre Vernant rightly recognized all the ploys, the tools of the trade—the status of the dead, the beautiful dead, the figure of Thanatos—as such, "as the means by which the living make their dead present," (1986:55), as social strategies that seek to place the dead into the collective memory, to domesticate death, to civilize it by placing each dead person within his or her own slot, part of a larger picture that constitutes each person's identity.

## KEEPING TIME

*Yia dhes kairó pou dhiálexe ho Háros na me páre*
*Tôra p' anthizoun ta klōniá kai vyázei hē gês hortári*

See the time that Charos chose to take me away
Now that the branches are blooming and the earth is sprouting grass

This distich is attributed by official Greek historiography to Athanássios Dhiákos, an Orthodox monk and hero of the War of Independence who was roasted alive on a spit by the Turks following his capture after the battle of Alamana. He was young, handsome, and brave, and his death took place in the springtime, around Easter. In this distich he is lamenting the untimeliness of his death.[8] Although his death was heroic, fetched him historical glamour, and probably (because of his fame) was envied by many, it cannot be classified as *kalós thánatos* (good death). It was undoubtedly a tragic one.

The image of kalós thánatos could be equated with Ariès' "tame" death (1981:605), a death one would like to die. The tameness of the death, however, is never fixed. There is never one prescribed mode of dying, but it changes over time, over space; it responds to economic conditions, to shifts in the understanding and relationship to religion, and naturally to historical factors such as wars, occupations, dictatorships, and the relationships between genders and generations. Hence there is not *a* preference of one kind of death over another, but rather a preference for the number of different configurations that are constituted as a "good death" over the number of the opposite configurations that are constituted as "not good" (*óchi kalós*) or even as a "bad death" (*kakós thánatos*). We should also not forget that what is optimal (kalós thánatos) and what is real change over time, being greatly influenced by how this reality changes. As Melanie Wallace says, we can see these changes only through a historical perspective (1984:43).[9]

Sally Humphreys in 1983 took us on an exploration through time of the various qualities of death. Moving temporally from the dying to the dead, she reviews the various dimensions of the experience of death that could be classified as temporal. In her scheme, there is a good time to die and a not-so-good time to die. She also explores the "temporal *structure* of death as a rite de passage" (1983:144), as the person passes from the state of dying to the state of being dead. Finally she examines the temporal factors of being dead. Moving vertically through Greek time and horizontally through European time, she examines the parameters of death in the archaic period where kalós thánatos was the death of a young warrior in battle.[10] She then proceeds to the teachings of Solon, who placed particular emphasis on the actual time of death, and through to the classical and Hellenistic ages, where everlasting old age was considered worse than death. Yet this scheme, however correct, is totally opposite to the Judeo-Christian appreciation for longevity, from Methuselah, "who lived for nine hundred and sixty-nine years," to Saint John the Evangelist, who lived between ninety and one hundred ten years. In this monotheistic and messianic tradition, longevity is viewed as a sign of the love of God, and death at a young age was again to be culturally appreciated only during the Romantic period (Humphreys 1983:145).

The desire for immortality, however, is always woven with the desire for eternal youth. No one, as Papayiorgis (1991) reminds us, wants immortality that would lock him or her in the age of infancy or in old age. If immortality was to be granted to an old person, that would be considered not the fulfillment of a wish but the fulfillment of a curse (as in the curse "Na sé xehásē ho Cháros," "may Charon forget that you exist").

## ARTICULATIONS

Other factors, though, beyond the temporal dimensions of death, concur in the classification of "good" or "not good" death. Hence, apart from the age of the individual, the cause and the circumstances of death are examined in order for people to decide whether one has died a good, or enviable, death. As David Counts informed us in his 1973 treatise on death in Kaliai, a "good death" there is one which comes to a psychologically prepared individual and family; it is a death accepted and not resented (see Counts 1980). This is also a position eloquently expressed by Maurice Blanchot, who, looking at the Rilkean approach to death, places it within the framework of accepting the impending fact by the dying person, hinging upon a sense of dignity and gallantry (1982:156). Panayês' death was caused by an accident; it was quick and, probably, as painless as a very rapid death can be. That fact, though, was of no consolation to his mother. His cousin, another Panayês, had died two years earlier of leukemia. He had been ill for many years and lived an almost reclusive life until the time of his death at the age of eighteen. Yiôta considered her young nephew's death a better death than her own son's. In her words: "You see, his parents had a long time to adjust to the idea. How can I believe that my son is dead when he left my house in his gray sweater, drove off, and was on his way home? In two hours he would have telephoned me that he was there. Instead I got the telephone call from the police. They told me that Panayês had had an accident and was seriously hurt. They lied to me. I did not believe it in the beginning; I thought it was only a mistake. And even now, Neni, I tell you honestly, I would rather have him still alive, even in a coma, if I could only see him, than know as I do that I will never see him again."

As I had seen so many other times, in so many other deaths, after one is considered "dying," as opposed to simply ailing, or is pronounced dead, efforts toward helping and care shift from the dying to the living, helping them make the transition as gently as possible. In the case of Panayês, his mother was pitying herself for not having been given time to adjust to the possibility of her son's death, but she was doing so only after it was certain that she could offer him absolutely no help. Panayês' death was not a "good death." He died in the prime of his life, *sto ánthos tês hēlikias* (Vernant's *la*

209

*fleur de l'âge* [1982:45]), the victim of a freak automobile accident, when he was still a soldier and unmarried. His death was horrifying because of its untimeliness, its unfairness, and its absurdity, and also because it reversed the natural course of things, where children outlive their parents. With his death, suddenly the symbolic and conceptual structure of life of those whose lives had been touched by his was altered and brutally disrupted. Not only did his mother, Yiôta, find herself still a mother but with one child fewer than before, but also his brother, Kôstês, was not a brother any longer. One of the variables of his social existence had been removed. It was a situation parallel to the one that all the children, grandchildren, and great-grandchildren felt after my grandfather died. The person who was the common referent of our lives was gone, and we were also nobody's children, grandchildren, great-grandchildren, any longer. We would not address anyone as Patéra or Pappou.

A good death in Inner Mani, Seremetakis notes, involves the ethic of an easy separation of the soul from the body (1991:69–79). This is also apparent in the story I have been repeatedly told by Dêmêtra, that involves the death scenes of her mother, Eléni, who died in 1942 in her midforties, and her father, Kônstantinos, who died in 1961. Regarding her mother's death scene, Dêmêtra always mentions the fact that she was not present. She says, "She didn't want me around because she didn't want me to watch the moment of her death. She thought it was inappropriate and that I would be scared. I was still young. So she sent me to get her some water. But she didn't want water from our own tap; she wanted me to go up on the hill and get her water from the municipal fountain. When I returned she was dead. She didn't suffer at all." In recounting her father's death, however, Dêmêtra does not stay as calm and content. Her father was about fifty-five years old when Eléni died in 1942. At the time Dêmêtra was a university student, living away from home in an apartment that she shared with a friend. A few years after Eléni's death, Kônstantinos married Regina, a spinster from the mountains of Achaia (in the Peloponnese, above Akráta), who was in her early forties. Regina always declared that God would take her in the same condition in which he had delivered her (namely, as a virgin), meaning that her marriage to Kônstantinos had never been consummated. As Kônstantinos lay dying (of cancer of the esophagus), Regina was by his side. Dêmêtra, by then, was teaching and had married. She and her husband had one daughter, and she was six months pregnant with her second child. Dêmêtra contends that Regina hid from her the seriousness of Kônstantinos' condition until death was very near. But the day that Kônstantinos finally died, she said, "Regina sent for me and Kostês, and we

The only existing photograph of Eléni and Kōnstantinos Tsákalos,
ca. 1920

went right away. I got into the house, and Regina had called her own doctor, Chrýsē. I walked into the house, and I saw my father lying in bed with all the covers drawn away from him. 'Why do you have the covers pulled away?' I asked her. 'So that his soul will leave him quickly,' she said. Do you hear that? The whore! She wanted him to die quickly, as if she had some place to go! I told her, 'Cover him up immediately, and don't you dare pull the covers away again or we'll have another Korean War in this house. My father will die when he's ready to die, and he doesn't need any help from you.' She covered him up without a word. He was shivering from the cold, the poor man. He died a few hours later."

I cannot claim that Regina's was a widespread belief, as I have never encountered it in any other case. When I asked Dēmētra about it and its validity as a cultural item, she said scornfully, "Come on now, if it was a cultural item then it was from Regina's personal culture. I'd never heard it before, and I haven't heard it since. She just wanted him to die." Ellen Badone, however, does mention a similar practice in Brittany, when she remarks that included in the Breton rites to aid the dying and ease the agony of the process is the upright seating of the dying, the removal of the shoes, and the touching of earth with the bare feet (1989:170).

If a death is not "good," is it then necessarily "bad"? No. The conceptual opposite of a "good death" is not a "bad death," for they do not both carry value judgments within them. A bad death is usually attributed to an unworthy individual who dies an unnatural or particularly painful and prolonged death, alone or surrounded by strangers. The potency of the fear of dying alone, or with no loved ones around, is enough to make a person reconsider and reevaluate relationships. Let me give one, final example. Nikē found out rather late in life that her husband of almost thirty years, Elias, had been cheating on her for at least fifteen years. She came to our house one day, drenched in tears, and told me, "I'm getting divorced." I said it was a wise decision, since despite the fact that both she and her husband came from upper-middle-class families and were well educated and financially independent of each other, they did not always see eye to eye. That was the explanation I gave her when she asked me why I was so ready to accept the possibility of her divorce. I did not tell her that it was common knowledge that Elias had been cheating on her. I asked about the particulars, and she started crying again, saying that it was not only the fact that he had struck up relationships with friends of hers and coworkers, but that he frequented the brothels of Athens as well.

Then she became enraged, recalling her latest encounter with him. Apparently Elias had it all figured out, the way he was going to live the rest of his life. He did not want a divorce, not even a separation, but wanted to live with her while carrying on with his affairs. Nikē said, "And he told me, 'When we get old, and all this has passed, we will sit out on the veranda, and I will explain to you what life is all about.' And then I told him, 'You are gravely mistaken, my friend, if you think that I will spend the rest of my life waiting for you to appreciate my friendship. Nor am I going to stick around and take care of you when you are dying. The whores that you love so dearly, they will be the ones that will cross your hands on your chest when you kick the bucket [*tha se stavroheriásoun oi poutánes ótan ta tináxeis*]. Nor am I going to let my kids come close to you. That's it. You want the whores, you'll have them on your deathbed." Probably the threat was potent enough, because Elias decided to abandon any plans of an experimental lifestyle and to devote himself to his relationship with Nikē and their children.

This is neither a heroic age nor a particularly romantic one. Now, as we have seen, "good death" is that which comes to an old person, full of years, at home (as opposed to the hospital or someone else's house), with the whole family present. It is a death which is not accompanied by pain or fear but is rather welcomed by the dying person. A good death is one like YiôrgoPanourgiás'.

Therefore, the spiritual and moral worth of a person is equated with the kind of death the person will have. Although the two parts of the equation cannot be transposed (that is, a good person will not necessarily have a good death, and vice versa), the specifics of the death are always discussed, and as we saw, there is a discursive attempt to draw possible moral and ethical conclusions, in the indefatigable attempts to explain, once again, the unexplainable logic of death.

## PARERGA

1. As Lemert and Gillan note, Foucault does not concern himself with "logical circularity but with the void," which constitutes a rapture in the logic. For Foucault, death is that void, and only naturalism has attempted to provide a "positive theory of death" (Lemert and Gillan 1982:120). Through his attack on positivism Foucault brings to the fore the inevitable shock that society experiences with the existence of death, thus constituting death as a legitimate object of analysis.

2. Black clothing is culturally prescribed for women in mourning, and it is usually worn, with adherence varying according to area of residence, social class, age, and relationship to the dead person (see Rushton 1983;

Alexiou 1974; Hirschon 1989; Pharos 1988; and Hatzisotiriou 1980). Also prohibited are jewelry and makeup (hence Violétta's comment about putting makeup on, after she saw some trace of it on Vétta's face at the funeral of YiôrgoPanourgiás). Risking oversimplification, I would say that generally the time frame for black attire is three years to the end of one's life.

Kyria Yiôta, an educated and still young woman living in Akráta, had lost her husband in 1980 and wore black until Easter 1983. Then Panayês urged her to start blending the black with gray and white, intending that after the next memorial of her husband she would stop wearing black. Of course Panayês' death put her back into black clothing, which her other son, Kôstês, insisted that she abandon after Panayês' fourth memorial. As Pharos writes regarding the historical role of black garments, "Mourning attire was a signifier noting that a person was in a period of mourning and it also showed the stage of mourning. . . . Thus it served as . . . a public announcement of the death . . . and as an external symbol of mourning it sets the time frame within which society obligates the bereaved to return to normal life" (1988:236–37).

Black clothing has been challenged by various feminist organizations in Greece. These groups, which find it sexist, impractical, and financially draining, advocate the abolition of the practice and its replacement with a more subtle marking of mourning (Pharos 1988). Naturally, the first question that arises is How can cultural praxis be abolished? Second, the proposition negates the possibility of the desire for a mourning attire. An eloquent statement about this came from Panayês' mother. She was on her way to Athens the summer that Panayês died, dressed in black, long sleeves and all. When I saw her next she complained to me about the self-contradictory feelings that her desire for black clothes was creating in her: "I felt so guilty, Neni, because, despite the fact that I did want my black clothes, it was so hot, and I was sweating and feeling so uncomfortable, and I started crying because I was feeling all this discomfort and Panayês could feel nothing." And here is exhibited the cyclicity of emotions stemming from death, the acknowledgment of the existence of a prescribed code of emotions, its rejection, and the consequent (so quintessentially Greek and Christian) self-imposition of guilt.

Mourning attire should also be considered within the framework of desire by the living to keep the deceased closer to them, not to expunge them from quotidian life. Thus black clothing can create an emotional and conceptual bridge between the two worlds which allows mourners a privileged negotiation of their loss, especially since this negotiation is unilateral, on the part of the living, now that their dead has no desires, rights, or existence.

Of course, black clothing also makes a conscious statement within the context of family politics. Siblings or synyphádhes striving for recognition, acceptance, rights, and attainment of rank within the family can, and very often do, manipulate this exoteric marking of emotions (existent or constructed) as the agent which will accord them the desired inclusion.

3. "May God forgive him/her" is the standard incantation whenever reference to a dead person is made. It is assumed that no one is free of sin; therefore there is always something, however small and trivial or great and important, that God would have to forgive. Thus, the incantation here has nothing to do with the preceding comments regarding black attire, with the specific dead person, or with the specific woman.

4. See Adorno 1973 for a critique of the Heideggerian position on death in the context of authenticity. The condition of the "inauthentic" has found its extreme expression in the professionalization of laments. Lest anyone think that professionalization of death rituals is the exclusive mandate of capitalist modernity, I should mention here that in ancient Athens an organized class of professional mourners apparently controlled death rituals to such an extent that Solon found it necessary to outlaw them (Humphreys 1983). In more recent times it has been widely known throughout Greece that professional mourners have existed in Mani.

5. Inevitably all this falls within the discourse of normal versus pathological mourning, especially as it has been formulated by Freud in his essay on mourning and melancholia. It is, thus, a rendering of a theoretical approach to the canons that organize responses to death, watered down through decades of interpretation, reinterpretation, and dissemination by the mass media and popularizing publications. See also Badone (1989:252) on precisely the point where the decoding of visitations to the grave changes from viewing them as beneficial for the bereaved to being criticized as excessive.

6. I do not intend to embark on an analysis of narrative or narratology, but I am presenting these accounts simply as an illustration of my subsequent discussion on sublimatory objects. I actually privilege Dhareshwar's proposition of an "epistemology of narrative," in which he attempts a breaching of the dichotomy between narrative and theory, following Rorty's recent "turn towards narrative," Jameson's theory on narrativity and the complication of "the relationship between theory and the narrative," and Proust's search (via Barthes) for a "third form" (1989:137–39). Taking as a basis Dhareshwar's interweaving of theory and narrative, I

attribute to narrative—concerning my position in this project overall—a double bifurcation. At first glance, this may appear to be a paradoxical thought, but in fact I am only following this interweaving of concepts through to its diacritical parts, to its threads. In these terms, then, narrative plays an operative role on the level of my own narration superimposed on the events in question (i.e., this text in its entirety), which can, and should, be seen also in its duplicate role as both theory and native text. Narrative also exists on an a priori subordinate and de facto contained level, where narration(s) within the narrative are used heuristically as explications of a native necrology and thanatology—among which, of course, my overarching narrative (namely, the narrative that I as author "command," the concrete materialization of which is this text) should also be included.

7. This narrative is taken from the account that Panayês' mother wrote a few days after his accident, which she distributed among his friends. I quote it here with her permission.

8. The play here is with the term *kairós,* which means both time and weather. As tragic as Dhiákos' death was, and as much as his memory has been preserved untarnished in the official Greek historiography, none of this has prevented students in the Greek schools from calling Athanássios Dhiákos "the most famous shish kebab in history" (*to pió dhiásēmo souvláki tēs historias*), thus interrogating and undermining both the notion of heroism and heroic death, and the construction of heroic personae by the hegemonic discourse of the state.

9. Wallace goes so far as to say that "these changes can only be gleaned . . . from urban Greece," a proposition which, as much as it might support my study here, I am not prepared to accept unquestioningly. Even a study of death practices in urban Greece cannot be totally illuminating if it is devoid of historical perspective.

10. Seremetakis also notes about Mani that in addition to the easy separation of the soul from the body, the challenging of death is also counted as good death, since the Maniat society "is a society organized around the ethics of war and revenge" (1991:243n).

# 9

# Epimythion (Resistance)

*HYPERCHÓMENOI*

Upon the death
of the parent
we took
the position of waiting.
—Hara T. Tzavella-Evjen, "Hyperchómenoi"

There is no closure in this endeavor. I cannot position this treatise to the past. I cannot say, "It's finished." As I was writing the preceding chapter, Dêmētra called me one night, around midnight. I was entertaining friends when she called. She asked what I was doing, who was at the house, what we had for dinner. Then, abruptly, she said, "You know, Dēmêtrēs died finally." I was stunned. Dēmêtrēs is an old friend of my parents, barely in his forties, and our two families had a friendship that straddled age differences. I didn't even know he had been ill, to have finally died. I said so. She replied, "He didn't die of an illness. He was in the car with Nikos and another friend of theirs. They had gone off to Páhē for dinner. Apparently they had been drinking, and Nikos had just bought a new Volkswagen GTI. They were going very fast, and they hit a lamppost, and they were trapped inside the car when the car caught fire. They found them charred."

I was hoping that between the final revisions of this text and the time it went to the publisher I would not have to face the death of another loved one. After all, it was only a year's time. This didn't happen. Every death that occurs is a disruption of normal time. It is not so much that death pulls us apart, bit by bit, by removing each one of us from the nation of

217

the living; it is more that each death makes the presence of the dying brutally felt. It is as if a strong current passes through us, shaking the links of the chain that keeps us together, bringing to the front a loved person through the realization of this person's death. Through the announcement of its own existence, death reminds us of a life that used to touch ours and reaffirms our own identity as living.

This reaffirmation of ourselves as living is necessary for the correct placing of identities into their respective spaces. The dead with the dead and the living with the living. And those who are in-between in a space of their own. Then the movements, actions, and praxes that surround death become processes toward an incorporation that will bring death into the magma of our personal, collective, and cultural psyche.

My father called me from Athens one day, very early in the morning. He wanted nothing in particular, just to see how I was doing. "Is everyone fine?" I asked. Indeed, everyone was fine. My grandfather still visited my grandmother's grave every Sunday after church. "Last Sunday he came by after his visit," my father said. "I could see him coming down the hill, crooked as he is, leaning on his cane. When he came in I asked him how he was. 'What is there for me, now, but the wait for death?', he asked me. Do you hear that? There is nothing else for Pappou to do anymore." My father, who has avoided the thought of death like death itself, laughed as he said that, thus placing himself at a conceptual distance from those who feel that their turn has come.

This study, then, has been about two things. First, it has explored how the praxis of anthropology and ethnography can be a matter of everyday life. I was interested to see how we (Athenians) negotiate our existence in our city and negotiate our existence with the prospect of death, and how we (anthropologists) can study this intersubjectivity. And it has been a reflection not only on the navigation of the living through a life that can only lead to death, but, even more, on the possibility that the difficulty of incorporating death itself (much like ethnography and anthropology) into everyday life might be the total and complete act of resistance to its finality.

ἐπάμεροι. τί δέ τις; τί δ᾽ οὔ τις; σκιᾶς ὄναρ
ἄνθρωπος.

ephemeral; who is he, then? who is he not?
man is the shadow of a dream.
                          —Pindar, *Pythian Ode* 8

# Bibliography
# Index

# Bibliography

Adorno, Theodor W. 1973. *The Jargon of Authenticity.* Translated by Knut Tarnow-
ski and Frederic Will. Evanston, Ill.: Northwestern University Press.

Adorno, Theodor W. 1985. "On the Question: What Is German?" Translated by
Thomas Y. Levin. *New German Critique* 36 (Fall):121–31.

Alexiou, Margaret. 1974. *The Ritual Lament in Greek Tradition.* Cambridge:
Cambridge University Press.

Alexiou, Margaret. 1984–85. "Folklore: An Obituary?" *Byzantine and Modern
Greek Studies* 9:1–28.

Altorki, Soraya. 1982. "The Anthropologist in the Field: A Case of Indigenous
Anthropology in Saudi Arabia." In *Indigenous Anthropology in Non-Western
Countries,* edited by Hussein Fahim, 167–75. Proceedings of a Burg Warten-
stein Symposium. Durham, N.C.: Carolina Academic Press.

Anastasiou, G. 1944. *Greek-Byzantine Liturgical Hymnal: Classical Minor, Major,
and Chromatic Melodies* (bilingual). 7th ed. Philadelphia: n.p.

Anderson, Benedict. 1983. *Imagined Communities: Reflections on the Origin and
Spread of Nationalism.* London: Verso.

Andrews, Kevin. 1967. *Athens.* Cities of the World 7. London: Phoenix House.

Andriotis, N. P. 1983. *Etymological Dictionary of Modern Greek* (in Greek). 3d ed.
Thessaloniki: Aristotelian University of Thessaloniki, Institute of Neo-Hellenic
Studies.

Anghelaki-Rooke, Katerina. 1986. *Beings and Things on Their Own.* Translated
by the author in collaboration with Jackie Willcox. Brockport, N.Y.: BOA
Editions.

Apostolidis, Panos. 1983. *Flower Rocks* (in Greek). Athens: Estia.

Ariès, Philippe. 1974. *Western Attitudes toward Death: From the Middle Ages
to the Present.* Translated by Patricia M. Banum. Baltimore: Johns Hopkins
University Press.

Ariès, Philippe. 1977. *L'homme devant la mort.* Paris: Seuil.

Ariès, Philippe. 1981. *The Hour of Our Death.* Translated by Helen Weaves. New
York: Knopf.

223

Ayliffe. 1726. *Parergon Juris Canonici Anglicani; or, A Commentary by Way of Supplement to the Canons and Constitutions of the Church of England.* N.p.

Badone, Ellen. 1989. *The Appointed Hour: Death, Worldview, and Social Change in Brittany.* Berkeley: University of California Press.

Badone, Ellen. 1990a. "Magnetism, Spells, and Pendulums: Alternative Healing and Biomedicine in Brittany." Paper presented at the 89th annual meeting of the American Anthropological Association, New Orleans.

Badone, Ellen ed. 1990b. *Religious Orthodoxy and Popular Faith in European Society.* Princeton, N.J.: Princeton University Press.

Bakhtin, M. M. 1981. *The Dialogic Imagination.* Edited by Michael Holquist. Translated by Caryl Emerson and Michael Holquist. Austin: University of Texas Press.

Balamaci, Nicholas. 1991. "Can the Vlachs Write Their Own History?" *Journal of the Hellenic Diaspora* 17, no. 1:9–37.

Balamaci, Nicholas. 1993. "The Vlachs of Albania: A Travel Memoir and Oral History." *Newsletter of the Society Farsarotul* 8, nos. 1–2 (Aug.):1–25.

Baltas, Aristides. 1993. "Greece Today: A Thriving Instance of Deep Communism; Providing a Framework for a Comprehensive Answer to All the Aporias of Friendly Aliens." Unpublished manuscript.

Barrington, Mrs. Russell. 1912. *Through Greece and Dalmatia: A Diary of Impressions Recorded by Pen and Picture.* London: Adam and Charles Black.

Barthes, Roland. 1975. *The Pleasure of the Text.* New York: Hill and Wang.

Baud-Bovy, S. 1936. *La chanson populaire grecque du Dodecanese.* Part 1, *Les textes.* Paris: n.p.

Behar, Ruth. 1991a. "The Body in the Woman, the Story in the Woman: A Book Review and Personal Essay." in *The Female Body: Figures, Styles, Speculations,* edited by L. Goldstein, 267–311. Ann Arbor: University of Michigan Press.

Behar, Ruth. 1991b. "Death and Memory: From Santa Maria del Monte to Miami Beach." *Cultural Anthropology* 6, no. 3:346–84.

Benizelos, Ioannis. 1986. *History of Athens* (1735–1807, in Greek). Edited by I. Kokkona and G. Bokou, with an introduction by Ioannis Gennadeios. Athens: Ekdotike Athenon.

Benjamin, Walter. 1968. *Illuminations.* Translated by Harry Zohn. New York: Schocken Books.

Benjamin, Walter. 1979. *Reflections: Essays, Aphorisms, Autobiographical Writings.* Edited by Peter Demetz. New York: Harcourt Brace Jovanovitch.

Benjamin, Walter. 1989. *Paris, capitale du XIXe siècle: Le livre des passages,* translated from the German edition of Rolf Tiedemann by Jean Lacoste. Paris: Editions du Cerf.

Bérard, Victor. 1893. *La Turquie et l'hellénisme contemporain.* Paris: Félix Alcan.

Bhabha, Homi K. 1987. "Interrogating Identity." *ICA Documents* 6:5–11.

Bickerman, E. J. 1974. *Chronology of the Ancient World.* Aspects of Greek and Roman Life. H. H. Scullard, general editor. Ithaca, N.Y.: Cornell University Press.

# Bibliography

Blanchot, Maurice. 1982. *The Siren's Song: Selected Essays*. Edited by Gabriel Josipovici. Translated by Sacha Robinovitch. Bloomington: Indiana University Press.

Bloch, M., and J. Parry, eds. 1982. *Death and the Regeneration of Life*. Cambridge: Cambridge University Press.

Blum, Richard, and Eva Blum. 1970. *The Dangerous Hour: The Lore of Crisis and Mystery in Rural Greece*. With a foreword by H.R.H. Prince Peter of Greece. New York: Charles Scribner's Sons.

Bosanquet, Mrs. R. C. 1914. *Days in Attica*. New York: Macmillan.

Bruner, Edward, ed. 1984. *Text, Play, and Story: The Construction and Reconstruction of Self and Society*. Proceedings of the American Ethnological Society. Stuart Plattner, proceedings editor. Prospect Heights, Ill.: Waveland Press.

Bruner, Edward. 1986. "Ethnography as Narrative." In Bruner and Turner 1986: 139–59.

Bruner, Edward, and Victor Turner, eds. 1986. *The Anthropology of Experience*. With an epilogue by Clifford Geertz. Chicago: University of Chicago Press.

Cadava, Eduardo. 1991. "Worlds of Light: Theses on the Photography of History." *Diacritics* 22, nos. 3–4:84–114.

Campbell, J. K. 1964. *Honour, Family and Patronage: A Study of Institutions and Moral Values in a Greek Mountain Community*. Oxford: Oxford University Press.

Campbell, J. K., and Ph. Sherrard. 1965. "The Greeks and the West." In *The Glass Curtain between Asia and Europe*, edited by Raghayan Iyer, 69–86. Oxford: Oxford University Press.

Caraveli-Chaves, Anna. 1980. "Bridge between Worlds: The Greek Women's Lament as Communicative Event." *Journal of American Folklore* 93:129–57.

Castoriadis, Cornelius. 1984. *Crossroads in the Labyrinth*. Translated by Kate Soper and Martin H. Ryle. Cambridge, Mass.: MIT Press.

Chouliaras, Yiorgos. 1991. *Fast Food Classics* (in Greek). Athens: Ypsilon.

Clifford, James. 1983. "On Ethnographic Authority." *Representations* 1:118–46.

Clifford, James. 1988. *The Predicament of Culture: Twentieth-Century Ethnography, Literature, and Art*. Cambridge, Mass.: Harvard University Press.

Clifford, James, and G. Marcus, eds. 1986. *Writing Culture: The Poetics and Politics of Ethnography*. Berkeley: University of California Press.

Counts, David R. 1980. "The Good Death in Kaliai: Preparation for Death in Western New Britain." In Kalish 1980:39–44.

Crapanzano, Vincent. 1980. *Tuhami: Portrait of a Moroccan*. Chicago: University of Chicago Press.

Crapanzano, Vincent. 1991. "An Epistle." *Anthropology and Humanism Quarterly* 16, no. 1 (March):31–32.

Cutileiro, José. 1971. *A Portuguese Rural Society*. Oxford: Clarendon Press.

Danforth, Loring. 1982. *The Death Rituals of Rural Greece*. Princeton, N.J.: Princeton University Press.

Danforth, Loring. 1989. *Firewalking and Religious Healing: The Anastenaria of*

*Greece and the American Firewalking Movement.* Princeton, N.J.: Princeton University Press.

de Certeau, Michel. 1984. *The Practice of Everyday Life.* Berkeley: University of California Press.

de Certeau, Michel. 1985a. *Heterologies: Discourse on the Other.* Translated by Brian Massumi. Minneapolis: University of Minnesota Press.

de Certeau, Michel. 1985b. "What We Do When We Believe." In *On Signs,* edited by Marshall Blonsky, 192–202. Baltimore: Johns Hopkins University Press.

Defner, Michael. 1923. "Greetings, Wishes, Curses, Oaths, and Songs of Tsakones" (in Greek). *Laographia* 7:25–40.

Derrida, Jacques. 1976. *Of Grammatology.* Translated by Gayatri Chakravorty Spivak. Baltimore: Johns Hopkins University Press.

Derrida, Jacques. 1987. *The Truth in Painting.* Translated by Geoff Bennington and Ian McLeod. Chicago: University of Chicago Press.

Dhareshwar, Vivek. 1989. "Toward a Narrative Epistemology of the Postcolonial Predicament." *Inscriptions* 5:135–59.

Dimaras, K. Th. 1985. *Neo-Hellenic Enlightenment* (in Greek). Athens: Ermis.

Dimaras, K. Th. 1986. *Konstantinos Paparrigopoulos* (in Greek). Athens: Educational Foundation of the National Bank.

Dimen, Muriel, and Ernestine Friedl, eds. 1976. *Regional Variation in Modern Greece and Cyprus: Toward a Perspective on the Ethnography of Greece.* Annals of the New York Academy of Sciences 268. New York: New York Academy of Sciences.

Dimitrakos, D. 1959. *New Orthographic and Exegetical Dictionary of the Totality of Greek Language* (in Greek). Athens: Pergaminai.

Dionisopulos-Mass, Regina. 1976. "The Evil Eye and Bewitchment in a Peasant Village." In Maloney 1976:42–62.

Dodwell, Edward. 1805. *A Classical Tour through Greece.* Vol. 2. London.

Domínguez, Virginia R. 1989. *People as Subject, People as Object: Selfhood and Peoplehood in Contemporary Israel.* Madison: University of Wisconsin Press.

Domínguez, Virginia R. 1991. "How the Self Stacks the Deck." *Anthropology and Humanism Quarterly* 16, no. 1 (March):12–15.

D'Onofrio, S. 1991. "L'atome de parenté spirituelle." *L'homme* 31, no. 118 (April–June):79–110.

Douglas, Mary. 1966. *Purity and Danger: An Analysis of Concepts of Pollution and Taboo.* London: Routledge and Kegan Paul.

Dreyfus, Nicole. 1969. *Les étudiants grecs accusent.* Paris: Les Editeurs Français Réunis.

Dubisch, Jill. 1989. "Death and Social Change in Greece." *Anthropological Quarterly* 62, no. 4:189–200.

Dubisch, Jill. 1990. "Pilgrimage and Popular Religion at a Greek Holy Shrine." In Badone 1990b:113–39.

du Boulay, Juliet. 1974. *Portrait of a Greek Mountain Village.* Oxford: Clarendon Press.

du Boulay, Juliet. 1982. "The Greek Vampire: A Study of Cyclic Symbolism in Marriage and Death." *Man* 17:219–39.

du Boulay, Juliet. 1984. "The Blood: Symbolic Relationships between Descent, Marriage, Incest Prohibitions, and Spiritual Kinship in Greece." *Man* 19:533–56.

Dundes, Allan, ed. 1981. *The Evil Eye: A Folklore Casebook.* New York: Garland.

Durand, Gilbert. [1969] 1973. *Les structures anthropologiques de l'imaginaire: Introduction à l'archétypologie générale.* Paris: Bondas.

Eco, Umberto. 1978. *Travels in Hyper Reality: Essays,* edited by Helen Wolff and Kurt Wolff, translated by William Weaver. New York: Harcourt Brace Jovanovich, Inc.

Eco, Umberto. 1984. *The Name of the Rose.* Translated by William Weaver. London: Picador.

Elias, Norbert. 1991. "Über die Einsamkeit der Sterbenden." *Leviathan* 9:23–47.

Fabian, Johannes. 1973. "How Others Die: Reflections on the Anthropology of Death." In *Death in American Experience,* edited by Arien Mack, 177–201. New York: Schocken Books.

Fabian, Johannes. 1983. *Time and the Other: How Anthropology Makes Its Object.* New York: Columbia University Press.

Fallmerayer, Jacob Philipp. 1984. *On the Origin of Today's Hellenes* (in Greek). Translated from German by Kostas Romanos. Athens: Nefeli.

Farnell, L. R. 1907. *The Cults of the Greek States.* 5 vols. Oxford: Oxford University Press.

Faubion, James. 1993. *Modern Greek Lessons: A Primer in Historical Constructivism.* Princeton, N.J.: Princeton University Press.

Favret-Saada, Jeanne. 1990. "About Participation." *Culture, Medicine, and Psychiatry* 14, no. 2:189–201.

Fernandez, James. 1977. "The Performance of Ritual Metaphors." In *The Social Use of Metaphor: Essays on the Anthropology of Rhetoric,* edited by D. J. Sapir and C. J. Crocker, 100–131. Philadelphia: University of Pennsylvania Press.

Feyerabend, Paul. 1975. *Against Method: Outline of an Anarchistic Theory of Knowledge.* London: NLB.

Firth, Raymond. 1951. *Elements of Social Organisation.* London: Watts.

Foerster, Heinz von. 1984. "Disorder/Order: Discovery or Invention?" In *Disorder and Order,* edited by Paisley Livingston, 177–90. Saratoga, Calif.: Anma Libri.

Foucault, Michel. 1972. *The Archaeology of Knowledge and the Discourse on Language.* New York: Pantheon Books.

Foucault, Michel. 1975. *The Birth of the Clinic.* New York: Vintage.

Fox, Richard G., ed. 1991. *Recapturing Anthropology: Working in the Present.* Santa Fe, N.Mex.: School of American Research Press.

Freud, Sigmund. 1950. "A Disturbance of Memory on the Acropolis" (1936). In *Collected Papers,* translated by James Strachey, 5:302–12. London: Hogarth.

Freud, Sigmund. 1984. "Mourning and Melancholia." In *On Metapsychology: The*

227

*Theory of Psychoanalysis,* translated by James Strachey, 247–68. The Pelican Freud Library, vol. 11. Harmondsworth: Penguin.

Freud, Sigmund. 1991. "Our Relationship to Death" (in Greek). Translated from the German "Unser Verhältnis zum Tode" (1946) by Vassilikê-Pêgê Christopoulou. *Leviathan* 9:11–22.

Friedl, Ernestine. 1962. *Vasilika: A Village in Modern Greece.* New York: Holt, Rinehart and Winston.

Friedman, Jonathan. 1987. "Beyond Otherness; or, The Spectacularization of Anthropology." *Telos* 71 (Spring):161–70.

Fry, L. J. 1974. *Practical Building of Methane Power Plants for Rural Energy Independence.* Santa Barbara, Calif.: Privately published.

Galt, Anthony H. 1982. "The Evil Eye as Synthetic Image and Its Meaning on the Island of Pantelleria, Italy." *American Ethnologist* 9:664–81.

Garland, Robert. 1985. *The Greek Way of Death.* Ithaca, N.Y.: Cornell University Press.

Geertz, Clifford. 1983. *Local Knowledge: Further Essays in Interpretive Anthropology.* New York: Basic Books.

Geertz, Clifford. 1988. *Works and Lives: The Anthropologist as Author.* Stanford, Calif.: Stanford University Press.

Gennadeios, Ioannis. 1935. *Kaisarianê* (in Greek). Athens: Privately published.

Gertsakis, Elizabeth. 1992. "A Glamorous Private History." *Third Text* 19 (Summer):49–56.

Giannopoulos, Perikles. 1988. *Collected Works* (in Greek). Athens: Eleftheri Skepsis.

Gordon, Deborah. 1990. "Embodying Illness, Embodying Cancer." *Culture, Medicine and Psychiatry* 14, no. 2:275–97.

Gourgouris, Stathis. 1989. "Flying to Byzantium: Namely, (Anti)Logos on Military Service, Allied Commissions, Common Alterities, and All Patrideologemes" (in Greek). *Skhedia* 3:41–44.

Gourgouris, Stathis. In press. *Dream Nation: Enlightenment, Colonization, and the Institution of Modern Greece.* Stanford, Calif.: Stanford University Press.

Grimm, Eleutherios R. 1990. "Egalitarianism and Productivity: Rhetoric and Reality in Greek Educational Reform since the Fall of the Junta in 1974." *Modern Greek Studies Yearbook* 6:81–96.

Harakas, Stanley Samuel. 1990. *Health and Medicine in the Eastern Orthodox Tradition: Faith, Liturgy, and Wholeness.* New York: Crossroad.

Hardie, Margaret (Mrs. F. W. Hasluck). [1923] 1981. "The Evil Eye in Some Greek Villages of the Upper Haliakmon Valley in West Macedonia." In Dundes 1981:107–24.

Hastrup, Kirsten. 1987. "Fieldwork among Friends." In Jackson 1987:94–108.

Hatzisotiriou, G. 1980. *The Folklore of Inland Attika* (in Greek). Athens: Privately published.

Hayano, D. M. 1979. "Auto-Ethnography: Paradigms, Problems, and Prospects." *Human Organization* 38:99–104.

Herzfeld, Michael. 1980a. "On the Ethnography of 'Prejudice' in an Exclusive Community." *Ethnic Groups* 2:283–305.

Herzfeld, Michael. 1980b. "Social Tension and Inheritance by Lot in Three Greek Villages." *Anthropological Quarterly* 53:91–100.

Herzfeld, Michael. 1981. "Meaning and Morality: A Semiotic Approach to Evil Eye Accusations in a Greek Village." *American Ethnologist* 8:560–74.

Herzfeld, Michael. 1982a. *Ours Once More: Folklore, Ideology, and the Making of Modern Greece.* Austin: University of Texas Press.

Herzfeld, Michael. 1982b. "When Exceptions Define the Rules: Greek Baptismal Names and the Negotiation of Identity." *Journal of Anthropological Research* 38, no. 3 (Fall):289–302.

Herzfeld, Michael. 1983. "Interpreting Kinship Terminology: The Problem of Patriliny in Rural Greece." *Anthropological Quarterly* 56:157–66.

Herzfeld, Michael. 1985. *The Poetics of Manhood: Contest and Identity in a Greek Mountain Village.* Princeton, N.J.: Princeton University Press.

Herzfeld, Michael. 1986. "Closure as Cure: Tropes in the Exploration of Bodily and Social Disorder." *Current Anthropology* 27, no. 2:107–20.

Herzfeld, Michael. 1987. *Anthropology through the Looking-Glass: Critical Ethnography on the Margins of Europe.* Cambridge: Cambridge University Press.

Herzog, Edgar. 1983. *Psyche and Death: Death Demons in Forklore, Myths, and Modern Dreams.* Translated by David Cox and Eugene Rolfe. Dallas: Spring Publications.

Hirschon, Renée. 1983. "Under One Roof: Marriage, Dowry, and Family Relations in Piraeus." In Kenny and Kertzer 1983:299–323.

Hirschon, Renée. 1989. *Heirs of the Greek Catastrophe: The Social Life of Asia Minor Refugees in Piraeus.* Oxford: Clarendon Press.

Hobhouse, J. C. [1817] 1971. *A Journey through Albania and Other Provinces of Turkey in Europe and Asia, to Constantinople, during the Years 1809 and 1810.* 2 vols. Philadelphia: M. Carey and Son; rpt., New York: Arno Press.

Homer. 1963. *The Odyssey.* Translated by Robert Fitzgerald. New York: Anchor Books.

Horkheimer, Max. 1972. *Critical Theory: Selected Essays.* Translated by Matthew J. O'Connell et al. New York: Herder and Herder.

Horkheimer, Max, and Theodor W. Adorno. 1972. *Dialectic of Enlightenment.* Translated by John Cumming. New York: Seabury.

Humphreys, S. C. 1983. *The Family, Women, and Death: Comparative Studies.* London: Routledge and Kegan Paul.

Humphreys, S. C., and Helen King, eds. 1981. *Mortality and Immortality: The Anthropology and Archaeology of Death.* London: Academic Press.

Huntington, R., and P. Metcalf. 1985. *Celebrations of Death: The Anthropology of Mortuary Ritual.* Cambridge: Cambridge University Press.

Irigaray, Luce. 1985. *Speculum of the Other Woman.* Translated by Gillian G. Gill. Ithaca, N.Y.: Cornell University Press.

Jackson, Anthony, ed. 1987. *Anthropology at Home.* ASA Publications 25. London: Tavistock.

Jones, Delmos J. 1970. "Towards a Native Anthropology." *Human Organization* 29, no. 4:251–59.

Jusdanis, Gregory. 1991. *Belated Modernity and Aesthetic Culture: Inventing National Literature.* Theory and History of Literature, vol. 18. Minneapolis: University of Minnesota Press.

Kaklamanis, Yerasimos. 1984. *The Eastern Mediterranean as European History* (in Greek). Athens: Privately published.

Kaklamanis, Yerasimos. 1986. *On the Structure of the Neo-Hellenic State* (in Greek). Athens: Privately published.

Kalish, R. A., ed. 1980. *Death and Dying: Views from Many Cultures.* New York: Baywood.

Karantonis, Andreas, ed. 1955. *Palamas, Sikelianos, Kavafis* (in Greek). Athens: Zacharopoulos.

Karp, Ivan. 1988. "Laughter at Marriage: Subversion in Performance." *Journal of Folklore Research* 25, nos. 1–2:35–52.

Kazamias, Andreas M. 1990. "The Curse of Sisyphus in Greek Educational Reform: A Socio-political and Cultural Interpretation." *Modern Greek Studies Yearbook* 6:33–54.

Kearl, Michael C., and Anoel Rinaldi. 1983. "The Political Uses of the Dead as Symbols in Contemporary Civil Religions." *Social Forces* 61, no. 3:693–708.

Kenny, M., and D. I. Kertzer, eds. 1983. *Urban Life in Mediterranean Europe: Anthropological Perspectives.* Urbana: University of Illinois Press.

Kluckhohn, Clyde. 1949. *Mirror for Man: The Relation of Anthropology to Modern Life.* Foreword by Ashley Montague. New York: McGraw-Hill.

Kollias, Aristides. 1990. *Arvanites and the Origins of Greeks: Historical-Laographic-Cultural-Linguistic Overview* (in Greek). 6th ed. Athens: Privately published.

Kondylis, Panayotis. 1988. *The Neo-Hellenic Enlightenment: Philosophical Ideas* (in Greek). Athens: Themelio.

Konstantellou, Eva. 1990. "The Myths of Modernization: Post-1974 Educational Reform in Greece." *Modern Greek Studies Yearbook* 6:55–72.

Konstantinidis, G. 1982. "Sarcomas of the Soft Tissues" (in Greek). In *Clinical Oncology,* 549–58. Athens: National Advisory on Oncology.

Kyriakidis, A. 1909. *Modern Greek-English Dictionary.* Athens: Anestis Constantinidis.

Lakoff, George, and Mark Johnson. 1980. *Metaphors We Live By.* Chicago: University of Chicago Press.

Lawson, J. C. 1910. *Modern Greek Folklore and Ancient Greek Religion: A Study in Survivals.* Cambridge: Cambridge University Press.

Lear, Edward. 1848. "Letter to His Sister Ann, 3 June 1848." In *Edward Lear, 1812–1888,* by Vivien Noakes. London: Royal Academy of Arts, 1985.

Le Goff, Jacques. 1981. *La naissance du Purgatoire.* Paris: Gallimard.

Lemert, C. C., and G. Gillan. 1982. *Michel Foucault: Social Theory and Transgression*. New York: Columbia University Press.

Leontis, Artemis. 1990. "Autochthony and the Greek Landscape." Paper presented at the Conference on Byzantine and Modern Greek Studies: The Next Wave, Ohio State University, Columbus, 12–14 October.

Leontis, Artemis. 1995. *Topographies of Hellenism: Mapping a Homeland*. Ithaca, N.Y.: Cornell University Press.

Lévi-Strauss, Claude. 1985. *The View from Afar*. New York: Basic Books.

Liddell, Henry G., and Robert Scott. 1871. *A Dictionary of the Greek Language*. Translated into Greek by Xenophon Michos, edited by Michael Konstantinides. Athens: Ioannis Sideris.

Limón, José E. 1991. "Representation, Ethnicity, and the Precursory Ethnography: Notes of a Native Anthropologist." In Fox 1991:115–35.

Lincoln, Bruce. 1991. *Death, War, and Sacrifice: Studies in Ideology and Practice*. With a foreword by Wendy Doniger. Chicago: University of Chicago Press.

Loukatos, Dimitrios. 1977. *Introduction to Greek Folklore* (in Greek). 2d ed. Athens: Educational Foundation of the National Bank.

Maloney, Clarence, ed. 1976. *The Evil Eye*. New York: Columbia University Press.

Marcus, George. 1982. "Rhetoric and Ethnographic Genre." In Ruby 1982:163–73.

Marcus, George. 1991a. "False Friends in a New Relationship: The Internal Critique of the Western Individual Self/Subject and Ethnographic Accounts of Other Selves." *Anthropology and Humanism Quarterly* 16, no. 1 (March):15–17.

Marcus, George. 1991b. "Introduction." *Anthropology and Humanism Quarterly* 16, no. 1 (March):10–12.

Marcus, George E., and M. J. Fisher. 1986. *Anthropology as Cultural Critique: An Experimental Moment in the Human Sciences*. Chicago: University of Chicago Press.

Mavrokordatos, Nikólaos. [1800] 1989. *Philotheou Parerga*. Compiled, translated, and annotated by Jacques Buchard under the title *Les loisirs de Philothée*, with an introduction by K. Dimaras. Athens: Association pour l'Étude des Lumières en Grèce.

McGann, Jerome J., ed. 1986. *Byron*. The Oxford Authors. Oxford: Oxford University Press.

McManners, John. 1981. *Death and the Enlightenment: Changing Attitudes to Death among Christians and Unbelievers in Eighteenth-Century France*. Oxford: Clarendon Press.

Medick, Hans, and David Warren Sabean, eds. 1984. *Interest and Emotion: Essays on the Study of Family and Kinship*. Cambridge: Cambridge University Press.

Megas, G. A. 1963. *Greek Calendar Customs*. 2d ed. Athens: Privately published.

Michael-Dede, Maria. 1987. *The Greek Arvanites* (in Greek). Ioannina: Foundation for North-Ipeirotic Research.

231

Michael-Dede, Maria. 1991. *The Immodest, Irreverent, Hybristic, in the Greek Demotic Songs* (in Greek). Athens: Philippotes.

Mikoniatis, E. 1990. "Nineteenth-Century Greek Funerary Sculpture" (in Greek). *Archaeologia* 36 (Sept.):42–53.

Mintsis, G., and M. Pitsiava-Latinopoulou. 1990. "Traffic Accidents with Fixed Roadside Obstacles: A Study of the Greek Rural Road Network." *Traffic Engineering + Control* (May):306–11.

Mintz, Sidney W. 1985. *Sweetness and Power: The Place of Sugar in Modern History.* New York: Penguin.

Mouzelis, Nikos. 1976. "The Relevance of the Concept of Class to the Study of Modern Greek Society." In Dimen and Friedl 1976:395–410.

Murphy, Robert. 1987. *The Body Silent.* New York: Holt.

Myerhoff, Barbara. 1978. *Number Our Days.* New York: Dutton.

Nikolaou, Nikos. 1984. "Hippocratic Philology and Korais" (in Greek). In *Two Days on Korais (29–30 April): Approaches to the Language-Theory, the Thought, and the Work of Korais,* 85–101. Athens: Center for Neo-Hellenic Research.

Nilsson, Martin Persson. 1969. *Greek Piety.* Translated by Herbert Jennings Rose. New York: Norton.

Orso, Evelyn. 1981. *Modern Greek Humor.* Bloomington: Indiana University Press.

Palamas, Kostes. 1925. *Poems.* Selected and rendered into English by Theodore H. Stephanides and George C. Katsimbalis. London: Hazell, Watson and Viney.

Panourgiá, Neni. 1983. "Laments of Maundy Thursday on the Island of Kalymnos." Field Recording. Indiana University, Archives of Traditional Music.

Panourgiá, Neni. 1990a. "Death by Cancer: Local and Unlocal Knowledge." *Psycho-Oncology Letters* 1, no. 3:24–28.

Panourgiá, Neni. 1990b. "On the Political and Symbolic Capital of Educational Reforms in Greece." *Modern Greek Studies Yearbook* 6:73–80.

Panourgiá, Neni. 1994. "Athens and the European Aesthetic: Neo-Classicism in the Project of Greek Modernity." Lecture given at the Center for Literary and Cultural Studies at the invitation of the George Seferis Chair of Modern Greek, Harvard University, 14 April.

Papadiamantis, A. 1988. *Collected Short Stories* (in Greek). Athens: Neo-Hellenic Library, Kostas and Eleni Ourani Foundation. ("A Soul" was first published in *Parnassos* 14 [Sept. 1881].)

Papayiorgis, Kostis. 1991. *The Living and the Dead* (in Greek). Athens: Kastaniotis.

Papazisis, D. 1976. *Vlachs (Koutsovlachs)* (in Greek). Athens.

Patilis, Yiannis. 1984. *Warm Midday* (in Greek). Athens: Ypsilon. Unpublished English translation by Stathis Gourgouris.

Pesmazoglou, Stefanos. 1987. *Education and Development in Greece: An Asymptotic Relationship* (in Greek). Athens: Themelio.

Petropoulos, Elias. 1988. *Corpses, Corpses, Corpses . . .* (in Greek). Athens: Nefeli.

Pharos, Philotheos. 1988. *Mourning: Orthodox, Folkloric, and Psychological Consideration* (in Greek). Athens: Akritas.

Piña-Cabral, Joao de. 1986. *Sons of Adam, Daughters of Eve*. Oxford: Clarendon Press.

Politis, Nikolaos G. 1884. "The Custom of Breaking Vessels during the Funeral" (in Greek). *Parnassos* 17:81–87.

Politis, Nikolaos G. 1893. "On the Breaking of Vessels as a Funeral Rite in Modern Greece." *Journal of the Anthropological Institute of Great Britain and Ireland,* pp. 28–41.

Politis, Nikolaos G. 1894. "The Custom of Breaking Vessels at the Funeral" (in Greek). *Laographika Symmeikta* B:268–83.

Politis, Nikolaos G. 1978. *Selections from the Songs of the Greek People* (in Greek). Athens: Vayionakis.

Pratt, Mary Louise. 1991. "Arts of the Contact Zone." *Profession,* pp. 33–40.

Prevelakis, George. 1989. "Culture, Politics, and the Urban Crisis: The Case of Modern Athens." *Modern Greek Studies Yearbook* 5:1–32.

Preziosi, Donald. 1990. "Oubliez la città." *Strategies: A Journal of Theory, Culture and Politics,* no. 3, 260–67.

Prior, Lindsay. 1989. *The Social Organisation of Death: Medical Discourse and Social Practice in Belfast*. London: Macmillan.

Psacharopoulos, G., and G. Papas. 1989. "From the General Lycées to the T.E.I." (in Greek). *Education and Profession* 2, no. 1 (March):9–19.

Rabinow, Paul. 1977. *Reflections on Fieldwork in Morocco*. Berkeley: University of California Press.

Rabinow, Paul. 1982. "Masked I Go Forward: Reflections on the Modern Subject." In Ruby 1982:174–85.

Richardson, Miles. 1990. *Cry Lonesome and Other Accounts of the Anthropologist's Projects*. Albany: State University of New York Press.

Richardson, Miles. 1991. "Point of View in Anthropological Discourse: The Ethnographer as Gilgamesh." In *Anthropological Poetics,* edited by Ivan Brady, 207–19. Savage, Md.: Rowman and Littlefield.

Rigatos, Gerasimos. 1985. *Introduction to Psycho-Social Oncology* (in Greek). Athens: Privately published.

Rigou, Myrto. 1991. "Thanatological Terminology in Modernity" (in Greek). *Leviathan* 9:57–73.

Rosaldo, Renato. 1984. "Grief and a Headhunter's Rage: On the Cultural Force of Emotions." In Bruner 1984:178–94.

Ross, Andrew. 1993. "This Bridge Called My Pussy." In *Madonnarama: Essays on Sex and Popular Culture,* edited by Lisa Frank and Paul Smith, 47–64. Pittsburgh: Cleis Press.

Ruby, Jay, ed. 1982. *A Crack in the Mirror: Reflexive Perspectives in Anthropology*. Philadelphia: University of Pennsylvania Press.

Rushton, Lucy. 1983. "Doves and Magpies: Village Women in the Greek Orthodox Church." In *Women's Religious Experience: Cross-Cultural Perspectives*, edited by Pat Holden, 57–70. London: Croom Helm.

Safilios-Rothchild, Constantina. 1976. "The Family in Athens: Regional Variation." In Dimen and Friedl 1976:410–18.

Said, Edward W. 1979. *Orientalism*. New York: Pantheon Books.

Sant Cassia, Paul, with Constantina Bada. 1992. *The Making of the Modern Greek Family: Marriage and Exchange in Nineteenth-Century Athens*. Cambridge: Cambridge University Press.

Sartre, Jean-Paul. 1963. *Search for a Method*. Translated by Hazel Barnes. New York: Knopf.

Schein, Muriel Dimen. 1975. "When Is an Ethnic Group? Ecology and Class Structure in Northern Greece." *Ethnology* 14:83–97.

Schizas, Yiannis. 1991. *Ho Hymēttós* (in Greek). Athens: Stochastis.

Schopenhauer, Arthur. 1974. *Parerga and Paralipomena: Short Philosophical Essays*. Translated from German by E. F. J. Payne. Vols. 1 and 2. Oxford: Clarendon Press.

Scott, David. 1991. "The Cultural Poetics of Eyesight in Sri-Lanka: Composure, Vulnerability, and the Sinhala Concept of Distiya." *Dialectical Anthropology* 16:85–102.

Scott, David. 1992a. "Anthropology and Colonial Discourse: Aspects of the Demonological Construction of Sinhala Cultural Practice." *Cultural Anthropology* 7, no. 3:301–26.

Scott, David. 1992b. "Conversion and Demonism: Colonial Christian Discourse and Religion in Sri Lanka." *Comparative Studies in Society and History* 34, no. 2:331–65.

Seferis, George. 1964. *Poems* (in Greek). 6th ed. Athens: Ikaros.

Seremetakis, Nadia. 1991. *The Last Word: Women, Death, and Divination in Inner Mani*. Chicago: University of Chicago Press.

Skiffington, Kerry K. 1990. "Scottish Women's Impact on the Shape of Local Health Care." Paper presented at the 89th annual meeting of the American Anthropological Association, New Orleans.

Sontag, Susan. 1969. *Against Interpretation and Other Essays*. New York: Dell.

Sontag, Susan. 1979. *Illness as Metaphor*. New York: Vintage.

Souliotis, Yiannis. 1986. *The Kóllyva* (in Greek). Athens: Kedros.

Stasinopoulos, E. 1973. *History of Athens: From Antiquity to Our Time* (in Greek). Athens: Privately published.

Stewart, Charles. 1989. "Hegemony or Rationality? The Position of the Supernatural in Modern Greece." *Journal of Modern Greek Studies* 7 (Oct.):77–104.

Stewart, Charles. 1990. "Social Mobility, Pedagogy, and Ideology in Early Twentieth-Century Greece." *Modern Greek Studies Yearbook* 6:23–32.

Stewart, Charles. 1991. *Demons and the Devil: Moral Imagination in Modern Greek Culture*. Princeton, N.J.: Princeton University Press.

Stewart, O. John. 1989. *Drinkers, Drummers, and Decent Folk: Ethnographic*

*Narratives of Village Trinidad*. Albany: State University of New York Press.

Strathern, Marilyn. 1987. "The Limits of Auto-Anthropology." In Jackson 1987: 16–37.

Sudnow, David. 1967. *Passing On: The Social Organization of Dying*. Englewood Cliffs, N.J.: Prentice-Hall.

Sutton, Susan Buck. 1983. "Rural-Urban Migration in Greece." In Kenny and Kertzer 1983: 225–49.

Taussig, Michael T. 1980. "Reification and the Consciousness of the Patient." *Social Science and Medicine* 14B:3–13.

Taussig, Michael T. 1987. *Shamanism, Colonialism, and the Wild Man: A Study in Terror and Healing*. Chicago: University of Chicago Press.

Taussig, Michael T. 1992. *The Nervous System*. New York: Routledge.

Taylor, Lawrence. 1980. "Symbolic Death: An Anthropological View of Mourning Ritual in the Nineteenth Century." In *A Time to Mourn: Expressions of Grief in Nineteenth-Century America*, edited by Martha Pike and Janice Armstrong, Stonybrook, N.Y.: Museum at Stonybrook.

Tedlock, Barbara. 1991. "From Participant Observation to the Observation of Participation: The Emergence of Narrative Ethnography." *Journal of Anthropological Research* 47, no. 1 (Spring):69–94.

Thumb, A. [1910] 1964. *A Handbook of Modern Greek Language*. Chicago: Argonaut.

Travlos, Ioannis. 1958. *The Development of Cityscape in Athens: From Historical Times to the Beginning of the Nineteenth Century* (in Greek). Athens: Kapon.

Trinh, T. Minh-Ha. 1989. *Woman, Native, Other: Writing Postcoloniality and Feminism*. Bloomington: Indiana University Press.

Tsaoussis, D. G. 1976. "Greek Social Structure." In Dimen and Friedl 1976:492–42.

Tsigakou, Fani-Maria. 1981. *The Rediscovery of Greece: Travelers and Painters of the Romantic Era*. With an introduction by Sir Steven Runciman. London: Thames and Hudson.

Tsiomis, Yiannis. 1983. "Athènes à soi-même étrangère: Eléments de formation et de réception du modèle néo-classique urbain en Europe et en Grèce, au XIXe siècle." Doctorat d'état, University of Paris X, Nanterre.

Tsiomis, Yiannis, ed. 1985a. *Athens: Capital City* (in Greek). Athens: Ministry of Culture.

Tsiomis, Yiannis. 1985b. "Athens and Washington: Cities with or without History" (in Greek). In Tsiomis 1985a:143–47.

Tsiomis, Yiannis. 1986. "The City as a Cultural Phenomenon" (in Greek). *15thêmeros Polites,* 3 March 1986, no. 74:34–36.

Tsitsipis, Lucas. 1993. "The Bakhtinian Turn in Linguistic Anthropology: Genre and Event." Unpublished typescript.

Tsoucalas, Konstantinos. 1975. *Dépendance et reproduction: Le rôle social des appareils scholaires en Grèce*. Paris.

235

Tsoucalas, Konstantinos. 1987. *Dependence and Reproduction: The Social Role of Educational Mechanisms in Greece* (in Greek). Athens: Themelio.

Turner, Victor. 1986. "Dewey, Dilthey and Drama: An Essay in the Anthropology of Experience." In Bruner and Turner 1986:33–44.

Turner, Victor. 1992. *Blazing the Trail: Way Marks in the Exploration of Symbols.* Edited by Edith Turner. Tucson: University of Arizona Press.

Tyler, Stephen A. 1987. *The Unspeakable: Discourse, Dialogue, and Rhetoric in the Postmodern World.* Madison: University of Wisconsin Press.

Tzavella-Evjen, Hara T. 1993. *On the Way* (in Greek). Athens: Nea Skepsi.

Tziovas, Dimitris. 1989. *The Transformations of Nationism and the Ideologeme of Hellenicity in the Interwar Period* (in Greek). Athens: Odysseas.

Velioti, Maria. 1987. "Le parrainage, l'adoption et la fraternisation dans un village arvanite du Peloponnese." *Études et Documents Balcaniques et Mediterranéens* 13:69–76.

Vergopoulos, Kostas. 1985. *The Agrarian Issue in Greece: The Social Incorporation of Agriculture* (in Greek). Athens: Exantas.

Vernant, Jean-Pierre. 1982. "La belle mort et le cadavre outrage." In *La mort, les mort dans les sociétés anciennes,* edited by Gherardo Gnoli and Jean-Pierre Vernant, 45–76. Cambridge: Cambridge University Press.

Vernant, Jean-Pierre. 1986. "Feminine Figures of Death in Greece." *Diacritics* 16, no. 2 (Summer):54–64.

Vernier, Bernard. 1984. "Putting Kin and Kinship to Good Use: The Circulation of Goods, Labour, and Names on Karpathos (Greece)." In Medick and Sabean 1984:28–76.

"Vlach Men and Women" (in Greek). 1852. *Nea Pandora* 3:282–83.

Vovelle, Michel. 1980. "Rediscovery of Death since 1960." *Annals of the American Academy of Political and Social Science* 447 (Jan.):89–99.

Vovelle, Michel. 1990. *Ideologies and Mentalities.* Translated by Eamon O'Flaherty. Cambridge, Eng.: Polity Press.

Vranousē, Era L. 1970. "The Terms 'Alvanoi' and 'Arvanitai' and the First Mention of This People of the Balkan Peninsula in the Sources of the XI Century" (in Greek). *Symmeikta* 2:207–54.

Wace, A. J. B., and M. S. Thompson. 1914. *The Nomads of the Balkans: An Account of Life and Customs among the Vlachs of Northern Pindus.* New York: Dutton.

Wallace, Melanie. 1984. "Death in Greece." *Journal of the Hellenic Diaspora* 11, no. 1 (Spring):40–46.

Wallerstein, Immanuel. 1991. *Unthinking Social Science: The Limits of Nineteenth-Century Paradigms.* Cambridge: Polity Press.

Wilford, J. N. 1990. "Anthropology Seen as Father of Maori Lore." *New York Times,* Science section, 20 Feb.

Winkler, Cathy. In press. *Raped Once, Raped Twice, and Raped a Third Time.* Albany: Sage.

Woodhouse, Christopher M. 1984. *Modern Greece: A Short History.* London: Faber and Faber.

Wordsworth, Christopher. 1855. *Athens and Attika.* London: John Murray.

Yang, Martin, 1945. *A Chinese Village: Taigou, Shantung Province.* New York: Columbia University Press.

Yang, Martin. 1972. "How *A Chinese Village* Was Written." In *Crossing Cultural Boundaries,* edited by Solon T. Kimball and James R. Watson, 63–72. San Francisco: Chandler.

Zanetos, John C. 1975. *Funeral Services in the Greek Orthodox Church* (Greek text with a rendering in English). Boston: n.p.

# Index

239

# Index

# Index

Nikolaou, Nikos, 84
Nilsson, Martin, 131–32

objectivity, 5; in analysis, 18–19; in anthropology, 6; and modernity, 11–12
*Odyssey*, xxiii, 140n9, 187
Orso, Evelyn, 183

Palamas, Kostis, 150
Papadiamantis, Alexandros, 115–16, 119, 122–23, 140n
Paparrigopoulos, K., 57
Papayiorgis, Kostis, 157, 200, 208–9
Papazisis, D. 63
*parerga*, xx–xxii
Parry, J., 178, 189, 199
Patilis, Yiannis, 151
patriline, 32, 91
Pharos, Philotheos, 80, 214
Piña-Cabral, Joao de, 100, 191
Pitsiava-Latinopoulou, M. 193
Politis, Nikolaos, 83, 108–9
Pratt, Mary Louise, 18
Prevelakis, George, 32, 58
Prior, Lindsay, 160

Rabinow, Paul, 6, 12, 16,
religion; fundamentalism, 112–15; *Kólasē* (Hell), 187, 196; Paradise, 186–88, 196; Purgatory, 98, 196
Richardson, Miles, 16
Rigatos, Gerasimos, 76
Rinaldi, Anoel, 160, 178, 194
ritual, xix; exhumation (*ektaphê*), 188–91; and Holy Week, 160–61; symbolism of the lily, 162
Robertson-Smith, William, 116
Ross, Andrew, 62
Rousseau, Jean-Jacques, xxi
Rushton, Lucy, 123–24, 213

Safilios-Rothchild, Constantina, 60, 67
Said, Edward W., 17
Sant-Cassia, Paul, 95
Sartre, Jean-Paul, 9
Schizas, Yiannis, 62, 192
Schopenhauer, Arthur, xxi
Scott, David, 16
Seferis, George, 3, 74, 83

Seremetakis, Nadia, 16, 17, 18, 101, 124–25, 169, 179, 192, 210, 216
Sherrard, Philip, 34
Schein, Muriel Dimen, 63
Simons, John Addington, 37, 59
*soi*, 24, 32, 137
Sontag, Susan, 6, 76
Souliotis, Yiannis, 130–33
Stasinopoulos, E., 53, 59
Stewart, Charles, 82–83
Strathern, Marilyn, 7–11, 15–17, 18
subjectivity: in analysis, 18; intersubjectivity, 18, 30–31, 218
Sudnow, David, 14, 30–31, 193
superstition, 73; and Greek literature, 83; leap year, 73, 82–83; *máyia* (witchraft), 78–79, 85; and social classes, 82

Tambiah, Stanley, 9
Taussig, Michael, 16, 137
Taylor, Lawrence, 192
Tedlock, Barbara, 11, 18
Thumb, A., 17
Tsaousis, D.G., 70
Tsiomis, Yiannis, 60, 196
Tsitsipis, Loucas, 19
Tsoucalas, Konstantinos, 16, 70
Turner, Victor, 7, 98, 206
Tyler, Stephen, 6–7, 16,
Tzavella-Evjen, Hara T., 217
Tziovas, Dimitris, 34, 59

Velioti, Maria, 62
Vergopoulos, Kostas, 57
Vernant, Jean-Pierre, 123, 207, 209–10
Vernier, Bernard, 95
Vlachs, 56, 62
Vovelle, Michel, 125–26, 133, 196, 207
Vranousē, Era, 26–27, 34

Wallace, Melanie, 208, 216
Wallerstein, Immanuel, 57
Woodhouse, Chris, 55
Wordsworth, Christopher, 37–38

Young, Martin, 7, 10, 18

Zanetos, John C. 140

New Directions in Anthropological Writing
*History, Poetics, Cultural Criticism*

GEORGE E. MARCUS
*Rice University*

JAMES CLIFFORD
*University of California, Santa Cruz*

GENERAL EDITORS